The Central Pacific War
16 Months – 3,500 Miles

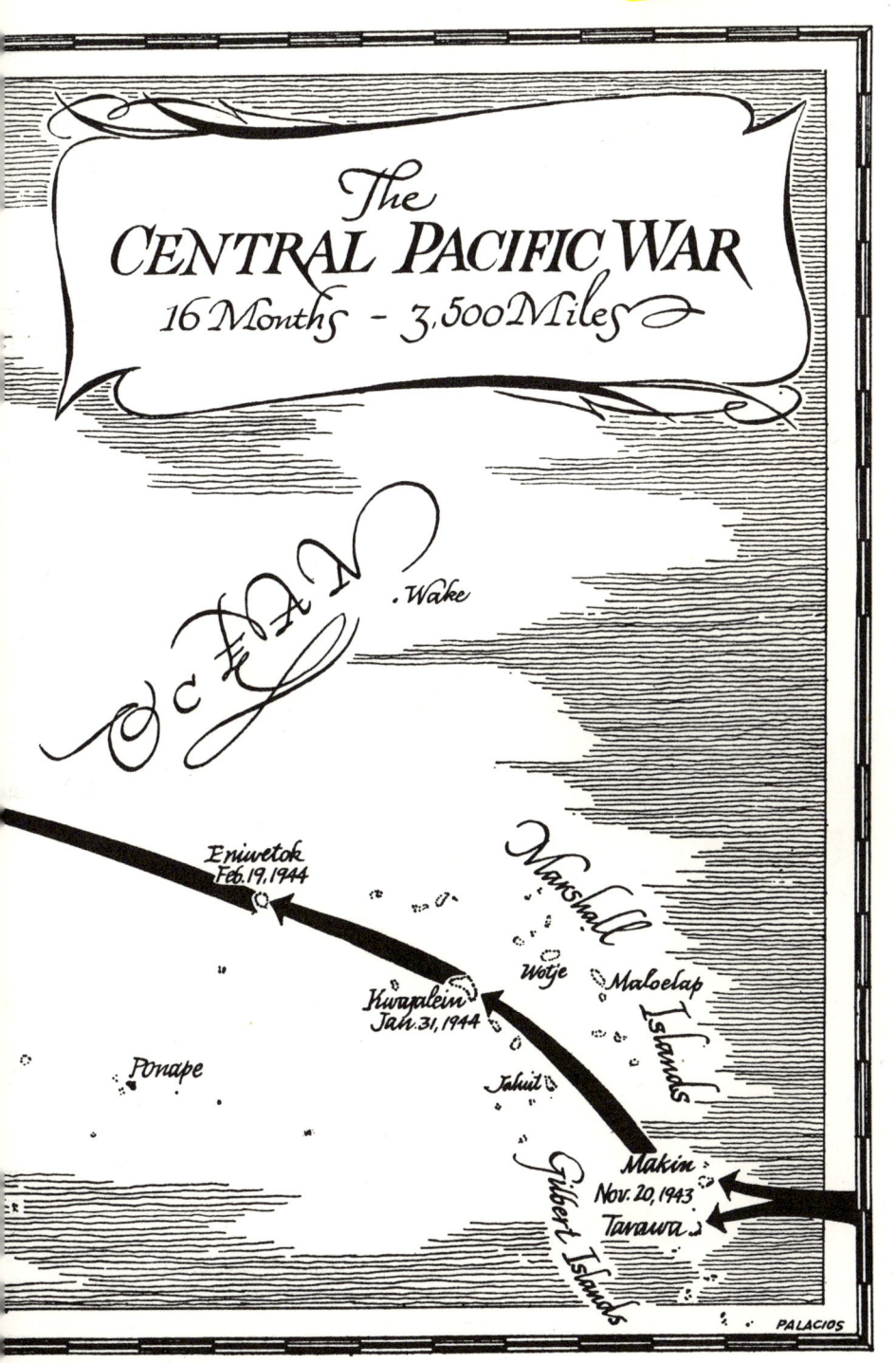

OCEAN

- Wake
- Eniwetok, Feb. 19, 1944
- Kwajalein, Jan. 31, 1944
- Wotje
- Maloelap
- Marshall Islands
- Ponape
- Jaluit
- Makin, Nov. 20, 1943
- Tarawa
- Gilbert Islands

PALACIOS

ON TO WESTWARD

GREAT
WAR
STORIES

Victory at High Tide
  by Robert Debs Heinl
The Battle for Guadalcanal
  by Samuel B. Griffith
Gallipoli
  by Alan Moorehead
The General
  by C.S. Forester
Rifleman Dodd
  by C.S. Forester
History of Marine Corps Aviation in World War II
  by Robert Sherrod
On to Westward: The Battles of Saipan and Iwo Jima
  by Robert Sherrod
Greenmantle
  by John Buchan
The Captain
  by Jan de Hartog
The Forgotten Soldier
  by Guy Sajer
Jubal Early's Memoirs
  by Jubal Anderson Early
'Boney' Fuller
  by Anthony John Trythall
Bugles and a Tiger
  by John Masters

On to Westward
THE BATTLES OF SAIPAN AND IWO JIMA

Robert Sherrod

 The Nautical & Aviation Publishing Company of America
Baltimore, Maryland

Copyright © 1945, 1990 by Robert Sherrod. Reprinted in 1990 by The Nautical & Aviation Publishing Company of America, Inc., 101 W. Read Street, Suite 314, Baltimore, Maryland 21201. Originally published in 1945 by Duell, Sloan and Pearce. All rights reserved. No part of this publication may be reprinted, stored in a retrieval system, or transmitted in any form by any electronic or mechanical copying system without the written permission of the publisher.

Library of Congress Catalog Card Number: 90-30894
ISBN: 1-877853-00-3
Printed in The United States of America
Second Edition

Library of Congress Cataloging-in-Publication Data

Sherrod, Robert Lee, 1909-
    On to Westward : the Battles of Saipan and Iwo Jima / Robert Sherrod.
    p.   cm.
    Reprint.
    ISBN 1-877853-00-3
    1. Sherrod, Robert Lee, 1909-   . 2. Saipan, Battle of, 1944. 3. Iwo Jima, Battle of, 1945. 4. World War, 1939-1945--Personal narratives, American. 5. War correspondents--United States--Biography.   I. Title.
D767.99.S3S52 1990
940.54'26--dc20   90-30894
                                                          CIP

DEDICATION

For Amy and Bill and Sonia and Marcia:
superior grandchildren all

CONTENTS

	Preface	ix
	Preface to First Edition	xi
ONE	The High Road to Victory	3
TWO	The Nature of the Enemy	15
THREE	Toward the Marianas	28
FOUR	The Invasion of Saipan	44
FIVE	The Price Goes Up	65
SIX	Midway on Saipan	94
SEVEN	The Semi-Finals	115
EIGHT	Battles End Banzai	133
NINE	We Leave For Iwo	151
TEN	Beachhead in Hell	168
ELEVEN	Japs Are Hard to Budge	183
TWELVE	The Ravines of Iwo	201
THIRTEEN	Division Hospital	216
FOURTEEN	The Top Brass	227
FIFTEEN	The Amphibious Brass	247
SIXTEEN	On to Okinawa	261
SEVENTEEN	The Unbelievable Landing	277
	Appendices	299

PREFACE

Having *On to Westward* reprinted forty-five years after it was first published is a gratifying and somewhat surprising turn of the publishing wheel of fortune. I wrote the book between April and September 1945, after I had returned to New York from Okinawa. Much of it came from notes I had taken on Saipan and Iwo Jima and Okinawa, with some between-battle jotting at CINCPAC headquarters at Pearl Harbor, later on Guam, and at the great anchorage of Ulithi.

I was racing the clock because I had a full-time job to do in the Time and Life Building, writing about the war, as I had done since 1942, until the next battle dictated that I take off again for the Pacific. The next time was to be just before the invasion of Kyushu, scheduled for November 1, 1945, where it was expected that every inhabitant would be defending the beaches with hand grenades and sharp sticks. I would accompany Major General Graves B. Erskine's Third Marine Divison.

The events of early August changed all that. I was writing a cover story about Major General Curtis E. LeMay, his portrait captioned, "Can Japan Stand Twice the Bombing That Germany Got?" I was halfway through the writing, on Saturday night, August 4, when we had a tip from Washington that a mighty bomb was about to be dropped on Japan, probably the atomic bomb that had been rumored. We had to tear up the magazine format, and turn the main job over to the science writers. We all had an uneasy feeling that the world never would be the same again. Meantime, I had a book manuscript to finish, so I ploughed ahead, squeezing the juice out of notebooks I had filled since the Tarawa battle of November 1943. Thank God for our youth, when we can work sixteen hours a day.

Since this edition must be printed by offset no changes have been made in the body of the text, so it is necessary to list corrections and other changes in an appendix. This procedure is unavoidable, considering the prohibitive expense of resetting the whole book. (see Appendix D)

Robert Sherrod
Washington, D.C.
March 12, 1990

To you, who lie within this coral sand,
We, who remain, pay tribute of a pledge,
That dying, thou surely shalt not
Have died in vain. . . .

. . .

When we with loving hands laid back the earth
That was for moments short to couch thy form
We did not bid a last and sad farewell,
But only "Rest ye well."
Then with this humble, heartfelt epitaph
That pays thy many virtues sad acclaim
We marked this spot, and, murmuring requiem,
Moved on to Westward.

PREFACE TO FIRST EDITION

THE TITLE OF THIS BOOK IS TAKEN FROM THE VERSE ON THE opposite page. These lines are inscribed on a plaque in the cemetery at Tarawa. Their Marine author is unknown, but he is said to be one who, experiencing the wrench of leaving Tarawa only five days after the landing, saluted the friends he left behind him.

Tarawa marked the beginning of a campaign which has no precedent in history, for the simple reason that the campaign across the biggest ocean could not have been fought except with very modern naval machinery. Such machinery did not exist until 1943, and it was not employed on a sizeable scale until 1944. By 1945, when the United States Navy was considerably larger than the combined navies of history, the full force of this mighty machinery was being exerted. Okinawa was the end of the islands campaign and, it turned out, the last battle of the war.

Sixteen months and one week elapsed between November 23, 1943, when the Second Marine Division secured Tarawa, and April 1, 1945, when soldiers and Marines of the Tenth Army landed on Okinawa. In between there were 3,500 miles and other battles on other islands: Kwajalein, Eniwetok, Saipan, Tinian, Guam, Peleliu-Angaur, Iwo Jima.

This is not the complete story of those battles, nor of the entire Central Pacific campaign. This is a sketch of the campaign, as it appeared to me, and the stories, in some detail, of the key battles I witnessed.

But the function of the war correspondent, as I see it, is not to write complete stories. He cannot write with the perspective which time alone can furnish. Leave that to the historians and their mountains of official records. At best, the war correspondent can write what he sees and hears and feels; he can perhaps reflect the mood of men in battle, as those men appear and talk and fight.

Of the millions of Americans who became involved in World War II, none were more fortunate than the war correspondents. Here were men privileged to witness history in the making, with no further duties than witnessing and recording, men who could come and go with a freedom barely restricted by military orders. The war correspondent could disagree with the admiral or general if he wanted to. He also could be (and sometimes was) cussed out by the private or the seaman third class. There was always censorship, of course, but in the Central Pacific I found most censors men of good will whose only interest was to protect the necessary military security. Working in the Central Pacific from late 1943 onwards was never made excessively difficult by the restrictions of censorship, even if some of those restrictions seemed absurd at times. (The worst thing about censorship is the mental block which confronts a writer before he even sits down to write.) Whatever a correspondent wrote had to be held within the broad outlines of the communique, but the communique, if sometimes slow, was nearly always honest and reasonable.

In the Central Pacific the correspondent was exceptionally privileged. He could witness a campaign as spectacular as it was successful. There have been bigger armies than the United States army, but no other nation ever dreamed of a navy such as the United States sent through the Central Pacific. The battles in the Central Pacific were easily defined. In addition, the nature of the Japanese enemy made him as unearthly—and, therefore, almost as newsworthy—as men from Mars.

But war correspondence was never an easy job. By the

middle of 1945 I had been at it for four years—so long that it sometimes seemed that I had never written anything except war. The more I saw of war, the more I realized how difficult it was for any one reporter to write absolutely accurate, perfectly balanced dispatches involving large bodies of men. What seemed true of one regiment or one division was not necessarily true of others. What looked good back at division headquarters was not good at the moment in the front lines, and the stilted division reports often told little of what the battle seemed like to the riflemen who fought it.

No one reporter could cover all the battles of the Central Pacific; none could have been in the simultaneous landings at Makin and Tarawa, for instance, nor at both Guam and Tinian. None could have attended all the first carrier strikes on the Japanese homeland and the simultaneous landings at Iwo Jima.

You can see, then, why nearly all of what I have written here is based on personal observations, as recorded in my notebooks, of the Central Pacific campaign. The nature of my job in battle made it necessary to spend some time at headquarters, so that I could keep up with the whole picture of the battle. At the same time, I, like other correspondents, wanted to know what the men under direct fire were thinking and doing. Therefore, this personalized story is largely an account of my wanderings from one headquarters or another to the front lines and back again. It is also an account of my wanderings from fleet headquarters at Pearl Harbor (later Guam) to such places as Ulithi, Saipan, Eniwetok.

In any battle involving more than one division, I usually stayed with a single division. Twenty thousand men are enough for one reporter to try to cover with any semblance of thoroughness. (If it had been possible, I always would have stayed with a single battalion of about 900 men, as I did about half the time on Saipan in order to get the story of Bill Jones's battalion.) But in battle I always tried to take a look at the other divisions involved. During my brief time on Okinawa (eleven days) not even that was possible. The Sixth Marine Division, to which I was attached, raced far to the north end of the island, and I saw nothing of the First Marine Division or of the Seventh and Ninety-Sixth Division which made the southern landings.

Most of this book concerns the amphibious landings. During the war I spent some time on 29 different ships, and I had hoped to write more about the war at sea, especially as seen from the aircraft carriers, the finest and most effective of our modern naval weapons. But the landing was the focal point, and even the aircraft carriers were only a means of destroying the enemy who stood in the path of our landing. Land is the solid evidence of success in war.

There is much in this book about the Marines; after Tarawa I spent most of my time with them. There were not enough Marines to fight their way from the Gilberts to the Ryukyus without invaluable assistance, at the various times, from five different Army divisions. But the Central Pacific war was essentially a war of beachheads, and that was what the Marines were trained for. The spearheading Marines bore the brunt of the Central Pacific land fighting; their casualties were about 65,000 against about 32,000 for the soldiers. It was natural that the Navy would assign its own soldiers, the Marines, to most (but not all) of the toughest jobs of the Navy's Central Pacific war. The toughest battles make the best stories. My job was writing stories, so I followed the Leathernecks.

In the dreary chores of camp life, or in the heat of battle, the Marines' *esprit de corps* rarely flagged. Generally, they lived as they died—with dignity, without complaint. Their average age was somewhere between twenty and twenty-two, which is the best age for fighting men. If, as General Eisenhower has said, morale is the most important factor in a war, the Marines had to a startling degree what it takes to fight a war. Their cockiness and assumption of superiority were sometimes resented by other services, but they paid off in battle.

Some day someone will write a book about the Marines which will adequately explain their superb *esprit de corps*. I never knew what caused it, unless it was this: From the time he underwent the severe discipline of "boot" camp until he died assaulting a Japanese pillbox, the Marine had it drummed into his head: "You are the best fighting man on earth, and you'd better never do anything to disprove it." His training included not only a thorough course in the use of weapons but also a stiff indoctrination in what Hanson Baldwin calls "moral superiority."

It may be that the atomic bomb and guided missiles will put war on a scientific basis, and hereafter wars will be won in the laboratories. In that case, this book may be taken as one reporter's record of the last campaign wherein raw courage played such a vital part.

ON TO WESTWARD

CHAPTER ONE

THE HIGH ROAD TO VICTORY

THERE WERE, AT VARIOUS TIMES, FIVE THEATERS OF WAR WHERE Americans were fighting Japanese. These included the China-Burma-India area, which served as an air base and a supply base only; and a jungle battleground where a few hundred American soldiers were engaged at one time.

Of the remaining four, the North Pacific looked promising to some in 1943 as a springboard from which we could pounce on the enemy. But the weather of the Aleutians proved too formidable, the strategic possibilities too slight. After the Japs lost Attu and pulled out of Kiska, the North Pacific lost its importance except as a staging area for a small force of surface ships and planes which occasionally shelled or bombed Japan's Kurile Islands.

The South Pacific was the first theater in which we attempted an "offensive-defensive" against the prowling Japs. This began as a shoestring operation in the grim days of August, 1942. Originally, the Guadalcanal landings had been planned for November, but the immediate threat to the United States-Australia supply line caused it to be stepped up to mid-August. At the last minute the operation was advanced another week because a breakdown of the Japanese code revealed that the enemy was about to reinforce his Guadalcanal garrison.

The malaria-ridden South Pacific never lost its tinge of desperation, throughout the Russell Islands, the New Georgia, and the Bougainville perimeter campaigns. After Bougainville (November, 1943) the principal objectives left in the South Pacific path were Rabaul and Truk. An attack on either would have been disastrously expensive. Rabaul was surrounded when the Green Islands and Emirau landings were made in February and March, 1944, and Truk was bypassed later in the year. As an offensive lever the South Pacific was abandoned; it remained a rehabilitation area for combat troops almost to the end of the war.

The two principal theaters of war were the Southwest Pacific and the Central Pacific. The Southwest was the older, having been established upon General MacArthur's arrival in Melbourne from the Philippines in March, 1942; the Central Pacific opened a year and a half later. One was essentially an Army affair, concerned with the conquest of the world's second largest island, New Guinea, and with the liberation of the Philippine Islands. The Central Pacific was the Navy's war, fought across more than 3,000 miles of blue water dotted with small, heavily defended islands. Some of these islands had to be seized as advance bases, in preparation for the next step forward. This book consists chiefly of one reporter's notes taken in some of the battles along that route across the Pacific.

Obviously, there was considerable conflicting opinion regarding the strategy of the Pacific war. General MacArthur stated publicly that he was opposed to "island-hopping" methods such as were employed in the Central Pacific. On the other hand, I have heard high-ranking officers in the Central Pacific argue that, militarily, the reconquest of the Philippines was unnecessary; American forces were already on Okinawa, nearly a thousand miles nearer Japan, before the Philippines had been completely regained.

It would have been interesting to see how the Pacific war would have been fought under a single Supreme Commander. Undoubtedly, the strategy would have been quite different from what actually evolved; neither MacArthur nor Nimitz was likely to take individually all the steps they took collectively. This, in spite of the fact that the Joint Chiefs of Staff in Washington theoretically ordered each step in both the MacArthur and the Nimitz wars. Neither the General nor the Admiral seemed to have much trouble getting the Joint Chiefs to approve whatever moves they advocated. Such was the power of the United States that we could fight Japan from any and all directions.

In terms of landings, the drive across the Central Pacific began late in 1943 at Tarawa and Makin, and ended in mid-1945 in the Ryukyus. This drive provided the bases from which the B-29's methodically destroyed the Japanese war potential, and provided most of the anchorages from which the Navy's planes and ships sailed to finish off Japan's Navy and merchant marine. The only pre-war Japanese possessions captured in this war were in the Central Pacific.

The atomic bombs were dropped by B-29's which flew from hard-won Central Pacific bases. These revolutionary missiles provided the Japanese Emperor with an excuse to "grant" outright the peace his ministers were already proposing secretly. Until the atomic bomb was produced, it seemed inevitable that we should invade the Japanese homeland; this undoubtedly would have cost scores of thousands of American lives, and probably millions of Japanese lives. The Emperor's capitulation-without-surrender, following the last-ditch Okinawa battle, came to the Pacific commanders, as it came to almost everyone else, as the greatest shock in a war of surprises. By August, 1945, our great power was geared for almost anything except a peaceable entry into Japan.

This Central Pacific was mostly a war of naval power; the Pacific, by its nature, was bound to be won by seapower and airpower, just as Europe had to be won by armies and airpower. Only eleven divisions of troops (six Marine, five Army) were involved in the battles from Tarawa to Okinawa, though often those divisions carried as heavy a responsibility as ever was placed on the men with infantry weapons. Usually the battles were short and severe; the Fourth Marine

Division fought four complete battles and suffered nearly 75 per cent casualties—yet it was in action only 61 days throughout the war.

The amphibious operations against the islands and atolls were one of the three most important factors in the success of the Central Pacific war; the others were the use of aircraft carriers, and the system of floating supply bases which included refueling and rearming at sea. In terms of men involved, the troops who did the landing were always less numerous than the sailors who manned the ships. But the troops paid the heaviest price: about 100,000 casualties in the eleven island battles of the six Central Pacific campaigns. These six were:

THE GILBERTS—The opening of the Central Pacific was originally planned as simultaneous landings on Nauru and Ocean Islands, southwest of Tarawa, and on Tarawa. Plans were changed so that the southern strike was made on Tarawa by the Second Marine Division, the northern on

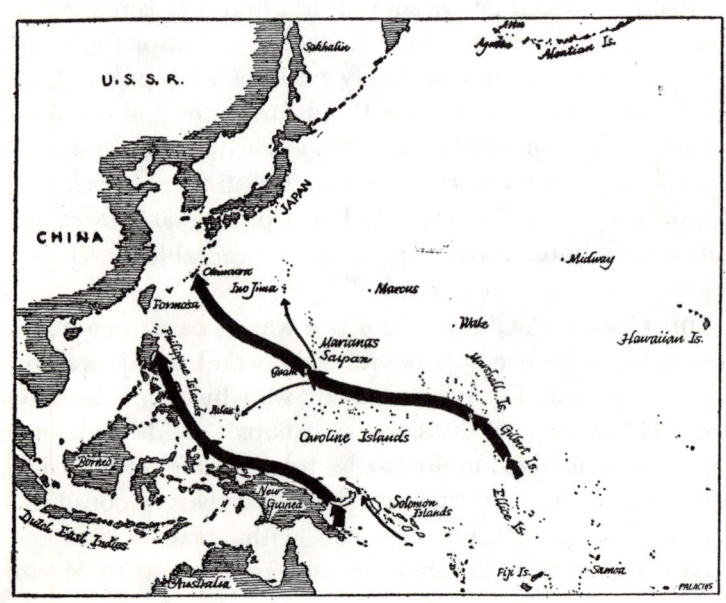

Makin by the 165th Regiment (reinforced) of the Twenty-Seventh Infantry Division. The date was November 20, 1943 (west longitude). The Makin landing encountered little opposition at first; the 300 Jap fighting men and 400 laborers put up a brief, stiff fight as the soldiers advanced inland. Of the Americans, 66 were killed, 187 wounded. Tarawa was another story.

Some hindsight observers believe that the invasion of the Gilberts was not necessary; that the Marshalls could have been invaded in the first battle of the new theater. But Admiral Nimitz was not prepared to risk his new, growing fleet in a head-on battle with the still strong Jap fleet, as might have been necessary if an advance directly into the Marshalls had been attempted; the Japs still had considerable airpower in the Marshalls and strong air reinforcements could have been called from the Marianas and Carolines. (One of the surprises throughout the Pacific war was Japanese plane production.)

Regardless of the advisability of attacking the Marshalls or the Gilberts first, we had to have a Tarawa. It was sad but true that we Americans usually learned the hard way about war and the weapons of war. Lessons had to be learned in attacking a heavily defended island for the first time. Although we poured 3,000 tons of high explosives on Tarawa's square mile, we found most of the 4,000 fanatical Jap defenders still firing from their pillboxes and concrete blockhouses as we waded ashore. We had to learn that heavier bombs were needed—nothing larger than 1,000 pounds had been dropped in the pre-invasion raids—that armor-piercing shells were needed to penetrate blockhouses when high explosives could not. We had to learn that we needed more and better-armored amphibious tractors to transport troops over coral reefs where ordinary landing barges could not navigate, that rockets would have killed many Japs, and saved the lives of many of our men. Tarawa led to the development of underwater demolition teams who thenceforth would explore reefs before the landings, blowing up obstacles in the water and determining the best landing beaches.

Tarawa remains, in my estimate, the supreme triumph of courage over adversity. But for the Marines' determination that they should not fail, Tarawa would have been lost. To uphold the shining reputation of their Corps and to save other men's lives in future operations, 988 Marines gave their lives, and 2,164 were wounded in Tarawa's 76 hours. Tarawa was the only battle of the Central Pacific which might have been lost after the landing had been made. But the Japs, for reasons probably not even known to themselves, did not counter-attack on the night of D Day when the Marines were crowded on a beachhead not more than 20 feet wide in most places.

THE MARSHALLS—The next step in the Central Pacific had been planned at Wotje and Maloelap (Taroa Island), 500 miles beyond Tarawa. After much debate among the tacticians at Pearl Harbor, these heavily defended islands were bypassed, and Kwajalein, the world's largest atoll (30-odd islands, 66 miles long, 18 miles wide), was selected as the target. Thus, not only Wotje and Maloelap, but also Jaluit and Mili in the Southern Marshalls, were bypassed.

Kwajalein was an almost perfect operation against an atoll. The Fourth Marine Division was assigned to the northern part of the atoll, the twin sandspits named Roi and Namur. The Seventh Infantry Division was picked to invade Kwajalein, the atoll's largest island, at the southern end. Neither division made a frontal assault. Each landed initially on smaller islets (February 1, 1944), and set up its artillery in preparation for the main assault. This time the Army troops took their time, killed 5,000 Japs in a methodical, six-day operation, and had 177 men killed, 1,037 wounded. The Marines rapidly overran their two assigned smaller islands—in 27 hours—killed 3,800 Japs while losing 229 in killed and missing, 797 wounded. Naval gunfire and artillery fire preceding the attack amounted to about five times the pre-invasion shelling of Tarawa. We had learned how to flatten an atoll.

Eniwetok, westernmost of the Marshalls, had been found by air reconnaissance to be less heavily defended than we suspected. Invasion came 16 days after Kwajalein, timed with Spruance's and Mitscher's first strike against dreaded Truk, where they sank 25 ships and destroyed 211 planes in one of the war's most successful, enemy-deflating raids. At Eniwetok the new 22nd Marine Regiment seized its northern island, Engebi, in 365 minutes, then moved down to the southern islands of the atoll to assist the 106th Infantry of the Twenty-seventh Division to mop up the Japs on Eniwetok and Parry Islands in the next three days. The Marines had 196 killed, 550 wounded, the Army had 70 killed, 228 wounded.

THE MARIANAS—At Eniwetok the atoll warfare ended, and the mountainside cave problem began. In his holes in the mountains the Jap proved even more formidable than in his blockhouses. The Second and Fourth Marine Divisions and the Twenty-seventh Infantry Division learned this at Saipan, which was captured between June 15 and July 9[1] with a total of 14,906 casualties. The Third Marine Division, the First Marine Provisional Brigade, and the Seventy-Seventh Infantry Division had been scheduled to land at Guam on June 18, but the severity of the fighting on Saipan caused a long delay, during which the Guam troops were finally sent back to wait in the Eniwetok lagoon. The landing finally occurred July 21, against some opposition. Fighting in the mountains farther inland was more severe; Guam cost the Marines 6,441 casualties, the soldiers 3,409. A Jap force of 18,500 was wiped out except for a few hundred who hid in Guam's hills and thick undergrowth; they surrendered a few

---

[1] By the time they reached the Marianas, American forces had generally adopted east longitude dates, such as those given hereafter in the text.

at a time for months afterward; some only after the Emperor declared the war over.

The Second and Fourth Marine Divisions rested only 13 days after suffering their heavy Saipan casualties. Then (on July 24) they moved across the four-mile-wide channel to establish a narrow beachhead on the northern shore of Tinian, where the Japs did not believe a landing possible. "We had the bastards surrounded before they knew where we were," said one officer of this model operation, of which little was heard because it was overshadowed by Guam. Total casualties on Tinian were 2,151, only 5.3 per cent of the force committed, lowest ratio of the Central Pacific war.

Seizure of the three Marianas islands for B-29 bases, only about 1,500 miles south of Tokyo, completed the first phase of the Central Pacific drive. American engineering skill, by no means the least factor in defeating Japan, eventually built enough airfields on these three islands (total, 309 square miles) to stage 800-plane B-29 raids—far more than originally anticipated. The Marianas cost the lives of nearly 6,000 soldiers and Marines (5,462 killed, 480 missing), but the loss of the islands precipitated the enemy into a decline from which there could be no recovery.

THE PALAUS—A plan to invade Truk had been discarded. In August, the First Marine Division boarded transports to sail nearly 1,000 miles beyond Truk for the invasion of Peleliu in the Palau Islands, while the Eighty-First Division proceeded to Angaur, next to Peleliu. The XXIV Army Corps (Seventh, Seventy-Seventh, and Ninety-Sixth Divisions) sailed to invade Yap, between the Palaus and Guam.

Even after the XXIV Corps was at sea, the Yap invasion was called off. General MacArthur's plans to invade the Philippines were advanced a full two months; the target was changed from Mindanao in the Southern Philippines to Leyte in the Central Philippines. The XXIV Corps was "loaned" by Nimitz to MacArthur.

By striking at Peleliu and Angaur in the Southern Palaus, the strategists had hoped to gain airfields which would complete the isolation of Japs in the Carolines and also serve as a connecting link between the Marianas and the Philippines. They hoped to do this without the excessive cost attendant upon the seizure of Koror or 25-mile-long Babelthuap in the Northern Palaus. But Peleliu, it developed, was defended by about 11,000 Japs instead of 8,000 as expected. And the terrain was six square miles of the worst the Pacific war had produced—precipitous coral cliffs, blazing hot rocks, muck-oozing swamps. "Bloody Nose Ridge" cost the First Marine Division most of its 6,024 casualties, 1,241 of them dead or missing. The Eighty-First Division killed about 3,000 Japs and secured Angaur in three days, then sent a regiment to help the Marines on Peleliu. Its casualties were 1,729. The division's 323d Regiment seized Ulithi to the northwest without opposition. Ulithi became the fleet's principal anchorage.

To the men who fought on Peleliu, the battle was a nightmare which seemed never to end—it lasted officially from September 15 to October 13, but mopping up continued a long time until 13,354 Japs had been killed, 433 captured, on the two islands. One Marine officer said: "It seemed to us that they called off Yap, then somebody forgot to give the order to call off Peleliu. That's one place nobody wants to remember."

IWO JIMA—Amphibious troops of the Central Pacific were out of combat from October, 1944 to February, 1945, while the Pacific fleet was engaged in and around the Philippines. When the Third, Fourth, and Fifth Marine Divisions returned to action at Iwo on February 19, they found an underground hell which tested them almost beyond human endurance.

This was no Tarawa. This was nearly a year and a half later, when we had perfected the instruments and methods of amphibious warfare, yet the Jap defenses were such that our superior firepower was all but nullified. If there ever was a place for an atomic bomb, it was Iwo, with its underground maze of caves and tunnels woven throughout the steaming rocks and ravines. But the atomic bomb was not ready, and men on foot had to conquer the bloodiest eight square miles of the Pacific war. Iwo cost the Marines 5,471 lives (4,238 killed, 1,233 dead of wounds, 46 missing), and nearly 15,000 others were wounded, but Iwo saved more than 20,000 B-29 flyers before the end of the war.

OKINAWA—This was the last stop on the Central Pacific route, slightly more than 300 miles south of the Japanese home island of Kyushu. Again the Japs were unpredictable. Our four divisions which made the Okinawa landing (the Seventh, Ninety-Sixth, the First and Sixth Marine Divisions) went ashore April 1, unopposed. In the first two weeks only a few thousand Japs were encountered, while nearly four-fifths of the island was occupied. Then, as the divisions moved south toward Naha and Shuri Castle, the Jap defenses turned the remainder of the island into another Iwo.

The four divisions in the original landing were joined by the Seventy-Seventh, which had been engaged in seizing smaller islands surrounding Okinawa, the Twenty-Seventh, and, finally, the 8th Marine Regiment (re-inforced) which came in for the final gasp. The Okinawa operation cost the Tenth Army 36,800 casualties (15,400 Marines, 21,400 soldiers). The island was defended by more than 100,000 enemy troops.

One of the remarkable things about the Okinawa operation was the great naval strength employed: more than 1,400 ships. Even so, the Navy had many ships left over. Except the ships for one division, the transports which took troops to Iwo were not used at Okinawa.

The Navy, too, paid here its highest price of the Pacific war. Off Okinawa the Japs sent their suicide flyers day after day to dive into the American ships. More than 250 ships were victims of the *kamikaze* pilots who exploded themselves and their planes against the American invaders. By the time

Okinawa had been secured, the United States Navy had incurred nearly 10,000 casualties there. But after Okinawa the war was all but over.

The fast carriers paced the Central Pacific war. Their operations were not, of course, confined to any single theater, and probably their most effective support was rendered in and around the Philippines during the landings on Leyte and Luzon. It is true that, except for the Hollandia operation in April, 1944, General MacArthur depended mostly on his own land-based bombers to support his hops up the New Guinea coast. During the second phase of his war—the liberation of the Philippines—he was largely dependent on the carriers as a strategic air force, since the carriers could muster more strength and length than the land-based planes of the Southwest Pacific.

In a sense, September 1, 1943,[2] might be said to mark the opening of the Central Pacific. Just as 1942 had been a year of hanging on, 1943 was essentially America's year of preparation, the year the carriers and planes were built and pilots were trained. The year 1943 was not, as some critics charged, the year we sent everything to Europe to the exclusion of the Pacific; the Navy's bald, iron-willed representative on the Joint and Combined Chiefs of Staff fought so hard for supplies that Winston Churchill was moved to refer to the Pacific as "Ernie King's beloved ocean."

No full-scale offensive could have been undertaken in 1942 or 1943 because the ships, especially aircraft carriers and transports, simply were not available. Any important offensive had to wait on the *Essex*-class carriers. They were sent to the Pacific as soon as they were ready. On September 1, 1943, the *Essex*, her sister the new *Yorktown*, and the first of the fast, light carriers converted from cruiser hulls, the *Independence*, struck at Marcus Island, about 3,000 miles west of Pearl Harbor. It was the first test of the new type of

[2] It was September 2 on the Japanese side of the international date line.

carrier task force, and, reported the enthusiastic flyers, 80 per cent of Marcus was destroyed. It was also the first time the carrier planes had carried 2,000-pound bombs.

Less than three weeks later, three more carriers were ready for combat. On September 18 the new *Lexington,* 27,000 tons of *Essex*-class ship, and two more cruiser converts, the *Princeton* and the *Belleau Wood,* made their first raid on Tarawa, Makin and Abemama in the Gilberts. On October 5 and 6 "the greatest carrier task force ever assembled" (as I called it in a story written from the *Lexington*) sailed due west from Pearl Harbor for Wake Island—all six carriers plus destroyers and some new and old cruisers which shelled Wake after the pilots had knocked out the air opposition.

From Tarawa onward, the carriers paved the way for the landings on islands across the Pacific. The formula was set: The carriers went ahead and burned up the enemy's planes, sank his supply ships, and kept his airfields useless. The old battleships, cruisers, and destroyers shelled the target, and the slow escort carriers delivered immediate support for the troop landings. When the airfields were prepared, the land-based bombers and fighters moved in (often before the island was secured), and the pattern was repeated in the next move. This system was carried across the Pacific, to the Marianas, to Iwo and Okinawa.

Essentially, the Pacific was an air war, and it was in the air that the Americans demonstrated their greatest superiority over the Japanese. But without the amphibious troops who had to seize the bases, in operations that required such a high quotient of sheer courage, the airmen could not have operated. It is true, by and large, that the United States won the Pacific war through its massive industrial power, which the Japanese could never expect to match—and it is easy to say so. But no man who saw Tarawa, Saipan, Iwo Jima, or Okinawa would agree that all the American steel was in the guns and bombs. There was a lot, also, in the hearts of the men who stormed the beaches.

CHAPTER TWO

THE NATURE OF THE ENEMY

THE CENTRAL PACIFIC CAMPAIGN EMPHASIZED WHAT WE HAD begun to expect earlier in the war—that we were fighting an enemy we knew only slightly. More than ever, we found that the mental processes of the Japanese apparently functioned in an altogether different manner from our own. Where we cherished life and living, the Japanese seemed to cherish death—so long as the Emperor gave no order to the contrary. "Common sense"—that is, occidental common sense—would have told the Japanese early in every one of our Central Pacific battles that they had no more chance of winning the the battle than of winning the war, that they had best stop before their forces were annihilated. Needless to say, no such halt occurred in any of the battles. The Jap always fought on, sometimes insanely, but more often skillfully and always bravely. The number of Japs who surrendered during any one battle was nearly always less than five per cent—at Okinawa it was slightly higher. (After organized resistance had ceased, and acute hunger had set in, the total sometimes rose above this figure). Usually, it was nearer one per cent. At Tarawa 17 Japs and 143 Koreans surrendered out of a total force of 4,000. (The Korean laborers were usually quite eager to surrender whenever their masters could not prevent it). In most battles the number of Japs who committed suicide was higher than the number who surrendered before organized resistance ended.

By refusing to give up, by hiding in caves behind our own front lines, the Japs could not hope to accomplish much. They could kill or wound a few of our own men before they were themselves killed. They could not change the course of a battle. But apparently they had no ambition to live to fight another day. The few who did surrender became traitors, and freely betrayed their own comrades.

It always seemed to me that one of the things prompting Jap fanaticism was this: The Tokyo war lords hoped that their bitter-end fighters might make the Pacific war expensive enough to cause Americans to recoil from their casualties, to be willing to settle for something less than unconditional surrender. They were wrong, of course, but what other plan could they have had? Before the war, Lieut. General Masaharu Homma put it thus to correspondent Clark Lee, who quoted the General in an article in *Collier's:* "We are prepared to lose ten million men in our war with America. How many are you prepared to lose?"

Sometimes it seemed that the Japs continued fighting on hope—hope that reinforcements were on the way. Everywhere we fought the Japs we were amazed at their ignorance, even among high-ranking officers. Early in 1945 Masaharu Homma was quoted by Radio Tokyo as saying: "It will be a fatal mistake for the enemy to expect our Navy to continue to lie in wait indefinitely . . . the enemy command in operating their convoys insolently in waters adjacent to our vital positions will sustain irretrievable defeat sooner or later at the hands of our Navy." Perhaps General Homma was rubbing a little salt in his Navy's wounds, but more likely the Jap Navy had not risked loss of face by telling Homma just what condition it was in—if the Tokyo admirals themselves knew. (Time after time we found evidence that admirals at sea and generals in the field lied outrageously to their superiors at home.) The general (and perhaps the admirals) probably did not know that when he spoke the Jap Navy was only a skeleton unable to defeat one of our task groups.

In an interview with an involuntary prisoner, written by Sergeant H. N. Oliphant in *Yank* Magazine's Western Pacific edition for February 16, 1945, a typical Japanese attitude could be found. Not many prisoner interviews got through censorship, but this Philippine incident did. Sergeant Oliphant questioned a Jap sailor through the interpreter, Jitter:

"Do you think Japan will win the war?"

"Of course, Japan will win the war."

"Why?"

"Japan can beat anybody."

"What makes you think Japan will win?"

"Japan never lost a war. She cannot be beaten. All of Japan is one mind."

"What do you mean by 'Japan is one mind?'" (In his answer the prisoner used a phrase that I had heard frequently throughout the questioning. It was *yamato damashi*. When I asked what it meant, Jitter said: "The phrase is hard to translate. There is no American word or phrase which means quite the same thing. The closest I can come to it is 'fighting spirit,' but to these people it means much more than that. If you think of a will power that no force on earth, short of killing its possessor, could discourage, and add to that the stubborn, cold belief of a bigot, you might get a little closer to its meaning." He went on with his questioning:

"Do you think Japan can beat America at anything—sports, for example?"

"Yes."

"How about baseball? Didn't the Americans beat your pants off at baseball a few years ago?"

"They got the highest score, yes."

"You mean that America didn't beat you?"

"Yes, Japan won." (Jitter looked at me with an expression of exaggerated patience, tapping his fingers on the ground as Oliver Hardy used to do when Stan Laurel tripped him into a trough of white plaster)."

"Look—first you said that the Americans got the high

score. And now you say that Japan won. What exactly do you mean by that?"

"*Yamato damashi.* You got the high score, but there are more important things. It's the way Japan plays the game." (Then the sailor burst into a flood of wild hissing chatter that lasted a good two minutes. When he finished, Jitter translated). You come over to play in a big baseball tournament. You hit the ball plenty, you make runs, but your players are not honorable. They were crude. They didn't bow and talk properly to people, and while they played they paid no attention to anything but the game. Also, they showed no *yamato damashi.* They wear uniforms with no American flags on them. Every Japanese player wears a uniform with the rising sun on it."

Before the war I knew as little about the Japanese as most Americans did. The embassy group in Washington consisted of amiable, correctly dressed little men who smiled politely and drank excessively. Some time after the Sino-Japanese "incident" of 1937, the popular ambassador Hirosi Saito, undertook, in a speech before the National Press Club, to explain how Japan had been forced to attack China in self-defense. He failed miserably, and it seemed to the audience that little Saito did not himself believe what he read from his manuscript. Saito died soon afterward, and his ashes were returned to Japan in the cruiser *Astoria.*

Certainly, there was nothing in the behavior of the Japanese in Washington to indicate the nature of the enemy we were one day to fight. The real nature of the Japanese—the super-race complex, the barbarism, the fanaticism—apparently was never revealed in foreign office and diplomatic circles. The Navy men to whom I talked before the war were deceived just as badly. They had no doubt that we could "polish off the little bastards" in a matter of three months—maybe six. In May, 1945, a very wise and honored admiral admitted to me: "We didn't have much conception of the Japanese before we fought them. We always planned to send our Navy out to sink their Navy, after which Japan would submit." The admiral granted that up to then he had never seen much evidence of submission as a Japanese characteristic. (Incidentally, it is no wonder that many Navy officers said much later that the attack on Pearl Harbor was the best possible thing that could have happened to the United States. If the old, slow battleships had been at sea, they would have been sunk beyond salvage. As it turned out, they could be repaired and used many times for naval gunfire support in amphibious operations.)

The first enemy Japanese I saw was a flyer who had been captured early in 1942 off the coast of New Guinea. We did manage to get a handful of prisoners in those early days in the Southwest Pacific. Beyond a few of these prisoners I saw no others until a year later, when we invaded Attu. Toward the end of that battle the intelligence officer of the Seventh Infantry Division, Lieut. Colonel Robert G. Fergusson, was tearing his thinning hair and offering prizes—an intelligence officer is desperate when he has no prisoners whatsoever. We knew we had already killed at least half the Japs on Attu, but not one had chosen to surrender.

By the evening of May 28 the fighting on Attu had virtually ended, except for wiping out the remaining Japs who fought in the bitter cold on Buffalo Nose, a high ridge overlooking Chichagof Harbor. Time had almost run out for the Japs on Attu. But at daylight of May 29, about three o'clock, the Japs pulled the first of many fantastic stunts that I was to witness in the long war ahead. They evacuated their remaining troops from the rear slope of Buffalo Nose, gathered for a counterattack from their last headquarters at the little port of Chichagof. Then they ran down the valley below and alongside Buffalo Nose, toward our line across the valley. They could not have chosen a more propitious time at which to hit. One of our companies was pulling out of line for chow, before being sent up Buffalo Nose.

The Japs streamed through the hole in the line. They fired wildly, shouting "Banzai!" and "Japanese drink Americans' blood!" They overran an aid station, bayonetting or shooting the wounded, the doctors, and a chaplain. Many men in this supposedly rear area were skewered in their sleeping bags. Men of the 17th Infantry rear command post were shot as they rushed out of their tents to meet the charge. Some of our men, including a corporal I had known well, had their heads bashed in by Japanese rifle butts. According to the best estimates we could make later at the cemetery, about 300 American soldiers were killed in this violent assault—almost half of the total lost on Attu.

The Japs penetrated as much as two miles behind our front lines. They almost reached our own artillery positions which presumably were the targets. They finally were stopped chiefly by the 13th and the 50th Engineers, who occupied a commanding hill further up the valley, and by the 7th Division Headquarters Company.

Up to this point, the Japanese counterattack made sense. It had been successful, probably beyond the Japs' own planning. By the time they were definitely stopped, the Japs had probably lost half the thousand men they threw into the last-man charge. Some of the remaining half were equipped only with bayonets tied to sticks—a favorite Jap measure—but most of them still had hand grenades, rifles (Japanese and American), and ammunition. Instead of trying to kill the Americans with the last bullet, or the last hand grenade, the little men began blowing themselves up, usually with hand grenades. A few were found who had fallen upon their own bayonets. Many who blew themselves to pieces had been wounded already; others, apparently not at all. In walking up the valley later to look with horrified fascination at this unearthly spectacle, I started counting the Japanese dead. I counted 425 before I quit; of these, 209 had taken their own lives, including many who had a dozen grenades left. It was not difficult to tell who had taken his own life; the missing right hand and the missing chest or stomach were the plainest of evidence. Some had held the grenades against their heads. These were even more gruesome.

It was evident that many of these Japanese had not killed themselves primarily to escape the disgrace they attached to capture. They had sought self-immolation for the sake, *per se,* of dying. ("I will gladly die today, for it is the anniversary of my father's death," one had written in his diary.) Suicide was, in their bizarre scheme of things, an honored Japanese institution. Suicide apparently guaranteed entry into the Yasukuni shrine (for those slain in battle) as surely as an American bullet. ("Seiji will gladly die with a smile.") One of the Jap doctors on Attu wrote, "Hand grenades were passed out to the patients," as if grenades were the panacea leading to the cure, death. His patients were the seriously wounded; all who could walk, even if only with splints, had been ordered into the final attack.

Not quite all the Japs on Attu went through with the plan of getting killed or killing themselves. Colonel Fergusson eventually could count 27 prisoners, the last of whom surrendered three months after the battle ended. We estimated that about 2,200 Japs had been killed on Attu; thus, those who were willing to admit defeat, and live, was slightly more than one per cent.

This suicidal pattern was repeated, in varying degrees, throughout the campaign across the Central Pacific. At Tarawa and Makin the percentage of suicides appeared to be lower than it had been on Attu, but many a Jap in the Gilberts pulled the pin of his grenade, tapped it on his helmet, and held it against his chest. Others lay in their foxholes, took off their shoes, pulled the triggers of their rifles with their toes, and shot themselves through the mouth or forehead. Our men who were in the Marshalls and at Palau and Angaur noted the same self-destructive performances. Officers of the Second and Fourth Marine Division said they believed the percentage of suicides was higher on Tinian than on any other island they had seen.

Perhaps the most fantastic suicidal performances occurred on Saipan. On the late afternoon of D Day (June 15) I saw the only attempt at hara-kiri disembowelment I ever saw. As I was digging a foxhole for the night, on the edge of the incompleted Charan - Kanoa airstrip, someone shouted, "There's a Jap in that hole!" and pointed to a log-covered sandhill about ten feet from where I was digging.

The words were hardly spoken before the Jap in the hole fired a wild shot over our heads and ran out: he was now armed with his bayonet only. A Marine tossed a concussion grenade at the tiny figure—the Jap was scrawny, and no more than five feet tall. The blast knocked him down. The Jap rose and pointed the bayonet not at his adversaries but at his own stomach. Before he could start carving himself, someone shot him, and nobody got to see the completed self-evisceration. For the Jap I will say this—he was tough. He rose again. The man with his carbine shot him again, then three more times. The last shot peeled off an inch of black-covered scalp and the Jap kicked, trembling in his death throes. We went back to digging our foxholes against the mortar barrages we knew would come throughout the night.

Probably the biggest counterattack of the Central Pacific war marked the finish of the Saipan battle (see p. 133), when about 2,000 Japs, maybe more, fell upon United States troops defending the west coast of the island. When it was over, the concentration of enemy dead was even thicker than it had been on Tarawa. In a space no more than 300 yards wide and hardly 2,000 yards long lay these estimated 2,000 Japs. (Figures on enemy dead were always guesswork.) In some places they were piled four deep. I estimated that one in four had killed himself; again the evidence was the missing hand and the missing chest.

In most battles where we were able to ascertain identity, we learned that the highest-ranking Jap officers had committed suicide. Sometimes they were surrounded by their staff officers, who also took their own lives when matters became hopeless. On Saipan, Lieut. General Yoshiji Saito attempted to lead the final *banzai* charge, but he was too old. Then he tried to kill himself but he was too clumsy, and his adjutant had to shoot him. But General Saito's final message to his troops furnished notable material for students of Japanese psychology:

"I am addressing the officers and men of the Imperial Army on Saipan.

"For more than twenty days, since the American devils attacked, the officers, men, and civilian employees of the Imperial Army and Navy on this island have fought well and bravely. Everywhere they have demonstrated the honor and glory of the Imperial Forces. I expected that every man would do his duty.

"Heaven has not given us an opportunity. We have not been able to utilize fully the terrain. We have fought in unison up to the present time, but now we have no materials with which to fight, and our artillery has been completely destroyed. Our comrades have fallen one after another. Despite the bitterness of defeat, we pledge 'seven lives to repay our country.'

"The barbarous attack of the enemy is being continued. Even though the enemy has occupied only a corner of Saipan,[1] we are dying without avail under the violent shelling and bombing. Whether we attack or whether we stay where we are, there is only death. However, in death there is life. We must use this opportunity to exalt true Japanese manhood. I will advance with those who remain to deliver still

[1] Actually, we had occupied about 65 per cent.

another blow to the American devils, and leave my bones on Saipan as a bulwark of the Pacific.

"As it is said in the *Senjikun* [battle ethics], 'I will never suffer the disgrace of being taken alive' and 'I will offer up the courage of my soul and calmly rejoice in living by the eternal principles.'

"Here I pray with you for the eternal life of the Emperor and the welfare of the country, and I advance to seek out the enemy. Follow me!"

The Americans on Saipan had learned to expect the "suicide-before-surrender" attitude in the Japanese soldier. What happened after the official close of the battle was something that nobody had anticipated; the civilians also started killing themselves. Like so many other actions of the Japanese, it had to be seen to be believed.

When we went into Saipan we did not know how many civilians were there. The 1935 population was given by one source as 23,000 of whom 3,000 were Micronesian Chamorros and Kanakas, the rest Japanese nationals, many of them peasants imported from the Ryukyu Islands (Okinawa) to work in the canefields. It seemed likely that even more civilians would have been imported since 1935 to help in the work on the fortifications. On the other hand, we knew attempts had been made to evacuate some civilians; just before the battle we sank ships from which women and children were rescued.

Therefore, the estimate of civilians was "20,000 to 30,000." We were curious to learn these civilians' reactions; would they be as fanatical as the soldiers? Would they attempt to arm themselves and fight? Would they destroy themselves rather than surrender? We hardly thought so. These we believed were not even Japanese from the home islands. They were from the Ryukyus, where hairy Ainu heredity predominated, where the culture was chiefly Chinese, where the Japanese had taken over completely only 65 years ago.

During the early stages of the battle, the Saipan civilians found their way through the Jap lines and surrendered in moderate numbers. On the eighth day 2,500 Japanese and Chamorros were in the civilian affairs stockade. The percentage of Chamorros was obviously higher, however, than their one-to-seven or one-to-ten ratio would warrant; the Chamorros surrendered eagerly. A week after the end of organized resistance on July 9 (the twenty-fifth day), there were 13,289 and six weeks later, after the civilians had streamed out of caves, 14,949 (Japanese 10,424, Chamorros 2,350, Koreans 1,300, Kanakas 875).

What happened to the other 7,000 or 17,000 Japanese civilians? Some, of course, were killed by artillery and bombs, but a tour of the island at various stages of the battle revealed surprisingly few of these. I did not believe I saw 100 civilians whom our fire had killed. Some were buried in caves where they had hidden with soldiers. Some men who might have been classed as civilians wore a sort of home-guard uniform—and a flamethrower made one uniform look about the same as any other.

A number that may never be determined committed suicide. From what I saw and from what other observers saw, I believe at least 1,000 Saipan civilians killed themselves. The number may have been much larger. Whatever it was, it was enough to indicate a fanaticism quite beyond the comprehension of Americans (See Chapter Eight).

A year after Saipan, Radio Tokyo quoted a poem from the newspaper *Mainichi* which paid tribute to school children on Aka, one of the small islands off Okinawa which had been seized by the Seventy-seventh Infantry Division. In the Japanese view, these children deserved the tribute because they "blasted themselves with hand grenades." Here are excerpts from the poem:

"Tears well up, involuntarily,
"Just to hear of them . . .
"Clutching tightly in their tiny palms
"Real fire-belching hand grenades . . .
"The tiny special attackers fell admirably,
"Like petals of a cherry blossom . . .
"The pitter-patter of their small army shoes
"Keeps pounding my breast, incessantly."

Part of the answer to the school children's attitude could be found on Okinawa. In a school house at Tokeshi village we found that each child in the now-abandoned classroom had been instructed to draw the same picture: a lean British Tommy lying prostrate on the floor, in two pieces, having been sliced in half by an eight-year-old Japanese child wielding a sword. Australian War Correspondent Alwyn Lee, noting the Union Jack which was the Tommy's armband, picked up one of the drawings and said, "My fellow Britisher is in trouble, I'll take him home with me." A week later some of these same children were waving at our tanks and jeeps, and shouting a new word they had learned—"Candy!"

Many of our high-ranking officers thought the trouble lay in our allowing the Japanese to have modern destructive machinery before we brought the Japanese concept of society beyond the Middle Ages, and at least one rueful admiral at Saipan privately advocated denying to the Japanese people for all time the use of the wheel.

To send the Japanese back to the Middle Ages was one solution—at least, they would be prevented from flying suicide planes into our ships. Bringing their concept of society up to date was the alternative, probably a more difficult alternative. During the war we learned that killing them was easier than teaching them. In talking to many Jap prisoners, in reading translations of many of their documents, I never saw or heard anything to indicate that the Jap had any conception of the rights or the freedom of the individual. It was all very well to say, So what? But we tried ignoring the loss of freedom in the rest of the world, and that attitude eventually dragged us into war, because the anti-freedom forces were able to muster great strength, with only a few voices raised against them.

The Japanese had to be re-educated against sadistic cruelty, against the totalitarianism implicit in Emperor worship, against presumptions of world domination. Their skill and their abilities had to be channeled for the right instead of the wrong. But to the man fighting the Jap this was an academic question. How can you re-educate a man who blows himself up before you can catch him? The suicide mania of the Japanese was symptomatic of their fanaticism. To the soldier or Marine who had to beat the Japs into submission (or suicide) the only trouble was that not enough of them killed themselves, or they waited in their caves too long. And they killed too many of our men first.

CHAPTER THREE

TOWARD THE MARIANAS

IT WAS JUNE 1, 1944, AND THE BRILLIANT SUNLIGHT OF HAWAII seemed to be made for a resort, not a great war base. I had just returned to the Pacific after five months in the States. From Tarawa and Makin the Pacific front line had already advanced 700 miles to Kwajalein, 400 more to Eniwetok. Now the longer hop, 1200 miles, was about to take us to the Marianas, to our own Guam, to the Japanese mandate capital, Saipan, to Tinian. In his office at Fort Shafter, outside Honolulu, Lieut. General Robert C. Richardson, the Army's Central Pacific commander, was saying, "This is where the serious phase of the war in the Pacific begins." The Marianas were nearer Tokyo in the north than to Kwajalein in the east, and Kwajalein had been ours only five months. Guam itself was like "an arrow aimed at the heart of Japan," an isolationist Congressman[1] had said in 1939 in arguing against the fortification of the island.

This was the plan for attacking the Marianas: On June 15 the Second and Fourth Marine Divisions would hit Saipan; on June 18 the Third Marine Division and the First Provisional Brigade (4th and 22nd Marines) were to attack Guam, 100 miles to the south. The Twenty-seventh Infantry Division was in floating reserve, and the Seventy-seventh Infantry Division, in area reserve, was to begin loading for departure on D Day plus 20. It was an ambitious schedule, and you will see how far we fell short of it.

I was already too late to board a transport in the Hawaiian Islands for either Saipan or Guam, but I could fly to Majuro or Eniwetok, the rendezvous areas, and accompany the troops

[1] Hamilton Fish, Jr.

from there. I chose to go to Eniwetok for the assault on Saipan.

June 4

The telephone operator at the Moana Hotel called me an hour after midnight. By 0130 I was in a taxi driving through the velvety, moonlit Hawaiian night toward the naval air station on Ford Island. At three o'clock the big PB2Y was grating over the water, pointing its nose upward and westward, and I was on the way to war for the fourth time since Pearl Harbor.

Five hours later we arrived at tiny, coral-dusty Johnston Island, and soon we were breakfasting on bacon and eggs in the excellent officers' mess at Johnston. Nine hours more, and the big seaplane was settling in the Kwajalein lagoon, off Ebeye Island, which the Seventh Infantry Division had wrested from the Japs in February. (On the southern Kwajalein islands the Seventh had killed 5,000 Japs at a cost of 177 United States lives.) A small boat took us five miles south to big (*i.e.*, three miles long) Kwajalein Island, where I received a blanket and a bunk was assigned to me in the transient officers' BOQ, a tent next to the power plant.

After supper I called up Captain Allen Rose of the 50th Army Engineers, whom I had known before the war and had last seen on Attu. Allen came by in a jeep, and we drove to Seventh Air Force headquarters to see Maj. General Willis Hale. We waited until General Hale came out of the B movie which was being shown under canvas next to his quarters.

General Hale had been in the war almost from its beginning. I had first met him on the way back from Australia in 1942, when his headquarters were in Hawaii. A year later I had seen him at Funafuti, in the Ellice Islands, his new headquarters, when I was returning from Tarawa. Now he was on Kwajalein, and was getting ready to move to Saipan as soon as that island had been cleared of Japs.

The Seventh was not a big air force, in terms of European

air power, or even of the Fifth and Thirteenth Air Forces in the Southwest Pacific. Hale's pilots (and the land-based Navy and Marine pilots) performed the vital but often dreary task of pinning down the Japs in the by-passed islands like Jaluit, Maloelap, Mili and Wotje in the Marshalls, and in the flanking islands like Ponape and Truk in the Carolines. These Army, Navy and Marine pilots also did most of the scouting and patrolling of thousands of square miles of the Pacific. They were the eyes of the immediate Pacific, just as the submarines were the eyes of the China Sea, the Philippine Sea, and the waters around Japan.

There was more glamour, more glory, and more danger in carrier duty, but Hale's men took their losses, too. Pictures of the by-passed Marshalls showed these islands as a series of overlapping bomb craters, but the tenacious Japs still shot down planes once in a while (a year later they were still at it). "What have these kids got to look forward to, except decorations and leave?" Willis Hale asked. A man had to have established leave policy. At one time the Seventh's losses rose to four per cent per mission. The general started giving his men leave (or relief from combat) after 30 missions, and losses dropped. Ten missions over the flanking islands, or twenty over the by-passed Marshalls, were worth an Air Medal to Hale's flyers.

General Hale—like most airmen, but unlike most foot soldiers—was contemptuous of the Japs: "Where is this face-saving of theirs? Of course, the Japs commit individual suicide. But what have they done to retaliate for all we've done to them in the past year? Where is their carrier strike against Honolulu? I don't think they've got anything to do it with. They can't retaliate after blows like the one the carriers made on Palau at the end of March [when at least 25 ships were sunk, 160 planes destroyed]. Besides, the Japs can't build like we can. They haven't got anything that can touch the bulldozer."

During the night, rain tumbled out of the sky as though a million buckets of water had been tipped over. In our tent, eight of us swore, sadly viewed our seabags and canvas suitcases, turned our mattresses over, and went back to sleep. Kwajalein was too hot in the daytime. At night it was pleasant—if no rain fell.

June 6 (East Longitude)

At 0730 the C-47 took off from Kwajalein, headed north. We were now traveling on one of the TAG (Transport Air Group) planes which shuttled between Kwajalein, Eniwetok, Majuro, and Tarawa. The fact that these planes flew every day past islands where Japs were still stranded rarely bothered anyone. "Let the bastards stay there until they rot and starve, if it is possible for a Jap to starve, if not, let them die of old age," said the Army captain who sat beside me. Then he added: "I don't know, though. Maybe they are inter-marrying with the natives and raising up a new generation of half-Japs."

It was only twenty minutes before we landed at Roi, which the Fourth Marine Division had taken (along with its twin sand-spit, Namur) in 27 hours in February, after killing the 3,472 Japs there and capturing 99 prisoners. About 200 white crosses near the Roi airfield told us that men had given their lives in order that we might land in the northern islands of the Kwajalein atoll.

As we waited beside the plane, a squadron of Marine-piloted F4U fighters took off on their morning patrol. A Ventura bomber followed them. After a while we took off again in Captain Maloney's shuttle plane, this time on a two-hour northwestward flight to Engebi, the northernmost island of the Eniwetok lagoon. On Engebi there were F4U's to intercept enemy aircraft (of which there had been some), and SBD's and a few B-25's for interception of enemy warships (of which there had been none). Engebi, said the Marine lieutenant who met our plane, had cost the 22nd Marine Regiment about 50 killed, as against 800 Japs. Some of the 22nd Marines also went into the southern Eniwetok islands to assist the 106th Infantry Regiment in cleaning them up.

The Marshalls were the best evidence of what we learned at Tarawa about assaulting atolls, though neither in Kwajalein nor Eniwetok were the Jap fortifications as formidable as they had been at Tarawa. Adding together the announced casualty figures for Kwajalein and Eniwetok produced the following figures: Jap dead 11,000; United States dead 666 (247 soldiers, 419 Marines), United States missing six (all Marines), United States wounded 2,612 (1,265 soldiers, 1,347 Marines).

Only a few minutes were required to fly the 20 miles from Engebi to Eniwetok Island. The OOD assigned bunks to us in the big double Quonset hut, where there were already 35 junior officers, most of whom were waiting for their ships to come in. (Ensigns and j.g.'s were always looking for their ships; I knew one ensign, earlier in the war, who had been looking all over the Pacific for eight months.)

About 1930, soon after dark, everybody turned out for the movies; there were half a dozen screens scattered about little Eniwetok Island. Before the movies started, a news summary was read to the audience, which at this particular screening consisted of sailors in blue dungarees and navy officers and Marines in khaki. The news announcer was Lieutenant Robb White, the Episcopal minister's son from my home town in Georgia, whom I was seeing for the first time in more than 15 years. Said White: "There was a lot of excitement stateside today. A 22-year-old English girl in the AP office in London was practicing on the teletype. She announced that the invasion of France had begun. It was denied, and everybody back home felt let down." White told of the fighting in Italy, and of the Biak peninsular battle where General MacArthur's soldiers were fighting. Then he said, "That's all the news I have, and the motion-picture operators are getting impatient."

It was a beautiful night. The moon was brilliant. The palm fronds rustled softly in the cooling breeze. There were few clouds in the sky.

This was the setting when White came back three minutes later and told the audience quite calmly, "Here is a piece of news that has just come in—the invasion of Europe has just been announced." The 400-odd sailors and Marines stood up and let out one great cheer. To them the beginning of the end of one war meant a step in winning their own particular war, half an earth away. Not that there was loud and prolonged cheering; the immediate war was the personal concern of the men at the movie on Eniwetok. But the distant European news meant, perhaps, that the Pacific war would be shortened, and the time when the sailors and Marines could go home was nearer at hand.

June 7

On this morning I walked around the island with Lieut. Commander William C. Mott, who was waiting to join Vice Admiral Richmond Kelly Turner's staff as flag secretary. Bill Mott had graduated from the Naval Academy, then he had resigned from the Navy to study law, and practice in Washington. The job he got when he went back into the Navy was a fine one; he tended the White House's super-secret map room. He knew, almost as well as Roosevelt and Churchill, what was going on in those early, critical months of the war. A man who could be trusted with secrets, Bill did not say much about what he learned. He did say that when Churchill came down to the map room after breakfast, his usual greeting was: "How's Hitler this morning, the bahstard?"

The Eniwetok airstrip was crowded with F6F Hellcats, which would be used as carrier replacement planes, and with B-24's and B-25's. Mott and I stopped at one B-24 (PB4Y in

Navy designation) named "Thunder Mug," which had literally dozens of bombs painted on it, one for each mission. "That's 'Bus' Miller's plane," said a sailor; "he's a madman."

Commander Norman Miller, an "old man" of 36, was indeed a "madman"—the sort of skilled madman who was doing so much to win the war against Japan. I never got to meet him, but I knew who he was because his fame had spread throughout the Pacific. "Bus" Miller's favorite objective was Truk, 800 miles southwest of Eniwetok. "Miller's Reluctant Raiders," as his squadron was called, sank 43 ships in seven and one-half months, and probably sank or damaged 91 others. Of these, Miller himself sank 20 ships totaling 35,500 tons, mostly cargo ships, but including one destroyer and one tanker. With the Navy pilot's ingrained contempt for high-level bombing, Miller flew over Truk at night at 50 feet or 100 feet, in spite of the size of his plane, which made it a prime target. He was wounded once by a shrapnel burst, but he stayed out only six days. Nobody begrudged Commander Miller his Navy Cross, his four DFC's and four Air Medals, nor his eventual reassignment home where his wife and five children were waiting for him.

The opening, in the afternoon, of the Eniwetok officers' club (beer and gin only) was a notable occasion. The Seabees, who made Eniwetok the neatest shipshape base I had yet seen in the Pacific, outdid themselves in building the two-story Quonset with screened-in porches, and long, elaborately-illustrated bar. Captain Edgar A. ("Bat") Cruise, the naval aviator who was the atoll commander, was proud of his club, prouder of his atoll.

His guests this afternoon included Admiral Raymond Spruance, the modest Hoosier who commanded the Fifth Fleet, Vice Admiral John S. McCain, who had come out to alternate with Vice Admiral Marc Mitscher as a fast carrier task force commander, and a lot of other rank. (Said Admiral Spruance: "This next operation is going to be tough ashore, but I've got a lot of faith in the Marines.") But more impressive than the admirals were a dozen nurses off the hospital ship *Bountiful*, the first white women to set foot on Eniwetok. To men hungry for the sight of a woman the nurses looked good, even if they wore unflattering slacks instead of frills.

June 8

The transports arrived today with the Saipan assault troops. The shooting looked closer. It always looked closer when Kelly Turner and Holland Smith showed up.

An amphibious operation of any size is a big undertaking. The Marianas operation, which involved 775 ships, more than 100,000 foot soldiers and nearly 250,000 sailors, was by far the biggest we had attempted in the Pacific. The chain of command will indicate, in skeleton fashion, just what the size of the operation entailed. It cannot indicate the amount of planning nor the amount of material necessary for us to take Saipan and Guam and Tinian.

Admiral Nimitz, at his desk in Pearl Harbor, bossed the whole show.

Admiral Spruance was on-the-spot commander of the land, sea, and air forces involved.

Under Spruance there were two vice admirals, Mitscher and Turner.

Mitscher, in charge of the fast carrier task force, had as his duty during the Saipan landings to range up and down the Western Pacific, knocking out Jap airfields at places like Iwo Jima, Rota, Guam, and Tinian. Still under Spruance's direction, he had to protect the landings against interference by Jap naval and air forces.

Turner commanded the amphibious landings. This meant he had to get the troops ashore, after his bombardment units (old battleships, cruisers, destroyers) had shelled the beaches. He also had to maintain supply for the troops ashore, and to protect them from outside interference which might get

35

through Mitscher. In addition, he had to furnish air support (from his small escort carriers, and from Mitscher's big carriers whenever necessary) and bombardment support after the troops were on the island. His was probably the most involved job of all, and only a demon for detail could do it, as he insisted on doing it, almost single-handed.

Under Turner the Number One man was a lieutenant general of Marines, Holland Smith. At the beginning of the Marianas operation old "Howlin' Mad" was in a transition stage. He was commanding the V Amphibious Corps, which meant the Second and Fourth Marine Divisions, plus whatever Army units were attached. But by now there was another amphibious corps under Maj. General Roy Geiger, the III, which included the Third Marine Division, the First Provisional Brigade, plus Army troops if it became necessary to call on them. (It was.) So, Smith was about to give up the V Amphibious Corps (to Maj. General Harry Schmidt) and take over Fleet Marine Force, Pacific, which would include both the III and V Amphibious Corps. But for the Saipan landing he was still commander, FIFTHPHIBCORPS, or VAC (V for five, A for amphibious, C for corps). Smith took charge of the troops after Turner got them on the beach.

Under Holland Smith at Saipan there were two division commanders, Maj. General Thomas E. Watson of the Marines' Second and Schmidt of the Marines' Fourth. If it became necessary to commit any other ground troops, these would also become Smith's responsibility. That was how the Twenty-seventh Infantry Division, commanded by Maj. General Ralph Smith and fighting as a division for the first time, came under his command, sooner than anybody expected. Because Saipan turned out to be very tough.

I had been assigned to the Second Marine Division, which I had accompanied into Tarawa. General Watson's assistant division commander, Brig. General Merritt A. Edson, was a friend from Tarawa, so I asked to be assigned to his troop transport. It was the *Bolivar,* Captain Robert Paul Wadell,

United States Navy, and it carried the commodore of Transport Division 28 (six ships, Captain Henry Clinton Flanagan).

The Second Division, which was my immediate concern, had three infantry regiments of about 3,300 men each (the 2nd, 6th, 8th), one artillery regiment (the 10th), and an engineer regiment (the 18th). The 2nd Regiment was commanded by Colonel Walter J. Stuart. His three 900-man battalions were commanded by Lieut. Colonels Wood B. Kyle, Richard Nutting, and Arnold F. Johnston. The 6th Regiment was commanded by Colonel James P. Riseley (battalion c.o.'s: William K. Jones, Raymond Murray, John Easley). The 8th, under Colonel Clarence R. Wallace, had as battalion commanders Lawrence C. Hays, Jr., Henry P. ("Jim") Crowe, Jack Miller, Jr. The artillery regiment was commanded by Colonel Raphael Griffin, the engineers by Colonel Cyril W. Martyr.

Aboard the *Bolivar* with General Edson and his ADC (assistant division commander) staff were Colonel Riseley's headquarters and the headquarters of the First Battalion, 6th Marines[2] and its A Company. It was with this battalion that I spent much of my time on Saipan.

June 9

Aboard Admiral Turner's flagship I saw General Holland Smith. Of him I will say this—throughout the Central Pacific campaign he estimated the enemy capabilities better than any other individual I talked to.[3] He said: "We are through

[2] A source of considerable confusion, especially for headline readers, was the custom of calling a Marine regiment "The Xth Marines." Thus, although the 1st Marines are in the First Division and the 2nd Marines in the Second, the 4th Marines are in the Sixth Division, the 5th Marines in the First Division, and the 6th Marines in the Second Division. To Marines "the 4th Marines" means the 4th regiment, not the Fourth Division, whose infantry regiments are numbered 23, 24, 25. Likewise, in the Army the "32d Infantry" refers to the regiment (which is in the Seventh Division), not to the Thirty-Second Division.

[3] Examples: "Iwo Jima will cost 15,000 men," and "Okinawa, 50,000 casualties"

with the flat atolls now. We learned how to pulverize atolls, but now we are up against mountains and caves where the Japs can dig in." Then he said slowly, "A week from today there will be a lot of dead Marines." Generals have to have confidence in their troops, just as troops must have faith in their generals, but Old Man Smith worshipped his beloved Marines.

June 10

Early this morning on his flag bridge aboard the *Rocky Mount*, Admiral Turner told me: "Yes, Saipan is going to be a tough one. But I think we have planned it well."

In the afternoon I went aboard the transport *Bolivar*, paid my respects to the commodore, Captain Flanagan, to Captain Wadell and General Edson. The *Bolivar*, the first new transport I had ever been aboard (one great naval shortage up to Saipan had been transports) had been commissioned about a year earlier, and stout, good-natured Captain Wadell had taken command in December after serving aboard the *South Dakota* at the Battle of Santa Cruz and aboard the recently rebuilt *California*. (She became an imitation *South Dakota*.) Wadell's able executive officer was one of the more interesting men aboard. James Linn Rogers had graduated from the Naval Academy in 1912, had been retired as a commander in 1928 because his hearing was faulty. He returned to active duty as a commander, but volunteered to take a reduction to lieutenant commander in order to go overseas. This despite the fact that many of his classmates were admirals.

My roommate was Lieut. Colonel William K. Jones, c. o. of 1/6, at 27 the youngest battalion commander in the Marine Corps. On a crowded troop transport (and the transports were always crowded) rank is very important, because it means the difference between being assigned to a cool, topside cabin or a stifling cabin on a lower deck. Having gone into Tarawa in a 100-degree room with seven junior officers, I felt promoted on going into Saipan in a topside cabin with only one roommate. (But war correspondents' promotions are fickle; months later, going into Okinawa, I had dropped a couple of ranks and was sharing a room with two others. Not that it mattered.)

The clang-clang-clang of "general quarters" sounded an hour before midnight. The Japs had made several fairly successful raids on Eniwetok, and they would never again pick a better time to catch a lot of ships in the harbor. On his bridge Captain Wadell yawned, and said, "All right, come on and drop your bombs, and let us go back to sleep." But the "raiders" turned out to be seven of our own planes.

June 11

General "Red Mike" Edson said: "This one is not going to be easy. Maybe I'm wrong and I hope I am, but you know I've got a reputation as a pessimist." I said that I hadn't seen anything since Tarawa, and I couldn't feel very optimistic myself; I had missed the "easy" victories of Kwajalein and Eniwetok, but some of the correspondents told me they felt that the Pacific war was a "pushover" henceforth; we had learned how to do it. Said Edson, with a fleeting smile, "The correspondents aren't the only ones in that frame of mind."

Today, four days before we hit the beaches of Saipan, we sailed out of Eniwetok lagoon. The sea was placid, the sunlight brilliant, and the force the most powerful we had ever sent against the Pacific enemy. As far as we could see, on the portside and on the starboard, there were American ships—transports, destroyers, cruisers, LST's, LSD's, small carriers, battleships. In our force, according to Captain Paul Coloney, the naval observer who lectured in the wardroom today, there are 506 ships.

Commander Saint Clair-Ford of the British Navy, who had come along to see how the Americans handled this amphibious warfare, wanted some instruction in firing the .45

pistol. Bill Jones, who handled weapons as effortlessly as a mother handles her third baby, offered to show him how to fire the gun. We went to the stern of the ship, threw bottles overboard, and fired for half an hour. I was much better than Saint Clair-Ford and told him so. He said, "Never mind; I picked up Mountbatten after his ship was sunk, and you never did that."

Commander Glenn English, the Sixth Regiment surgeon, who left Indiana to practice medicine in Hollywood, undertook to administer to me those evil necessities of war, booster shots of tetanus and smallpox vaccine. Yes, he said, the troops would get steak and eggs for breakfast before they went into battle; the 6th, like all Second Division regiments, had learned in New Zealand to like steak with eggs. "No good for punctured guts," he said, "but excellent psychologically."

June 12

Shortly after noon, fire broke out in Number 5 hold. Nothing frightens men at sea as does fire. Somebody had dropped a cigarette on a rope cargo net, setting it afire. The Marines jeered at the sailors who ran along the decks, "Ain't he pretty—helmet and everything!"

Today's lecture in the stifling wardroom concerned the Japanese possibilities on Saipan. The division language officer, bespectacled Captain Eugene P. Boardman, said: "We are going to run into Japanese civilians for the first time in this war. There are about 20,000 or 30,000 of them, and we believe about 3,000 of the men form a sort of home guard." Captain Thomas C. Dutton, ADC-2 (assistant division intelligence officer) told as much as he knew about enemy fortifications from studying aerial photographs; how many coastal guns, how many anti-aircraft guns, probable troop strength (estimated total: 19,000).[4]

After Tom Dutton had finished, blonde Lieut. Colonel

---

[4] It turned out that there were about 30,000.

Rathvon McC. ("Tommy") Tompkins, the assistant division operations officer, got up and said: "This is going to be a tough one; there's no use kidding ourselves. But here's the good side of it: we've got the biggest fleet in history with us—new battleships, new carriers, new special equipment." He was followed by Edson: "We have got to be able to take command of the division, in case anything happens to the division commander and his staff. From the time we leave the ship until the commanding general gets ashore, we will be in command. We have to go in early and pick the initial division command post. Every man knows his own particular job, but he may be called upon to take on other jobs, because we have to count on casualties among the staff as well as the infantry command."

Bill Jones told me there were two men aboard who had stowed away at Pearl Harbor. They were old 6th Marines who had been transferred to rear area duty; now they wanted to be with the outfit when it went into combat. "Yes, they're supposed to be disciplined, but what can you do with men like that?" he asked. There were others from the rear echelon who had done some "arranging" to make the trip to Saipan: Major Charles Janvier, of New Orleans, the division legal officer, had had himself designated graves registration officer. Captain Orien W. Todd, the division recreation and morale officer, who had managed the San Diego baseball team before the war, came along as Janvier's assistant. Janvier and Todd actually knew little about graves registration, but they had competent sergeants who did, and they actually had to work as hard as anybody else on Saipan. They took considerable "ribbing" from other officers. "How can you tell if a man is dead?" someone asked Todd. "It's simple," he said; "wave a picture of Betty Grable in his face, then a bottle of Scotch, then say 'here's a stateside ticket.' If he doesn't respond, we'll know he's dead."

June 13

Today was D minus 2. The news from Mitscher's carriers, which were preparing the way for the landing, was good. The Hellcat pilots had knocked down 124 planes off Saipan, while losing eleven planes and eight pilots from one group; one Hellcat and two SBD's from another. West of Pagan Island, between Saipan and Iwo Jima, a Japanese convoy was caught while steaming south; ten ships sunk, ten damaged. Another group reported that it caught five ships, four destroyers, and one cargo ship: "sank all." The canefields on Saipan, which might afford cover for Jap snipers, were reported "burning merrily." Mitscher's message was full of an airman's enthusiasm: "Keep coming, Marines, they're going to run away." The Marines were grateful for the magnificent work of the carrier men; their landings could never have succeeded if the Jap planes hadn't been knocked out. But they had been in this war long enough to know that the Japs were not going to run away.

A brief episode in the vast, tragic panorama of war: A destroyer brought along mail for the troops, but mistakenly unloaded a sack which should have gone to the Third Battalion, 8th Marines. I couldn't help thinking: "A lot of men in 3/8 will die without ever having read that last letter from home."

General Edson asked me if I wanted to go ashore with him. I said I did. He planned to leave the ship as soon as the assault troops were unloaded, and go to a patrol boat to await a signal to land and set up a command post.

June 14

Final communion services were held. About 100 men sweltered through Protestant services in the troop messing compartment. Not many more attended Catholic services on the breeze-cooled deck later in the afternoon. This day before D day was less tense than it had been at Tarawa. An air of quiet confidence permeated the conversation of these veterans. Every man, I suppose, considered the possibility of death, but nobody spoke of it. Death is something that happens to the other fellow. If men did not believe that, they would be more reluctant to go into battle. Many times throughout the war I heard of men who had a premonition of death but I never talked to one. I never heard a man say that he felt he was going to get it.

Before they go into battle men always build up their own spirits. It had to be that way. Even Colonel Riseley, who had to be prepared for any eventuality, took part in the general enthusiasm. Before midnight he came in and said: "I've just got a hunch this is going to be the easiest one of all."

CHAPTER FOUR

THE INVASION OF SAIPAN

WE WERE UP AT 4 O'CLOCK. AT CHOW, 45 MINUTES LATER, there was an air of tense alertness. Back packs were scattered about the wardroom; men who were eating their last hot meal in many days—and some men who were eating their last meal—piled helmets, pistol belts, knives, canteens, on the deck. There was a report that the transport *Monrovia* almost ran over a group of Japs whose ship had been sunk. A destroyer picked up all the Japs it could find. The Navy had been at work before the Marines arrived.

At 0530 Saipan was dead ahead, a shadowy land mass purple against the dim horizon. Two fires were burning brightly south of the mountain. Already some sailors were in their boats (LCVP's) which would haul the Marines to the transfer point. The amphtracs (LVT2's, Buffaloes) which would take them the rest of the way in, were ready to be lowered whenever the *Bolivar* stopped. Their engines were coughing as if to protest against so early arousing. From the bridge I noticed the flag fluttering briskly in the D Day dawn. Came the signal "Execute! Speed zero!" The signal flags were swung aloft, and the transports of our division settled to a halt.

At 0545 the rumble of the big guns crashed the quiet. The battleships, cruisers, and destroyers—already at work for two days—had begun their final softening up of the beaches. The great, explosive shells arched through the sky, and exploded against the land mass. Like so many flies the Marines began crawling down the cargo nets into the lowered boats. The thud of the battleship guns was jarring, even at 18,700 yards from the island.

From our transport, Saipan in profile looked like a low-lying prehistoric monster, whose spine rose in the center to 1,554-foot Mount Tapotchau. On our maps Saipan was shaped like a pistol pointing northward toward Tokyo (see map on p. 49). We were attacking on the west side, along the top of the butt of the pistol. The Second Division was to land on a 1,500-yard beach north of the sugar-mill town of Charan-Kanoa (one-time population: 2,500), the Fourth Division on a similar front south of the town. There would be a 500-yard gap between the two forces, at Afetna Point, and this gap must be closed as soon as possible, because the Afetna Point pier with its deep water channel was needed for the landing of heavier supplies. Until we seized pier and channel all our troops and all our equipment except tanks had to be sent ashore in amphtracs which must climb over a jagged reef extending unevenly 350 to 1,750 yards offshore. This reef was barely under water, and no boats except tracked vehicles could cross it.

Over the loudspeaker came Chaplain Cunningham's voice: "With the help of God we will succeed . . . most of you will return, but some of you will meet the God who made you . . . Repent your sins . . . those of the Jewish faith repeat after me [here he read some lines from the Hebrew service manual] . . . now Christian men, Protestants and Catholics, repeat after me . . ." When the chaplain said: 'Some of you will meet God," Lieut. Colonel Colonel "Tommy" Tompkins, who was standing beside me on deck, said "Perish-the-thought department."

By 0630, about half our troops were loaded into amphtracs, or into LCVP's which would take the later waves part of the way prior to the amphtrac relay. This was different from Tarawa. Now there were enough of the amphibious craft to take everybody ashore, so the reef around the island held no peril such as the Tarawa reef had held. Nobody would have to wade ashore except men who survived the hits on their amphtracs in the water. This was not the only improvement since Tarawa—here were many more planes and many more big guns to blaze the way for the men who must go ashore. But we all reserved the suspicion that the additional firepower would be partially nullified by the mountainous nature of the Jap hillside and cave defenses which no explosives could reach.

At Saipan we knew already what the reef and beach were like. For this we could be grateful to a small band of gallant men, the underwater demolition men. The correspondents could not write about underwater demolition teams at Saipan; the first public mention I ever saw of them appeared nearly a year later in Admiral King's official report. But we quickly learned how valuable they were.

The underwater demolition teams at Saipan were in charge of the officer who was their leading exponent, Lieut. Commander Draper Kauffman, son of the admiral commanding cruisers and destroyers in the Pacific. Draper Kauffman was lean, heavily sunburned, and an expert swimmer. He was an Academy graduate, but he had resigned from the Navy because he had weak eyes; he wore thick-lensed glasses. When war brought him back into the service he unhesitatingly jumped in with both feet.

After Tarawa, it was obvious that we needed to know more about the immediate approaches to these islands we had to invade. Draper Kauffman began gathering (at Fort Pierce, Fla.) expert swimmers who were not scared of anything. The plan: A day or two before we attempted a landing these men would leave their minesweepers or LCI gunboats and get into rubber boats; then they would move to within a couple of thousand yards of shore. There they would get out of their little boats and swim in the rest of the way, diving to find out the depth of the water and the condition of the reef. They would also take demolition charges to blow up obstacles; the Japs had a habit of planting concrete or steel posts offshore to keep our amphtracs from reaching the beach.

All the time, of course, the underwater demolition men were under fire from the Japs on the shore, even though heavy gunfire from our own ships helped to keep the Japs in their holes. At Saipan, Kauffman had 80 men and 24 officers. Only 16 were killed or wounded—which was a miracle. Kauffman had both sailors and Marines in his teams; he thought the volunteers he got among eager-beaver Seabees were as fine as any. As the war progressed we learned more and more about underwater demolition. In my estimation the UDT men rated as high as the submariners or the assault troops of the first waves.

Time after time the Jap radio would announce, just prior to the invasion of an island, that "an American attempt at landing was repulsed with heavy casualties to the enemy." That meant that on D minus 1 or 2 or 3 the underwater demolition men had gone in and had come back with the information we needed before the real landing took place.

Following the ships' bombardment, the air strikes began at 0700. It was a thrilling sight to see the waves of planes appear out of the east and the north, sweep down on the island (which was now burning in several spots) and loose their bombs. Seeing them reminded us that we had accomplished two of the prerequisites: Complete air and naval superiority. From the transport we could only judge by the thump of bombs and the clouds of smoke and dust which were left in the wake of the bombs. Within a very few minutes the whole of the area back of our landing beaches was obscured by these columns. One trouble about pinpointing land targets is this—the smoke and the dust cover the target, and the pilots cannot always see what they are trying to hit. After a while they can only let go in the general area of their targets, and hope that they get hits. Anyway, I wrote in my notebook at the time, "I fear all this smoke and noise does not mean many Japs been killed."

At 0745 I climbed into LCVP Number PA-34-25 with General Edson and his staff. In a few minutes we transferred to Subchaser Number 1052, and started rolling in toward the rendezvous point. It was still several hours before we would start for shore, but the old feeling of anxiety was already there: "Will I ever see this ship again; will I ever make it all the way down that long, watery road from ship to shore?"

Sergeant Albert Tardiff, who had been with General Edson ever since Guadalcanal, was manning one of the radios we had loaded onto the SC. He looked up at 0805 (25 minutes before H Hour) and said, "The planes say there is no sign of life on Aslito Airfield [three miles south of where we should land], but the light and heavy anti-aircraft guns along the railroad track have not been touched yet." Saipan was still only an outline—we were six miles offshore—but it began to look like a furnace seen through a haze. The warships were closing in, belching fire as they went, until the ships themselves seemed to be surrounded by the orange smoke which poured out of their gun barrels. Admiral Turner radioed an order that H Hour be postponed until 0840.

Captain Tom Dutton read a report he was receiving over one of the radios: "The first waves are 2,000 yards from Beaches Blue and Yellow (Fourth Division) and 1,000 yards from Red and Green (Second Division)." The 2d Marines were in Second Division reserve behind the 6th and the 8th which meant only that they would lie offshore until General Watson ordered them to land on one beach or another. Likewise in the Fourth Division, the 23rd and 24th Marines were the assault regiments, with the 25th in reserve.

Dutton kept repeating what he heard on the radio: "There is enemy machine-gun fire on boats going into Red Beaches"; "The boats are climbing the reef on Red Beach Two"; "Now laying down the first protective line 1,500 yards inland from Red Beach Two."

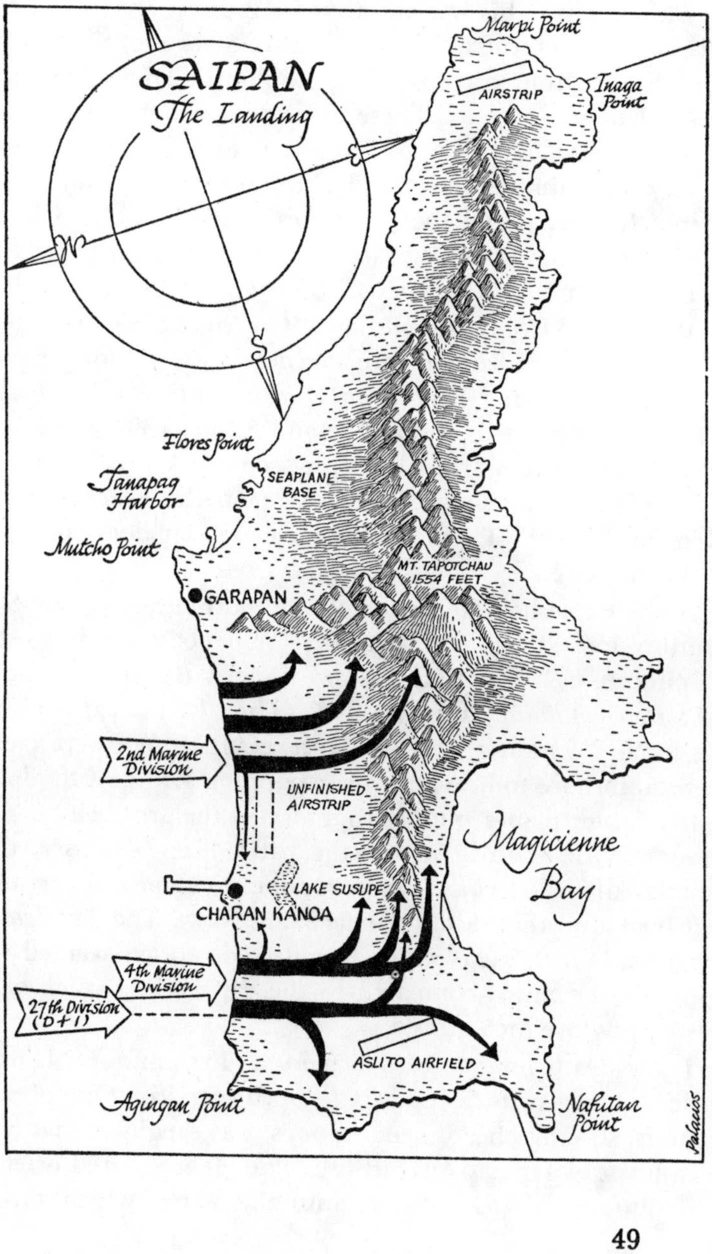
SAIPAN
The Landing
N
S
Marpi Point
AIRSTRIP
Inaga Point
Flores Point
Tanapag Harbor
SEAPLANE BASE
Mutcho Point
GARAPAN
MT. TAPOTCHAU 1554 FEET
2nd Marine Division
UNFINISHED AIRSTRIP
Magicienne Bay
LAKE SUSUPE
CHARAN KANOA
4th Marine Division
27th Division (D+1)
ASLITO AIRFIELD
Agingan Point
Nafutan Point
Palacios

This was it. This was the time of greatest anxiety in the lives of several thousand men, the assault waves of the Second Division in front of us, and of the Fourth Division a mile and a half south of us. These men were facing a crisis such as man should not have to face often in a lifetime; within a very few minutes they would be dead or alive—and only a thin line separated the two states. Some lived, and some died; fate alone made the decision; a man could not stand it if he did not believe that to be true.

We were 3,000 yards offshore. The smoke and the dust of the beaches of Saipan were so thick it was no longer possible to see towering Tapotchau. Dutton continued his chant: "They are 200 yards from Blue and Yellow, 300 from Red and Green; planes are still getting some AA fire."

At 0845 1/2 he shouted: "They're on the beaches; both Red and Green!" Then, "Anti-boat fire so far does not seem to be effective."

A shell splashed 150 yards off the port beam of our SC. Dutton looked up and grinned: 'Somebody seems to be sniping at us." From its size, we judged the shell to be a 37-mm. or 40-mm. anti-boat shell. Then he turned back to his radio: "Landing seems to be successful." We were close enough inshore to hear the grease-popping sound of the low-flying fighter planes' guns as they strafed the area behind the beaches. Our SC drifted past the battleship *Tennessee*, the veteran old *Blisterbutt* whose gunners claimed she could outshoot any other ship in Uncle Sam's Navy. The *Tennessee* let go a 14-inch salvo which, I reflected, always seemed incongruously muted compared to the ear-rending crack of a destroyer's five-inch guns.

I saw death for one of our men, at four minutes before nine. It was a swift death, and I hoped merciful. One of our fighters, strafing ahead of our troops, was caught at 700 feet by a burst of Jap anti-aircraft fire. The Hellcat flared briefly, and plummeted just offshore into the water, which extinguished the flame as quickly as it did the life of the pilot. But other men in other planes came behind the man who had died, flying even lower and strafing angrily to avenge their comrade.

By nine o'clock the tree-dotted foothills of Tapotchau were burning fiercely in spots. The second and third and fourth waves were reported ashore. Colonel Wallace had already left for the beach, we were told from the patrol boat as we went alongside. There was more anti-boat fire on either side of our SC, but nothing within 200 yards. "Troops are advancing standing up on Square 170." "Have just located gun position on Square 170." We moved within 2,000 yards of the beach, inside the line of battleships and cruisers.

"Third battalion, 6th, is 100 yards inland, and 2/6 is all ashore, but don't know how far. Lieut. Colonel Jack Miller, battalion commander of 3/8, has been hit, but we don't know how badly. Colonel Jones of 1/6 has been ordered to the transfer area [where the troops moved from LCVP's to amphtracs]" Bill Jones' battalion was in regimental reserve; 2/6 and 3/6 were Colonel Riseley's assault battalions.

At 0940 General Edson pointed to the island and said, "Nice gasoline fire over there." But I noted that there were only two fires still visible on Saipan by this time. The sugar mill at Charan-Kanoa, a prime target, was a smoldering ruin, but that was all, and Jap snipers could hold out a long time inside a smoldering ruin. The ships' guns and the bombs had wrought whatever damage they were going to work. From now on until we got a firm toehold on the beach the immediate job of killing Japs was up to the rifleman, the machine gunner, and the man with the flame thrower.

Three miles to the north, off Tanapag Harbor, we could see the destruction already accomplished by the carrier pilots. Four big Jap ships had been sunk; two of them had settled on the bottom, with their decks awash; two of them were sunk in water so deep that only their tall masts were

51

showing. Three smaller ships were flopped over on their sides, nearer inshore. What a shame that we had not found a way to dispose of Japs on land as efficiently as we knocked them out of the water!

By 1000 hour we could assemble the pieces of the jigsaw puzzle and construct some kind of picture of what was happening ashore, although up to then we had been forced to rely mostly on air observers' reports. It was evident that the early waves had got ashore without too much difficulty. Some amphtracs had turned over on the reef. Some had been hit, and their occupants killed in the water. One was visible on the reef three hundred yards to our left. Several more were reported knocked out and burning on the beach; they had been hit as soon as they reached shore. Eight of these exploded on Green Beach 1. Requests were pouring in for LVT's (amphtracs) to bring ammunition and to evacuate casualties. There was no doubt that the beach was hot, and it looked as though it were going to become hotter. (2/6 had just reported to 3/6 that "We are 75 to 100 yards from the road and are meeting heavy machine-gun fire"). But there was no doubt, either, that our landing had been successful.

An amphtrac crawled up to our little ship and asked permission to put aboard a man who had died as he was being evacuated from the beach. Permission was refused. Said "Tommy" Tompkins, "We couldn't do anything but haul him around all day." He paused, and added, "If I ever catch it, I want 'em just to push me over the side."

Bill Jones' 1/6 battalion was ordered to land at 1015 in support of the other two 6th Marine battalions. By this time, mortar fire on the Red Beaches was heavy, and both commanders of the assault battalions, Ray Murray and John Easley, had been wounded; casualties inshore were rising rapidly. The beachhead, which air observers reported variously as 200 to 500 yards deep, was actually little more than 100 yards. The time they picked to send in Jones approximately coincided with the time when the Japs recovered from the bombardment and began finding the range on the amphtracs as they rolled through the water.

Jones' battalion caught hell as it approached the shore. He wrote me about it much later: "The Jap mortar and artillery fire registered on the reef knocked hell out of our formation, and the companies became widely separated. Instead of landing on Red Beach 2, as ordered, we landed C Company on Red 1, A on Red 2, and B on Red 3. Incidentally, no outfit had landed on Red 3, so B Company found themselves with a virgin bunch of Nips wanting to play. This private party kept B Company interested for about an hour. The fascinating part of it for B Company's Captain Claude G. Rollen was that he had no contact on either the right or the left, and his radio was wrecked in the landing. This was not so fascinating to me—since, while this 'increment' was having himself an exclusive picnic, I was trying to find out where the hell he was, or even if he still 'was.' In the meantime, somehow, Captain Charles R. Durfee (A) and Captain Joseph T. Golding (C) collected their scattered companies from among the hundreds of men of the other two battalions on the beach, reorganized them, and reported ready for action 20 minutes after they landed. To me this was one of the greatest feats of leadership and cool thinking I have ever seen. Golding had been wounded in the hand and arm, but refused to be evacuated. After getting through the mortar and artillery fire on the reef, several of his amphtracs were knocked out by that damn Jap light tank that hit my amphtrac and killed my Bn-3 (operations officer), Captain Charles H. Triplett, Jr., one of the finest officers who ever wore the uniform. Durfee's company was also shot up by the tank, and Rollen lost his executive officer and a couple more amphtracs from direct hits by mortar on the reef. In fact, the battalion had over a hundred casualties before even reaching the beach and losses of equipment due to men swimming in from wrecked amphtracs were terrific. This equipment, of course, was replaced by equipment no longer needed by the dead boys who had preceded us.

"We had orders to pass through the Third Battalion immediately, to give them a chance to reorganize. So, with me making believe that Tony [Pfc. Tony Toscano, Jones's orderly] was my lost B Company, and praying the Nips wouldn't hit my open right flank, I tacked my left flank onto the Second Battalion and started a swinging-gate movement to the left with two companies. In a little while, Rollen and his 'Dead End Kids' came popping out of the woods on my right, licking their chops and asking for more Nips. Tony was told to quit looking like B Company, and everything was *ting-hao*. [Chinese for 'very fine.'] We deepened the beachhead 700 yards before Golding was killed. By that time it was getting dark, my right flank was still flapping in the breeze, and we were on a good defensive position. So we dug in for the night, after passing B Company through C Company, which had been pretty well shot up fighting their way in from the beach.

"The speed with which these three company commanders reorganized and attacked indicated the initiative and guts shown by every officer and man in my outfit. The communications officer was knocked out, so a noncommissioned officer took charge; the Bn-3 was killed, so my exec, Major James A. Donovan, Jr., took both jobs; the Sergeant Major, Howard Lyon, took charge of evacuating the wounded, and several platoons were reorganized and led off that beach by sergeants, and, believe it or not, by corporals. All this, remember, in a period of 20 minutes. This will always be incredible to me because I'm damned if I know how they did it. As the old gunner used to say, 'It ain't ethical, it ain't even logical, but by God, it's Marine Corps, so we'll do it.'"

Concerning this action by Bill Jones's battalion, all we knew at the time aboard the SC was contained in a one-line radioed report, "Jap artillery is giving the Red Beach boats hell." It is not difficult to see that there are a hundred dramas in a battle for every one that finds its way into print.

But from our 111-foot sub-chaser (Captain, Lieutenant Arthur Phillips, of Detroit) we could tell that the Japs had stepped up their fire aimed at the oncoming amphtracs. Three hundred yards away, LVT's were getting direct hits; big plates of steel flew into the air; men could be seen swimming. Around our own craft, shells exploded more frequently. A plaintive radio message told the story: "Request air [bombs] on mortars." If we had known a way to find well hidden Jap mortars, so we could drop bombs on them, we could have stepped up the war by months and saved men's lives by the thousands. All we could do was the best we could without knowing just where the murder was coming from. The radio message added: "It's pretty rugged." "This," I noted at the time, "looks like a real crisis."

At 1100 the Second Division's "spare battalion,"—First Battalion, 29th Marines—was ordered to land on Green Beach 1. This outfit, whose nucleus was made up of men from all Second Division units, was commanded by Lieut. Colonel Guy Tannyhill, and was intended to become a part of the 29th Marines which would join the new Sixth Marine Division. At 1101 the Red Beach control boat reported that 2/6 was 400 yards inland, and its left flank was now receiving fire from our own planes and guns—a complaint that is repeated a hundred times in every battle. The delayed news from the Fourth Division was sparse, but it was good: Troops on Yellow Beach 1 were already 1,200 yards inland, and on Yellow 2 they were half as far. Schmidt's Fourth Division, whose combat experience had been limited to the fierce, 27-hour Roi-Namur battle, was cocky, and it was intent upon bowling over the Japs without any delay.

At noon, just after a report said, "Heavy mortar and artillery fire throughout Red and Green beach areas," General Edson asked, via radio, the division commander's permission to land. Superfluously, Edson turned to me and asked: "Been on her long enough?" I swallowed and said, "Any time, think we'll leave soon?" He said, "Wouldn't be surprised." We moved over toward the Green control boat, but the four amphtracs we had requested to take us ashore were misplaced somewhere in the confusion of battle. The line of boats steadily plowing alongside us were filled with artillery and ammunition. After some of the most effective swearing I ever heard, General Edson preempted four amphtracs. We piled into them.

Bobbing into the beach, we saw, every now and then, artillery fire in the water around us. The sharp crack of detonation on the water, following the soft "whoosh" through the air, was almost deafening as we reached the reef, which was about 1,000 yards offshore at our point of crossing. Fifty yards to our portside an amphtrac had just been hit, and men were swimming in the breakers, some trying to make the shore, some struggling seaward whence they had come. Others undoubtedly were beyond movement of any kind.

As we closed in toward the shore Edson ordered everybody in our boat (Number 410) to get down, though he himself continued to stand and look ahead. I noticed that I was crouching on boxes containing 81-mm. mortar shells, and I figured a direct hit on this boat would preclude the necessity of deciding which way to swim. Actually, no shell hit closer to us than fifty yards as we approached the beach.

It was 1430 when the amphtracs crunched ashore; that is, three of them went ashore. The fourth landed somewhere farther up the beach, and was not heard from for a long time. We in the general's amphtrac jumped over the side, and ran to a tank trap a few yards inland. We had arrived on Saipan, 1,500 miles from Japan.

Whether we should ever leave there alive was in considerable doubt for the rest of the day and night. An artillery shell or a mortar shell—I have never found anyone who could definitely tell them apart as they exploded—landed near us every three seconds for the first twenty minutes. Most of them were in the water, 100 yards and more offshore, but some of them hit the beach itself. None hit inside the seven-foot deep trap which the Japs had built for their protection and which we were now using for our protection.

Inside the trap the battalion aid station for 2/8 (Lieut. Colonel H. P. Crowe) had been set up. There were a half dozen men lying on the sand; they were already bloodily bandaged and awaiting evacuation by amphtracs. On the inshore edge of the trap there were five dead Jap soldiers lying beside their dismantled machine gun, which they apparently had been moving inland when they were hit. As the artillery and/or mortar fire continued heavily, a medical corpsman said, "Hell, I'm going back up front; it's safer." "Up front" meant about 500 yards across the incompleted coral strip which was just beyond the tank trap.

With General Edson, I walked a few yards south. There, in a shellhole, lay the battalion commander, "Jim" Crowe himself, the old, red-mustached Jim who had been a legend in the Marine Corps for twenty years. Jim was breathing hard, but his steely blue eyes were bright as ever. Around his chest there was a wide bandage. On his left arm there were five smaller bandages. He had been shot through the lung by a machine gun bullet. Mortar shells which had killed a corpsman and wounded a doctor had done the rest. Now Doctor Otto Henry Jantan was finishing the patching, and giving Jim morphine. Jantan shook his head and murmured, aside, "Not much chance, I'm afraid." But there was nothing defeatist about 44-year-old Jim, no more than there was when I landed on his section of hell at Tarawa. Said Jim, "I hate like hell for this to happen, general, but I'll be all right." The crack of an exploding shell sounded behind us. "Keep your head down, general." Then he shifted his eyes toward me, and said: "I'll see you stateside. We'll throw a whizdinger." As we turned away Edson said, "No man in the shape he's in has a right to look so well and talk so normally." As a matter of fact, the report spread throughout Saipan that Jim Crowe was dead, and the report was accepted as fact by all but old Marines, who insisted, "You can't kill Jim Crowe gradually: if he's got a fighting chance he'll come through." The last time I heard of him, in the spring of 1945, he had completed his months-long tour in the San Diego hospital, had taken a rousing trip around the United States, and had returned to duty overseas.

Crowe's battalion was taken over by his executive officer, Major William C. Chamberlin, a reserve officer who resembled Crowe about as much as a bullfrog resembles a blue heron. Big Jim Crowe was rip-roaring and profane; one of the world's finest rifle shots, and a great Marine football player until he got so old he could make only half the tackles on his side of the line. Bill Chamberlin was 28 years old. Bespectacled, soft-voiced, he had been an economics teacher at Northwestern University until he went on active duty in the Marine Corps in 1940. Both Crowe and Chamberlin had received the Navy Cross for Tarawa.

Back at Colonel Wallace's regimental command post, just beyond the tank trap, we heard that the line in front of us was reported 600 yards inland. Wallace walked over to a corpsman who was removing the bayonet from a dead Jap's scabbard. He stormed: "You'll get yourself mixed up with a booby-trap. Now, God damn it, leave him alone." Somebody shoveled sand over the dead Nips, who were beginning to smell. The most cheering sight I had seen since arriving was a line of our tanks moving in through the water, one medium and 18 lights. A Marine with a badly shattered leg was brought in and blood plasma was given to him. Colonel

Wallace put down his telephone, and turned to the surgeon, "Doctor, the third battalion is badly in need of litters and litter bearers." The Japs opened up again, and the artillery shells "whooshed" overhead like hot blasts that ended when they burst on the water. Fortunately, nearly all went into the water, but even there I did not see another amphtrac hit all afternoon. On Saipan the Japs had not learned much about the proper use of artillery.

I looked around to see what my corner of Saipan looked like. Along the beach, between the sand and the coral air strip, there were many small trees which looked like pines and scrub oak. Occasionally there was a flame tree in brilliant orange. Beyond the air strip the small trees, including some palms, fresh fruit trees and pandanus, were even more dense, but nowhere was there anything resembling a jungle. Saipan was semi-tropical, but there was nothing of the South Pacific; in fact, the map showed that Saipan was almost as far north as Hawaii. I decided it might be a nice place if it were properly fixed up by the Seabees and the engineers.

About four o'clock I was sitting in the ditch next to the dead Japs, talking to a Marine who said his name was David Swanson; he was a captain from Iowa. "I'm a 155 man," he said, "and I'm waiting for my guns. Let's take a walk up the beach." Swanson's LVT had been hit as it reached the beach. Of his own four men, three were lost; one killed, one wounded, one "went batty." We started south along the water's edge, but the mortar fire was very intense, so we retraced our steps and walked about a mile north.

We saw two dead Marines lying on the sand, then two dead Japs. A third Marine, a few feet farther north, had had the top of his head neatly carved out, evidently by a shell fragment, and his brains had run out on the sand. Near one of our 1,000-pound bomb duds there were three Japs. A Marine named Robert Forsberg, a Catholic whose blood had been Type O, according to the dogtag which lay on his chest, had died of many wounds; he was bandaged in fifteen places. A little farther on, H. R. Walters was unconscious, but he was still breathing. Beyond him another Marine lay in a position I had seen many times at Tarawa; when death struck him down he had been charging forward across the beach; his legs were still in a sprinter's crouch, and his M-1 rifle was still held in his extended right arm. Scattered along the beach were numerous Japanese "tape-measure" mines, discs about ten inches in diameter.

An amphtrac named "Beast of Denver" had been knocked out ten feet inland. A small white goat had taken cover under its curved bow. A Jap 75-mm. pack howitzer, mounted on wagon wheels, sat a few feet farther inland, beside two small ammunition wagons. Not far away was a Marine who had had his leg blown off at the hip. Beyond the "Beast of Denver" another amphtrac, curiously named "Abattoir," lay in the water's edge. In the 300 yards separating the two vehicles I counted 17 dead Marines. Several others who had been treated by corpsmen lay quietly, awaiting evacuation to transports where they would be hospitalized.

Near the invisible line dividing the 6th and 8th Marines, W. J. Worblewski (according to the name stamped on his canteen cover) had given his life toward his country's capture of Saipan. He had captured the 15 feet of sand which lay between the water and the spot where fate caught up with him. Two more dead lay next to amphtrac Number A-36, which was still burning with a color which strangely matched that of the exotic flame tree nearby. Under a small tree that looked like a cedar someone had planted a tiny American flag, which fluttered bravely in the breeze. The sight of it brought a hard lump to my throat, because I could see, all around me, men who had made the ultimate payment so that the little piece of bright cloth might wave there. And I knew already that many others within my view would also die before the Japs stopped contesting our presence on this island.

The 29th Marines were advancing across the airstrip, to pass through a battalion already fighting on the other side. Three amphtracs had been knocked out over there, and the sharp staccato of rifle and machine-gun fire told us that the battle was not far beyond the strip. In a big shellhole next to the airstrip the Japs had evidently registered a powerful direct hit, killing about six Marines who had taken cover there. Their bodies were sprawled about the hole. They were terribly mangled; no more than half of any one man was left. One man's hand, ten feet from the hole, still held the trigger of his piece. Said Captain Swanson, "That man loved his rifle."

We walked back to the division CP, part of the way along the airstrip, part of the way on the sand. I was amazed to note how many men evidently had been wounded, only to be killed by a second or a third explosion. Two intelligence officers were questioning the first live Jap I had seen, a gold-toothed little fellow with a bullet hole in his leg. Near some blasted amphtracs a big Marine officer was shouting orders, though he had a thick, blood-stained bandage slung around his chin, which made shouting difficult.

A dozen wounded now lay in the aid station-tank trap where I had landed, and the puddle of water which had seeped through the sand was dark brown with the blood of many men. The amphtracs were evacuating the wounded as fast as possible, but they had difficulty in keeping up with the stretcher bearers who were bringing men from the front line back across the airstrip every few minutes. As I began to dig my foxhole for the night, I estimated that I had seen in this piece of the battleground about 100 dead Marines, and only about 20 dead Japs; the last one had been killed a few minutes before, not far from where I was digging (see p. 22).

That first night was a succession of artillery and mortar shells in my particular area. From 8 until 9, from 11 until

1, and from 4 until 5, the shells burst on the beach and in patterns for 500 yards inland, one shell every five seconds. Around the old command post—General Watson moved the CP 1,000 yards north during the night, but I stayed in my original foxhole—perhaps 20 shells burst within 25 yards, but so far as I could find out, nobody was hit in the immediate vicinity of it. Men in holes are hard to hit.

For me there was none of the terror of the first night on Tarawa. Partly, I told myself, this was because I had become used to getting shot at; any man in combat begins to adopt a sort of "Is it mine or ain't it?" philosophy, after a while. But, also, we kept the front lines lit up with star shells, so that we could anticipate Jap counterattacks. Most of the night was like daylight; even the Japs used star shells. And there was a solid 500 yards between the front lines and my hole in the sand. That was better than the 20 feet we had at Tarawa. This time I got a few hours of sleep.

June 16

All night there was some rifle and machine-gun fire in front of the old CP, but on the left flank of our beachhead there was a great deal more firing. And for a good reason: The Japs had mounted a counterattack down the beach road leading from Garapan. The Second and Third battalions of the 6th Marines were ready. In the morning about 700 dead Japs attested the state of their readiness.

Soon after dawn our artillery opened up, directed by spotter planes which were already picking out Jap artillery positions. The naval gunfire joined the thunder, and soon we were throwing many tons of steel onto the slopes of Tapotchau.

I walked north to the new division CP, located beside a Jap ammunition dump, and the news was not good. Casualties had been much heavier than anybody had expected. Captain John W. Thomason III, assistant division public relations officer and son of the famed Marine Corps author, had hit the beach with Bill Jones's 1/6 battalion, He said the battalion had had nearly 50 killed and 150 wounded already, which estimate turned out a little high, but no more than initial casualty estimated usually do. An artillery shell had hit Thomason's amphtrac, killing three men and wounding six others. Between the chatter of machine guns and the firing of our own 75's nearby, General Edson said: "Will we have to call in the Twenty-Seventh Division? Sure we will, and we may need the Guam force, too, before this thing is over." Half of the Second Divisions's ten original battalion commanders had already been wounded; Crowe, Murray, Miller, Easley, and Johnston. Big Ray Murray's own battalion had had four commanding officers within ten hours. Two hours after Murray had been hit, his executive officer, Major Howard Rice, had caught a piece of mortar in his back and had been evacuated. An observer, Lieut. Colonel William Kengla, had taken command temporarily until Major Leroy Hunt, Jr., took over. He lasted throughout the battle.

It was no trouble at all to find out why our casualties were so high. The Japs from their mountainside dug-outs were looking down our throats. Not only our front lines were being pounded. Our beaches were still crowded with shore parties unloading supplies. In a 1,500-yard walk down the beach Captain Thomason and I hit the sand four times. First came the "whoosh" of the shell. We threw ourselves sprawling on the sand. Then came the explosion on the water. All the shells exploded offshore, but that was our luck, which was better than the luck of the many newly wounded men who lay on the beach while corpsmen attended them.

On the way we saw civilians for the first time, three women and four children aged about one to five. Two children were crying. Two others were being nursed by their stoical mothers, who never moved as shells burst not far away. An allegedly tough Marine lieutenant looked at the scene and said, "God damn; does war have to come to this?"

Major Bill Chamberlin's battalion was on the Second Division's right flank. He wiped his forehead and said: "We're doing better now. G Company is on the pier. We haven't made contact with the Fourth Division yet, but we expect to, soon." We moved on to Afetna Point, where rifle fire was still intense, and tanks moved about, firing their 75's into Jap dugouts. A wide-eyed private on the northern side of the point said: "I am a bazooka man, but our amphtrac got hit. I lost my buddy; shot through the head. My bazooka and all my ammunition were blown up at once. Now I'm just getting water and chow up to the troops."

At 1155 Major Chamberlin was breathing easier: "The pier has been taken and we've made contact with the Fourth Division." The Second's intelligence officer, Lieut. Colonel Thomas Jack Colley, was more emphatic: "Things are looking up now," he sang. I had a deadline to make, so at 1300 I boarded an amphtrac for the ship to write a story on the first day and a half on Saipan.

CHAPTER FIVE

THE PRICE GOES UP

June 17

BY RETURNING TO SHIP I MISSED THE FIRST REAL TANK ATTACK the Japs had ever mounted against the Marines. But aboard ship I saw new evidence that Saipan was becoming a very expensive operation; already 243 casualties had been brought to the *Bolivar* and this figure was increased to 290, near capacity, as more amphtracs bearing torn bodies came alongside during the night. The six transports of our division took aboard a total of 627 wounded during the first day and a half, of whom 21 had already died of their injuries. The doctors said there were few bullet wounds, and shell fragments generally made bigger gashes than bullets.

The tank battle I missed was a spectacular affair. I was able to reconstruct it later: We had expected the Japs to use tanks on Saipan, perhaps 100 of them, maybe 200. The 6th Marines had destroyed four tanks on D Day, but the counterattack that night was an infantry charge. On this early morning of D plus 2 the Japs decided to try another counterattack, this time with tanks. Just why they had not tried a co-ordinated push in the first place was one of those inexplicable things about Japs. Maybe naval gunfire kept them under cover on D night.

B Company of 1/6 bore the full weight of the tank attack, aided only by a bazooka team from A Company, and, in the mop-up, by men from K Company and some halftracks from Regimental Special Weapons. Captain Rollen of B Company reported at 0330 that tanks were coming toward him from the hills which sloped off Tapotchau; the Japs evidently expected to gain surprise by avoiding the road from Garapan.

Within a few minutes, the tanks were upon the front lines of B Company. One of the company's 60-mm. mortar positions was overrun. Another 60-mm. position was overrun by a tank that was leaking oil; a Marine in the foxhole had oil-covered dungarees to show for it. Captain Rollen rose from his foxhole and fired his carbine, which was equipped with a grenade launcher. The tank kept going past him. The confusion that attends any battle was multiplied a hundredfold in the B Company area, where star shells lit up the sky, tracer bullets arched overhead, the clanging of Jap tanks was mixed with the explosion of anti-tank grenades and bazooka hits. Captain Rollen had his ear drum burst by an explosion, but he continued to direct his company until his relief was ordered and he was evacuated. Captain Norman Thomas, his relief, a hero of Tarawa, was himself killed before the relief was affected.

What did the men of B Company do? They stayed there and took it. Some men waited in their foxholes ("well built holes, they were") until the Jap tanks rolled over them; then they hit the tanks in the vulnerable rears with bazooka rockets and anti-tank grenades. Private Robert S. Reed of Cabot, Arkansas, according to his Navy Cross citation "accounted for four hits on four different tanks with his rocket launcher, and, then after running out of rockets, climbed upon a fifth tank and, with utter disregard for his own personal safety, dropped an incendiary grenade in the turret, thereby disabling the tank."

Pfc. John Kounk, of Sheboygan, Wisconsin, in spite of heavy enemy fire, moved among the tanks, firing his bazooka at very short range. He and his teammate, Pfc. Horace Narveson, of Oberon, North Dakota, hit three tanks with four bazooka charges. Corporal John E. Watson, of Lake Charles, Louisiana, threw two incendiary grenades into a tank, then killed the Japs as they tried to escape from it. Despite intense machine-gun fire from another tank, Watson carried a wounded pal to safety. Sergeant Alex B. Smith, of Lake Providence, Louisiana, directed the fire of his machine-gun squad against three tanks, but it was ineffective. So Smith took his carbine-grenade launcher, moved to a more advantageous (but more dangerous) position and put all three tanks out of action.

Perhaps two first class privates, Charles D. Merritt of Greenville, South Carolina, and Herbert J. Hodges, of Anchorage, Kentucky, established some kind of world's record: They got out of their foxholes, moved first to the right and fired their bazooka there, then to the left and fired again. Time after time they repeated this. The Jap tank gunners and riflemen who followed the tanks were shooting all the time, but they did not faze Merritt and Hodges. Their score: Tanks fired at, 7; number of shots, 7; tanks hit, 7.

Partially, the Japs' tank losses were due to their own ineptness. The tanks were followed by some infantry, mostly after the second wave. But B Company's four heavy machine guns cut them down. Then the tanks, both blind and confused, ambled aimlessly toward the beach instead of penetrating B Company's lines farther, until the bazookas or anti-tank grenades stopped them. One of the Marines told me later about the enemy antics: "The Nips would halt, then jump out of their tanks. Then they would sing songs and wave swords. Finally, one of them would blow a bugle, jump back into the tanks, if they hadn't been hit already. Then we would let them have it with a bazooka."

Not all the tanks had been knocked out by the hits scored on them. K Company of the Third Battalion helped to finish off seven tanks after it relieved B Company at daylight. The Regimental Special Weapons Company's halftracks were also called out, and their 75-mm. guns polished off the cripples or caught the remnants which were attempting to flee back to the hills. About 0700 one last tank was seen struggling back toward the Jap lines. A destroyer fired 20 salvos. The tank burned all day. A total of 29 Jap tanks had been accounted for, and, in the words of General Watson: "I don't think we have to fear Jap tanks any more on Saipan. We've got their number." At 0735 the 6th Marines, including B Company, jumped off in the attack up the slopes of Tapotchau.

About noon of the 17th I got in a small boat and went over to the *Rocky Mount* to find out how things looked from the command ship. Lieut. General Holland Smith's wall chart was incomplete, but it told enough: Casualties in the assault battalions were marked: 2/8 and 3/8, 40 per cent; 2/6 and 3/6, 197 enlisted men and seven officers; 23d and 24th Marines, "very heavy, especially in the 23d." The latter regiment had rapidly seized the area near the sugar mill, but had been driven back during D night. It was reported that two patrols of 12 to 15 men had been sent out that night to make contact with the Second Division, and no man had been heard of since. The Twenty-seventh Division had been called in from reserve; the 165th Regiment, which had taken Makin, had started landing behind the Fourth Division on D plus 1 night, and the 105th and 106th Regiments were being ordered to land. The invasion of Guam, scheduled for tomorrow, had been postponed because nobody had any idea how much this Saipan thing might cost before it was finished, whenever that might be.

At 1430, when I landed alongside the coveted pier at Charan-Kanoa, the sugar mill had long since been retaken by the 23d Marines. It was a mass of rubble, pounded by hundreds of tons of high explosives, its vats stinking in the sun and drawing millions of flies. The big smokestack had been pierced a thousand times, but it still stood. A smaller refinery next door (wistfully designated as a probable rum distillery by a Marine) was as completely wrecked.

I walked a mile south from the little town, down the road that was already a foot deep in dust which had been ground to fine powder by tanks, trucks, and jeeps. At General Schmidt's Fourth Division CP, a deep sandbagged dugout of two rooms, there was no spirit of pessimism. The Fourth's casualties were 2,200 men. Eighty-six men had been buried, 70 more awaited burial, though collection of the dead had hardly begun. Even the artillerymen had been hit fairly hard; six guns had been knocked out the first day by counter-battery fire. By now four had been repaired. Lieut. Colonel Maynard Schultz, commanding the First Battalion, 24th Marines, had been killed. But troops of the division had almost crossed the island. Aslito Airfield had been partially captured on D Day, but the Marines had pulled back to a defensive line for the night, and now they were bypassing the airfield on its northern side, leaving its capture and the securing of the southern part of the island to the Army troops which were already fighting their way back to the field. After the Fourth had crossed the island it would swing north on the eastern side as the Second swung north on the western side. The Army division's troops would come up the center, along the eastern slopes of Tapotchau.

Captain William McCahill, public relations officer of the Fourth, had set up headquarters in foxholes between General Schmidt's CP and the beach. "Have a foxhole," he said, passing the shovel, and I began digging alongside Frank Kelley of the New York *Herald Tribune*. When the word "Condition Red!" was passed, (meaning that Jap planes were on their way) Kelley and I, slow diggers, found refuge in a poncho-covered foxhole with the division provost marshal, Lieut. Colonel Melvin Krulewitch of Albany, New York. The colonel found—of all things—a bottle of bourbon.

June 18

With Kelley and Lieutenant Jim Lucas, McCahill's assistant, I started across the island to the Fourth Division front line. We walked through neat little farms which grew sugarcane, corn, peas, a sort of cantaloupe, and potatoes. This southern end of the island was low and fertile. But the Jap farmhouses indicated sad indigence. They were sorry little one-story affairs with tin roofs that would shame a tobacco road sharecropper. But nearly every farmhouse had a cow which was badly frightened or dead.

Half a mile inland there were three amphtracs which the Japs had knocked out. Next to one of them lay a dead Marine, fallen on his face in a small rice paddy. Farther up the road 50 old men, women, and children plodded patiently toward the civilan enclosure which had already been set up on the beach. They were directed by two MP's. Nearly all the women of child-bearing age had babies strapped to their backs. Many of the babies were asleep, their heads rocking loosely in the hot morning sun. I recalled reading somewhere that Saipan had one of the highest birth-rates on earth; women between 15 and 45 bore babies at the rate of 300 per 1,000 per year, of whom more than 200 lived. The lame were carried in American stretchers by Japs who wore uniforms but who, we were told, were merely South Seas Development Corporation workers.

Near a farmhouse which had four cows and many chickens, Colonel Franklin Hart, commander of the 24th Marines (he was said to be the only Marine in the Dieppe raid), had set up his regimental CP. We remarked to a staff officer that we had seen very few Japs since arriving, and he assured us there were about 2,000 of them only 500 yards ahead. But we saw no more than a couple of dozen near the path we walked along.

We could see the airport, Aslito Field, 800 yards to the south, surrounded by what looked like blockhouses. As we passed a radio jeep we could hear the tired chant: ". . . Perky will move up on the right of Percheron. Don't get fouled up." "Perky, Perky, this is Percheron, your mortars are firing on our front lines." "Percheron, this is Perky. Message received. Our mortars have ceased firing."

On the last hillside but one until the island was crossed we stopped in the 1/24 CP where Lieut. Colonel Austin R. Brunelli, of Washington, had just taken command of the battalion from Major Robert N. Fricke, who filled in after Colonel Schultz had been killed. The battalion had had 210 casualties, about one-fourth of its strength, but only 27 were dead. Destroyers were firing air bursts over a cornfield 1,000 yards to the north. Sometimes the shells burst 200 feet above the ground, sometimes only 50 feet. They drenched the field with fragmented steel until no Japs could have stayed above ground and lived. But the Japs long ago learned to get underground.

On the way back across the island we stopped at a farm shack next to a cornfield, where some doctors and corpsmen had set up the battalion aid station. It was hot; Kelley and I took off our helmets and sat in the shade of the little porch. We had not been there five minutes before two bullets rattled against the wall, no more than six inches from our heads, We hit the dirt, and crawled around to the other side of the house. A sniper in the canefield next to the house had apparently lain in wait several hundred yards behind our lines, patiently expecting somebody, eventually, to sit on that side of the house. But even at 30 or 40 yards his patience had exceeded his aim; he had missed. Some Marines went into the canefield to flush him, but they found nothing.

Another farmhouse had been taken over by the Jap Military, whose clothing and picture albums were scattered about the ten-by-ten-by-six rooms, of which there were three. In one room about 20 cases of beer and *Mitubisichampne,* a sort of lemon pop, were stacked. The beer was excellent (Japs are good brewers), but the non-alcoholic lemon soda was even better; it was cooling, and the Saipan sun was becoming unbearably hot.

Another farmhouse farther back was even more interesting. The whole house, propped up by small, crooked poles, was no more than 12 by 15 feet, but one of the three small rooms was two stories high, with shelves for sleeping. In the rear there was a crude kitchen, lined with earthenware. In the six-foot-square "parlor," fishing nets were hung on one side. On the other wall was tacked an incongruous set of pictures, all in rotogravure. Mostly they were religious pictures; the occupant was evidently a Christian Chamorro. But there was one clipping showing a Jap anti-aircraft gun crew at maneuvers. And another of Hitler and Goering. What confusion must have existed in the mind of the man who pasted those pictures on his wall! Were some of his pin-ups intended to appease his Japanese masters? Or did he believe he could be Christian and pro-Hitler at the same time? Perhaps he pinned up the only pictures he could find.

Whatever his reasons, he would never tell them. He lay dead on the floor of his lower sleeping shelf. Beside him, on a red cassock, lay a year-old baby, neatly covered. Both had been killed apparently by the bullets of a strafing plane which had punctured the tin roof in many places. They were two of the comparatively few civilian Japs I saw on Saipan who did not die by their own hands.

As we neared the beach, in what had been the hard-hit 23d Marines' D-Day sector, we saw about 50 dead who were now becoming heavily covered with dust. Their bodies were hugely bloated, and they were turning black in the hot sun. The only way to distinguish Jap from American was by the helmets, leggings (Jap, wrap-around; American, canvas), or belts (black leather or khaki web). There were about two dead Marines for three dead Japs.

On the beach the civilian internees were now grouped in three large enclosures. About half were Chamorros or Kanakas, half Japs. None seemed too unhappy, and the MP's allowed them to wander in and out of the barbed-wire fence, and go down to the water in groups to bathe. One intelligent Chamorro named Mike showed up in Marine clothing. He was cheered by the darker-skinned natives. Saipan had been his home; he had been taken away by the Japs and we had brought him back when he had escaped from the Marshalls, to help us to deal with his countrymen.

Lieut. Commander Claude R. Bruner, one of the doctors who had arrived on the *Bolivar,* had helped to set up a civilian hospital in a partially bombed-out Japanese headquarters. There were about 15 civilians lying on cots, and a four-year-old boy who was being operated on; he had three bullet holes in his arm. A buck-toothed Chamorro woman grinned broadly ("She hates the Japs, and won't speak to the Jap woman in the next bed.") Two of the Japs were soldiers, including a 28-year-old corporal under guard ("a tough bastard; he shot 11 Marines before they got him.")

When I returned to the Second Division CP (a mile north) about dusk, a dogfight was going on, said to be between two of our carrier planes and three Jap planes. All I could see were some planes swirling about at 5,000 feet. We saw one plane go down in flames, and a parachute floated over the horizon. It was reported to be a Jap, who landed behind his own lines. Within two hours there were four "Condition Reds!" but this was the only evidence of enemy planes we saw from the CP.

June 19

It was quite a night. There was spasmodic firing around division CP during most of it. Some Japs infiltrated from the Lake Susupe area, and the Marines around headquarters fired long bursts every time they saw something move. (Front-line troops invariably tell you it's safer up there, because the infantrymen on the line are not trigger-happy.) The CP was set up not far from the division's 105-mm. artillery, which fired all night. The sequence was repeated every few seconds: The "whoosh" overhead, then the explosion as the shells left the guns, then the detonation on the distant hillsides. Worse than the artillery noises were the mosquitoes. After I had slept four hours my supply of "Skat" wore off, and I was at the mercy of the beasts the rest of the night. I had no intention whatsoever of walking around in the dark to find some more repellent. In addition to the mosquitoes, the artillery fire, and the spasmodic rifle fire, there was the rain, which came about 0300. Then what turned out to be a land crab got into my foxhole, but when he first bit through my sock I was positive I had been infiltrated; the night before, 30 saber-waving Japs had penetrated into a battalion CP of the Eighth and had caused some casualties before they were killed. Naturally, I could not turn on a flashlight, so the land crab and I played tag until dawn, by which time I had conceded the match.

Halfway up on the slopes of Tapotchau I found the 6th Marines CP of Colonel Jim Riseley. His regiment had suffered nearly 35 per cent casualties, but he had acquired the Third Battalion, 2d Marines, when it had landed, and had swapped his own 2/6 to Colonel Stuart of the 2d Marines. "Nowhere but in the Marine Corps could you switch battalions around like that, and still have them function with the same efficiency," he said proudly. Stuart's regiment now occupied the Second Division left flank, from the beach inland (eastward). Riseley's three battalions were lined up as follows: Jones's 1/6 , then 3/6 (Major John "Monk" Rentsch had taken it over when Easley was wounded), and Arnold Johnston's 3/2. On Riseley's right flank were the 8th Marines, who had swung northward and, with 1/29 attached, were beginning the assault of Mount Tapotchau. Lieut. Colonel Guy Tannyhill of 1/29 had been wounded and evacuated, and "Tommy" Tompkins had been called from staff work to take command.

"We had some bad luck this morning," said Riseley; "one of our best company commanders was killed by rockets from one of our own planes. The pilot must have been crazy. He came smashing into our front lines, and got a direct hit, then he fired wild, then he fired again, killed the captain. The artillery has been off, too. One of our 105's hit a bunch of our own men, killing three and wounding seven or eight. It seems like a long way to come and get it from your own men. It has always happened, though, and I guess it always will." Riseley added: "You know, I've got the best battalion commander in the Marine Corps—Bill Jones, and the best tank commander, Captain Frank Stewart. Stewart's always ready; he supports B Company, then C Company, anywhere he's needed."

Everywhere I went on this morning I heard the same report: Japan had declared war on Russia (*not* Russia on Japan). So far as I could find out, it had originated yesterday in the Fourth Division ("Colonel X confirmed it.") A staff officer of the Second Division told me flatly he got it from another officer who had heard it on the radio. The "scuttlebutt" spread rapidly throughout the island, and I had come to believe it myself. From what I had seen of the Japanese, it would not have been inconsistent with their suicidal nature to try to lick the whole world, then to pull a *Gotterdammerung* which would make Hitler's look pallid. By the time I had heard San Francisco radio news I knew the report was not true, but it persisted throughout the Saipan battle.

I hopped on a Sherman tank which was going up the slopes to the front. After half an hour's ride up and over, I got off when I saw Bill Jones set up beside the road. His battalion had lost 287 officers and men, about one-third of its total strength, but Jones was proud of his boys; they had done well and their spirits were high as ever. He had incurred another severe loss when Captain Charles R. Durfee of A Company, a Navy Cross winner at Tarawa, had been killed while directing a flame-throwing light tank against Japs in a cliffside cave. Durfee's senior lieutenant, Albert

Wood, was severely wounded about the same time; another lieutenant, Joseph Palmer, assumed command but was wounded a little later. Now Second Lieutenant Raymond M. Graves was commanding A Company (he was wounded later in the battle).

Having lost five of his captains (Golding, Triplett, Thomas, Durfee, and Rollen), Jones looked at Don Calkins and George Azud, his supply and intelligence officers, respectively, and said drolly, "I guess the only thing to do is to bust the other two to lieutenant."

In the afternoon I walked the length of the Sixth Regiment front lines with Lieut. Colonel Kenneth McLeod, a young Naval Academy graduate from Wyoming who was Riseley's executive officer. The line ran along the top of a 100-foot cliff, then across the crest of a hill to the east. The Marines were stringing barbed wire in front of the line, though I could not see how the Japs could counterattack such an impregnable natural position in any case.

There was a good view, from this cliff, of the smashed town of Garapan (pre-war population 10,000), about a mile and a half to the north and west. The pleasant lowlands between the cliff and Garapan stretched below us. Already the Second Marines were patrolling part of this nearby level ground. Said McLeod: "We are ready to move forward any time, but we are waiting for the Eighth to move up on our right, and the Eighth is waiting for the Fourth Division to move up on the east side of the island, on the other side of Tapotchau."

McLeod paused beside some rocks in which the Japs had cut caves and then camouflaged them almost perfectly with small trees and underbrush. "Why on earth would they leave impregnable fortifications like these?" he asked. There were five dead Japs and three Marines laying near a Jap CP, a little house on top of Hill 650 where silk underwear and fine (but tiny) black boots had been left behind. A knocked-out Jap tank also stood nearby. On top of this hill it was cool, because a soothing breeze seemed always to blow from the east.

On the way back downhill we saw some MP's shepherding a group of 300 civilians, mostly Chamorros, some Japs, who had been fetched out of caves. It was enough to make a man weep to see the desperation with which little children drank the first water they had had in four days. One of the Marines carried two Jap babies, one in each arm.

June 20

During the night there was no excitement around Jones's CP. I lay awake for a long time, watching the stars through the trees, and listening to two 23-year-old Marines in a nearby foxhole discuss whether or not the war would last so long they would be so old they couldn't get married and raise families. About 0600, mortar shells began splashing on the slope of the hill behind us. After a few minutes the Japs stopped firing, even before Lieutenant Graves had got the counterfire he called for. Nobody was hurt. And Sgt-Major Lyon was happy. His casualty list was down from 287 to 247; forty men, slightly wounded or exhausted by heat, had returned to duty. (This happened frequently. The strangest case in 1/6 occurred toward the end of the Saipan battle, when Lieutenant Paul M. Dodd of C Company, listed as missing, returned from a hospital hundreds of miles away, whence he had been evacuated. Dodd had been in an amphtrac which had been hit on D Day. The man next to him had been blown to pieces, and Dodd had been wounded by a bone from the man's body.)

The carrier planes were busy before 0800. Many of them fired rockets 1,000 and 2,000 yards ahead of us. "You know what firing rockets sound like?" Colonel Colley had asked. "It's like a giant in the sky tearing enormous silk sheets." As we watched the rocket planes dive over and beyond Tapotchau, some of the Marines were commenting on the peculiarities of the Japs. "They don't know how to use artillery," said one, "they fire three or four bursts from their old, antiquated guns, then they stop. After a while they fire three or four more bursts in the same spot." I thought it good when an outfit which had lost one man in three could still disparage the enemy.

Somebody said that a Japanese woman had been found who had carried her dead baby three days. Her story was that she had hidden in a cave where there were two Jap soldiers. When her baby had started to cry the soldiers had choked the breath out of it, lest its cries reveal their position to the Americans. One Jap civilian, it was reported to headquarters, had cut the throats of his wife and child, and had told the Americans, boastfully, "That is what we will do when you get to the empire." Lieut. Wolff, commander of the engineer platoon attached to Jones's battalion, said: "The other day up here we were covering a cave. They heard us call for a flamethrower. When the Japs in the cave heard the word 'flamethrower' they all blew themselves up. There were six of them in there."

On the way down the hill, I stopped again at Riseley's CP. A Catholic chaplain of the artillery regiment, Father C. C. Riedel, of Chicago, was talking to Riseley and to Lieut. Colonel Presley M. Rixey, also of the 10th Marines. Father Riedell said bitterly, "The Second Division dead will run to 500 already; it's going to be more costly than Tarawa." It was the first time I had thought of Saipan in terms of Tarawa, which was (and remained to the end of the Central Pacific war) the acme of all personal horror. Perhaps it was because Tarawa had been my only battle which I ever thought we were going to lose; perhaps it was the nature of that long trudge through the water in the face of machine gun-fire; maybe after Tarawa I got used to battles.

But every man has his Gethsemane. Probably one incident

of one battle stands out above all others in every man's mind, just as most men can recall instantly the greatest act of heroism they ever saw.[1] But regardless of the total casualties, there are no easy battles in the minds of men who lose eyes or arms, nor in the minds of the next of kin. That is why comparing one battle with another, while interesting, is futile.

At Division CP, General Edson was impatient because the division had to wait for other units to move up: "It will be at least two days before we'll be able to advance. During that time the Japs will dig in, the way they like to fight defensively. Then it may settle down to another Guadalcanal." But Edson thought prospects looked better as a whole. The Twenty-seventh Division should be able to clean up the southern end of the island in another day and a half; the 106th, last of the Twenty-seventh's regiments, had completed its landing, and there was now lots of manpower and firepower on Saipan.

In mid-afternoon I went to the *Cambria,* flagship of Rear Admiral Harry Hill, deputy force commander to Admiral Turner. There Hill confirmed the naval engagement which had been rumored ashore. Last night one of our submarines had put three torpedoes into one of Japan's new carriers. Yesterday a large part of the Jap total carrier force had attacked Admiral Mitscher's carriers, and had lost more than 300 planes[2]: "no Naval Air Force can afford to lose 300 planes." Hill thought the Japs might have been heading for Guam, intending to refuel before socking us again. But Mitscher's planes had been busy tearing up the airfields on Guam, so whatever planes got through probably cracked up, on landing. The action Hill was describing was the initial stage of the First Battle of the Philippine Sea. In the past two days around Saipan, Admiral Hill said, we had shot down 12 planes. They may have come from Tinian, just four miles

[1] My choice: the inspiring leadership and indomitable courage of Lieut. William Deane Hawkins on D Day at Tarawa.
[2] The revised figure, 402; we lost 17.

away, where the Japs were suspected of sneaking planes in. He expected another raid at any time from Iwo Jima, where he thought the Japs had had time to land planes from the home islands.

There was no doubt that we had plans for Saipan. Commander Sam King, whom I had known in Washington as Congressional delegate from Hawaii, had arrived by seaplane to take charge of the Saipan Naval Base. Sam King even had extra clothing. (Even if they were too large, the clothes he gave me were blessedly clean.)

I wrote two more stories before I found that no news at all had been sent out excepting a first-day pooled press-association dispatch, transmitted by the *Rocky Mount's* radio. When the possibility of a big Jap raid had arisen Admiral Turner had pulled out with most of the ships that were in the harbor. Meantime, the PB2Y seaplanes which were to fly our dispatches back to Kwajalein or Pearl Harbor for radio transmission had been held at Saipan for search patrols.

During the night the Japs had blown up one of our ammunition dumps. Some Jap sampans had attacked a destroyer offshore and had wounded nine sailors. Planes which raided Rota yesterday (between Saipan and Guam) found quite a few planes there.

In the LCVP returning to shore there were two torpedo bomber pilots. Their planes, plus a third which had made a crash landing on Saipan, had been shot down by anti-aircraft over Tinian, and they had bailed out. "That gunner is damned good; three TBF's in one day by the same gun," said one of the pilots.

I stopped briefly at the civilian hospital. One of the doctors said a wounded Jap soldier had tried to escape yesterday; the sentry had shot him. "These Japs are rugged people," said the doctor; "a girl was picked up 20 miles at sea by a destroyer. She had been in the water at least two or three days. But after a day in the hospital here she was all right. We sent her to the civilian stockade."

With Australian Correspondent Denis Warner, I went over to Aslito Field, which had been captured on D plus 2 by the 165th Regiment and renamed Conroy Field in honor of the regiment's colonel, Gardiner Conroy, who was killed during the capture of Makin. The doughboys already had a sign painted, CONROY FIELD. (On June 30 Admiral Nimitz renamed the field Isely Field, following a recommendation of Admiral Mitscher and an old custom of naming fields for flyers. Commander Bob Isely, a Kansan, had been skipper of Torpedo Squadron 16, aboard the new *Lexington* in the attacks on Wake, Tarawa, Kwajalein, Palau, Woleai, Truk. He was killed June 12, leading an attack on the field which was to bear his name.)

The airfield was a remarkable sight. Its broad, hard-surfaced runways had hardly been touched. Its huge frame hangar had been partly wrecked, but somehow the 20 Jap planes, bombers and fighters, inside the hangar and parked outside had been damaged slightly if at all. Just why the Japs had withdrawn from the field without destroying their planes we did not know. "I could get in any one of a dozen and fly it away," said a naval aviator who inspected the planes in wonder.

Colonel Gerard Kelley, a slight, blue-eyed New Yorker who had graduated from West Point, had resigned from the Army and had re-entered through the National Guard, was now in command of the 165th. The 165th (prior to the last war, 69th) was the Twenty-seventh's favorite regiment, and Kelley its favorite regimental commander. His present CP had been the airfield's ammunition dump; its doors were steel, its walls two-foot-thick concrete. With Colonel Kelley, Warner and I climbed a ladder to the roof of the CP, where a well sandbagged spotter's nest had been set up. The preliminary bombing and shelling had done no damage to the building beyond chipping off a few pieces of concrete.

Colonel Kelley said his troops had had some sharp, bitter

fighting before they reached the airfield, but the capture itself was quite uneventful. Except for a few snipers, the Japs had withdrawn. His regiment's casualties were 28 dead, about 150 wounded.

At the eastern end of the airfield Lieut. Colonel John F. McDonough, c.o. of the Second Battalion, 165th Infantry, had set up his CP in a revetment. He said his men had killed quite a few Japs, but the enemy was dragging his dead back as he withdrew; this was indicated by the large number of blood-stained Jap rifles found in the areas the enemy had evacuated. McDonough had had six men killed (two by land mines) and 26 wounded. The southern end of the island was tough; the coral-rock formations provided natural caves, and the last 1,400 yards were laced with these jagged rocks and caves. Some of the caves, said Colonel McDonough, had sliding doors and artillery pieces on tracks. The Japs would open the door, run the guns out, fire, then withdraw to the cave.

Tonight the *Rocky Mount* and other ships returned.

June 22

The correspondent's house, a small, slightly bombed dwelling in Charan-Kanoa village, had woven mats which we unrolled on the floor and used as mattresses. Three newsmen could sleep under each mosquito net, which seemed quite civilized. There were three air raids between 0130 and 0430, which, although puny, caused everybody to pile into log-covered, bug-infested dugouts the Japs had built in the front yard. After a few nights, everybody either slept through the air raids or went to the back yard to watch the anti-aircraft fire.

Lieut. General Holland Smith, who had set up corps headquarters on the next street, held a press conference this morning. He said 15 tons of 81-mm. mortar shells had been captured; they were already being fired back at the Japs. We had also captured two eight-inch mortars, three six-inch coast defense guns, 41 75-mm. guns, one 70-mm. gun, two 47-mm. anti-tank guns, 15 40-mm. anti-aircraft guns, and about 50 assorted, smaller artillery pieces. The Japs had dropped twelve 500-lb. bombs during their raids last night, which had killed one man, wounded two seriously and two slightly. Propaganda leaflets urging the Japs to surrender had been dropped again this morning. The net yield of propaganda leaflets thus far had been one Jap seaman, who came into our lines waving the printed message, as instructed. He reported that the Jap soldiers picked up the leaflets and read them, but their officers took them away.

Total American casualties on Saipan up to now were 6,000, of which the Fourth Division had suffered about 3,800. One of these casualties was a grasshopper plane (artillery spotter) which landed on one of our ammunition dumps and blew up plane and pilot.

At the Second Division cemetery, where Major Janvier and Captain Todd were working much harder than they had ever expected, the evidence of the casualties was much more impressive than any mere figures could indicate. (Already buried: 420, including 12 unidentified.) "If people back home could see the condition of these bodies when they are brought in here," Todd said, "I wonder if they would want to keep on fighting."

"The real heroes were six corpsmen I've got here. They bring in the soggy corpses which were lying in the water. The Second Division had 300 to 325 killed in the beach area and in the water. These corpsmen retch and puke when gas escapes from the bodies. But they poke and search until they find some kind of identification, then they go ahead with the burying after the bulldozer has scooped out the graves."

By now it had been possible to bring the civilian internees half a mile inland from the beach, where two stockades had been set up for them. The civil affairs section attached to the Corps had taken over from division detachments, and we were dealing with large groups of Japanese nationals for the first time in two and a half years of war.

The civilians were first taken to a small stockade, where they were screened. Japs were separated from Chamorros, and a few soldiers who had put on civilian clothes were weeded out. Then they were taken to the big stockade, a fenced-in area about 500 yards square which contained some small houses and leantos. Inside the enclosure there were trees, pine, palm, papaya, and banana, which furnished some shelter. Captain Geoffrey Sage, a naval officer, was civil-affairs deputy under Maj. General Sanderford Jarman, the Army officer who would become island commander after combat had ceased. Under Captain Sage were several officers, including Lieut. Colonel Donald Winder, a Washington lawyer, Captain Wynne Van Schaick, an old World War I Marine. Facilities for civilians were naturally limited, since the battle had hardly begun. But the Japs were being directed to build cooking facilities and toilet facilities for themselves, and were being divided into groups of about 50, for whom leaders were selected. At least, there was now some semblance of order among the civilians, of whom 2,500 were already in custody. And we had captured much rice and other Jap supplies, which would preclude our having to dig deeper into our own stores. Among these docile Japs there was little indication of the fanaticism and suicides which came after organized resistance ended.

Only the slightest hint: One Jap had snarled at Father Cho, the Korean Catholic priest, and pointed north: "You may have part of this island, but there's the empire back there." Said Cho, sadly: "Once a Jap, always a Jap."

June 23

I spent the night at the new CP of the 2d Marines, commanded by Colonel Walter Stuart (after Tarawa, Colonel David Shoup had moved up to become divisional chief of staff). Besides Colonel John Griebel, who was Stuart's executive officer, I found there several old friends from Tarawa, Captains Hicks and John Giachetto and John Schwabe. There were only two air raids during the night, and the bombs seemed to fall near Aslito Field, three or four miles south.

Bill Jones had moved his CP a few hundred yards forward, and had perched it on the side of a hill near a Shinto shrine. Roaming around the area which Jones's Marines had recently occupied, I found a one-room house, a sort of crib, with a strange assortment of relics, religious and otherwise. For some reason, someone—evidently a priest—had stored his sacred paraphernalia there—a four-foot statue of Christ, a glass-enclosed statute of the Virgin. But also stacked in the little storehouse were oriental dancing dolls, a Yamaka piano, invalids' roller chairs, a toolbox, a package of "Mascot" cigarettes, a Panama hat, a broken movie projector. On the piano there were several pieces of music with English words, published in Japan. "Hit Jazz Piece" was the name of one; others were "Moonlight on the Colorado," and "Old Man River." Among the books were Barnes's *Second Reader* and Elson's *Second Reader* and the *Third Catholic Reader*.

This material had evidently involved an English-speaking Chamorro. Written on the fly-leaf of one thin volume was, "This book belongs to David D. Reyes, Guam Institute, Second Grade." One of the notebooks contained this writing lesson, dated Agana, Guam, October 9, 1934: "Dear Friend, here one little fellow not saw fat, not saw thin, not saw big, not so smal he first swat white bud the other is block he where shoes & short hear and he was a black hear his nose not saw pointe. Can you guess who it is. Your living friend, David D. Reyes."

David D. Reyes also had received a postcard written in

Japanese, dated "Tokyo, October 12, 1934." In his fifth-grade notebook he had written, "A literature is a written record of man's best thought and feeling." What had since happened to this student I never learned, but I often wondered.

At Jones's CP, Lieutenant Donald Seibert turned up, in a pair of sailor's blue dungarees. He had been wounded in the leg by a mortar fragment on D plus 1. Now he had been discharged from the transport sick bay, was ready to return to duty. Said Jones: "I want you to take over a platoon of A Company, but for God's sake get yourself some greens. You wouldn't last five minutes in that sky-blue lingerie."

Jones, like all Marine officers, was a strong believer in patrolling. He always had small groups of men probing into the dense undergrowth to find out where the enemy was. It was dangerous work; patrols frequently ran into ambush. But it was necessary. Now one of the patrols, led by Lieutenant Peter Lake, had located a Jap artillery piece, and Jones was talking to Lake by radio: "Hold up until we call you back."

Then he turned to one of his staff officers: "Tell those God damn 105's to quit firing; we don't want 'em unless they've got an f.o. [forward observer]." He looked up and said: "These God damn inaccurate maps . . . look at this; we're on top of a hill 600 feet high, but the contour map shows us on a rolling plain." (Later in the battle we switched from our own aerial photograph maps to captured Japanese maps.)

A machine-gun nest was now holding up the patrol. Jones ordered the rest of Lake's platoon to go forward and help to knock out the nest. He said, jokingly: "You'd better get that artillery piece, too. If I let my brother get wounded 'way back in the rear area, mother would never forgive me." (Jones's brother Jim, captain of the corps reconnaissance company, provided the security patrol for corps headquarters, guarding against infiltrating snipers, three of whom had already been found under a house near Holland Smith's quarters. Ordinarily, the corps recon outfit was engaged in extremely hazardous missions, such as night landings on enemy beaches, but just now it was only a rear-area guard. Bill considered that a joke on Brother Jim.)

Late in the afternoon I reached the *Rocky Mount,* where some reports had arrived about the naval battle in the newly named Philippine Sea on the 20th (east longitude date), the day after Mitscher's forces had shot down the 402 Jap planes. On the 20th the retreating Jap ships had not been located until late afternoon, and to launch our planes late in the afternoon meant that they would not get back to their carrier bases until after dark. This was the action which was partly and vividly described by Lieut. Commander J. Bryan III and Philip Reed in *Mission Beyond Darkness.*

The story we heard then was this: The Japs had finally been caught late in the afternoon on the 20th; they had lost at least two aircraft carriers, two destroyers, and a tanker, had probably lost two or three more aircraft carriers, a battleship, and three cruisers. In spite of this great victory, the observers were growling when I went aboard the *Rocky Mount.* They thought we could have sunk the whole Jap fleet if our force had been farther westward; some Jap ships did get away. What they did not know at the time was that the whole Jap fleet was not in the Philippine Sea; Admiral Spruance had been careful to keep his forces within range of Saipan. He figured that if he had gone dashing far to the west on June 19 the Japs might have enough extra naval force to shuttle down from the home islands and play havoc with our Saipan landing. Whether or not he was right will probably be a matter for debate at the Naval War College for several decades; we shall not know until we can assemble all the pieces of the puzzle after the war, providing the Japanese left any historical record. Admiral King told me nearly a year later that he had nothing but praise for Admiral Spruance's action: "His primary mission was to protect the Saipan landings." (That also seemed important to us who were on Saipan. We certainly would not have wanted the Japs to come down and try to knock us off.)

But, as a matter of fact, the men ashore heard almost nothing, for a month, about the great air and naval engagements, just as the men aboard ships had little actual knowledge of the land fighting. It is remarkable how men separated by as little as a mile of water can be as far apart as two worlds. Here, aboard this ship, the food was hot and excellent, and there were baths to be had. At night it was comfortably cool. There were movies (Ginger Rogers in *Kitty Foyle* tonight). Ashore the soldiers and Marines were dying by the hundreds, they were filthy and bearded and miserable, and itchy with heat rash. They were still eating those abominable calorie-packed C and K rations, cold.

But that was the way things were, and I never knew anything that could be done about it except to sympathize with the man on foot who, in the final analysis, had to win the Saipan battle.

June 24

This was the day when Lieut. General Holland Smith relieved the Army's division commander, Maj. General Ralph Smith, thereby setting off an argument which probably would continue for many years. I first learned about it at corps headquarters; two Army regiments had swung northward and up the center of Saipan; the Second Marine Division was still on the left (west coast) and the Fourth Marine Division was on the right. The Army division had only a 2,000-yard front, with six battalions to cover it, but its progress was too slow for Marine tactics. ("We've got to win this battle quickly, so these ships can get out of the harbor and get on with the next operation.") Last night, I was told at corps headquarters, one Marine outfit had taken a hill in front of the lagging Army troops, "rather than risk losing it back to the Japs." The third Army regiment, the 105th, was still stalled in the coral-packed southeast corner of the island (Nafutan Point). Holland Smith had ordered two of the regiment's battalions out of this area, on the theory that one battalion should be able to clean out the Japs down there, where three had not yet succeeded.

"We cannot attack Mount Tapotchau until the Twenty-seventh Division moves up," said a staff officer at corps headquarters, "and we've got to have that high ground so we can look down the Japs' throats instead of letting them look down ours. Besides, if we don't keep pressing 'em, they'll reorganize and dig in deeper, and casualties will shoot up higher. We can't sit back and expect artillery and naval gunfire to blast 'em out of those caves."

I saw General "Howlin' Mad" at his headquarters; he was nervous and he was remorseful. "Ralph Smith is my friend," he said, "but, good God, I've got a duty to my country. I've lost 7,000 Marines. Can I afford to lose back what they have gained? To let my Marines die in vain? I know I'm sticking my neck out—the National Guard will try to chop it off—but my conscience is clear. I did my duty. When Ralph Smith issued an order to hold after I had told him to attack, I had no other choice but to relieve him." (Technically, Admiral Spruance had issued the order for General Ralph Smith's relief, and Holland Smith had carried out the order.)

The Marines had other harsh words for the Army's officers, particularly for the National Guard hold-overs; the Army officers, on the other hand, spoke bitterly of Marine General Smith (the Army's Smith was popular with his officers and men). But there was no disposition among the correspondents at Saipan to write a story which might stir up the situation. In the first place, the friction between two services which had a common enemy was regrettable; in the second place, Admiral Nimitz's censors would never have passed a story about inter-service conflict. Nobody had to be told that.

The story about the conflict might never have been printed; numerous divisional and even corps commanders were relieved during the war without a line ever appearing in print about them. The late Lieut. General Lesley McNair, commander of the Army Ground Forces, mentioned this to me in a conversation in early 1944, sorrowfully adding: "I had to relieve the man I had picked as the best corps commander in the Army—but you can't always tell until they have been in combat."

Ironically, the relief of Ralph Smith was first publicized by one who sought to defend him. On July 8, just before the end of the Saipan battle, Hearst's San Francisco *Examiner* carried a front-page story, under a Washington dateline: "Allegedly excessive loss of life attributed to Marine Corps impetuosity of attack has brought a breach between Marine and Army commanders in the Pacific . . . Maj. General Ralph Smith, United States commander of the famous Twenty-Seventh Division, has been transferred summarily to Honolulu from the Saipan battlefield at the instigation of Lieut. General Holland 'Howlin' Mad' Smith . . . The controversy hangs upon Marine tactics versus Army tactics, the Marines seeking a swift decision at high cost, while the Army moved more deliberately—at lesser cost."

Naturally, the Marines blew sky-high when they saw that story. They knew they had had to take the beachhead losses, whereas the Army had been able to land later with safety; the Marines also knew that they had had to do most of the fighting on Saipan. They knew they had to take early initial casualties in any island operation, but they believed an enemy who was kept reeling would inflict fewer total casualties than one who was given time to come back.

Hearst continued his attack. In the New York *Journal American* for July 17 he editorialized: "The American people were shocked by the staggering casualties on Saipan, even before the fall of the island.[1] The Army's advocate of more cautious tactics has been relieved of his command . . . The supreme command in the Pacific should, of course, be logically and efficiently entrusted to General Douglas MacArthur." Next day the *Journal American* again editorialized: "There were 15,053 casualties in all categories of killed, wounded, and missing . . . This was a high and dreadful price . . . The important and significant thing the American people DO know is that equally difficult and hazardous military operations conducted in the Pacific War under the competent command of General Douglas MacArthur have been successfully completed with little loss of life in most cases and with an obvious MINIMUM loss of life in all cases."

This was enough to make many Navy and Marine commanders see red, since they considered that they had done a pretty good job in moving the Central Pacific front line from Hawaii to Saipan, 3,700 miles, with a loss of only 4,277 lives. Heavily defended small islands and atolls were bound to exact a certain cost in lives, but they had to be captured if air bases and advance supply bases were to be used in pushing the war through the Central Pacific toward Japan.

On July 19 it was announced at Army headquarters in Honolulu that Major General Ralph Smith had received command of another division. This action on the part of Lieut. General Richardson seemed to be a vindication of the Army general and a condemnation of the Marine general who had fired him.

In the next two months there were a few "dope" stories concerning what had happened at Saipan, but reportorial curiosity had almost abated when, on September 9, Lieut. General Holland Smith returned to Washington and held

---

[1] When Hearst ran his first story on July 8 he did not know that Army losses, because of the counterattack of July 7, had shot up nearly as high as either Marine division's.

a press conference. One high-ranking Navy Department official, knowing full well what questions would be asked of Holland Smith, doubted the wisdom of this. "Maybe we can control him," said another official. "Yeah," said the first official, "about as well as you can control a land mine after you've stepped on it."

Inevitably, the press conference turned to the Saipan battle. "I knew someone would ask that question," snorted Holland Smith, who went on to say: "One of the many prerogatives and responsibilities of a commanding officer . . . is the assignment and transfer of officers commanding subordinate elements . . . Unfortunately, circumstances forced me to exercise one of these prerogatives. I did relieve General Ralph Smith." For further details "Howlin' Mad" Smith referred reporters to the War Department (because Ralph Smith was an Army general). The War Department referred them back to Holland Smith (because he had made the change in command).

The cat was, finally, officially—and unfortunately, out of the bag.

The Twenty-seventh's misfortunes on Saipan were complicated at the end of the battle by the *banzai* counterattack which broke through the lines of the division's one regiment which had not been in action in a previous battle, the 105th. (The 165th had fought at Makin, the 106th at Eniwetok.) The Marines had had it drummed into their heads repeatedly that they must button up their lines at night, must prepare for the final charge which was bound to come. The 105th was caught on the early morning of July 7 with a gap between the two battalions it had placed in the line on the previous afternoon; the regiment had no patrols out in front, so that the full weight of the Jap attack fell on the line like a brick wall; the terrain chosen by the 105th was open ground favorable to the Jap attack (whose fault this was I never learned). Whether two Marine battalions could have stopped the heaviest Jap counterattack of the Pacific war (perhaps by 2,000 men) will never be known—but the Marines thought they could have done so. Many brave men of the 105th gave their lives in trying to stop the Japs; the Medal of Honor citations of two of them are printed in the appendix of this book. One burly corporal was found dead, his rifle and BAR empty, with 30 Japs piled in front of him. A pfc. had killed almost as many Japs before he went down. But more than 100 men backed into the water and swam out to the reef, where they were picked up by small boats. The Marines who heard of this incident did not know that the soldiers had no more ammunition; they did know that the Jap counterattack was finally stopped in the area of a Marine artillery battalion 2,000 yards back of the front line. (Whether the artillery Marines stopped the counterattack, or whether Army troops of the 106th finally stopped the remnants was a disputed point; the credit probably should be equally divided).

You can see, then, why there was considerable bitterness on Saipan, between the soldiers and the Marines. The former thought the Marines were claiming more credit than due; the latter thought the soldiers had let them down. It was most unfortunate that this state of affairs existed, but to say it did not exist is to lie. In most battles of the Central Pacific where Marines and soldiers were thrown together, particularly at Guam and Okinawa, they got along together very well.

If the counterattack had not occurred at the very end of the battle, the chances are that this bitterness on Saipan would have been avoided. Many Marines were especially warm in their praise of the 165th Regiment, which had the very difficult assignment of taking some tortuous terrain in the center of the line, just east of Mount Tapotchau.

CHAPTER SIX

MIDWAY ON SAIPAN

June 25

BY THIS DATE, THE SECOND DIVISION HAD SETTLED DOWN TO small patrol action, which amounted to little more than sitting and waiting for the other two divisions to straighten out the line. "We are having a hard time holding these boys back," said Colonel Shoup, the division's chief of staff, when I talked to him in the morning. "They want to go ahead, but it would be bad tactics to push too far ahead of the others." (The Fourth Division, which had a lot more ground to cover, including the big Kagman Peninsula—the trigger of the Saipan pistol—soon caught up, and the only sag in the line was in the middle.) Colonel Shoup guessed the battle would require 15 more days, which turned out to be a very good guess. We had captured nearly half of the island, excepting small pockets here and there, but many Japs remained to be killed. A prisoner had told us that Jap casualties remained fairly light, though he estimated 500 had been killed by artillery night before last.

The Second Division's left flank had advanced into Garapan early this morning, as far as Eighth Street (according to our numbering). Although there was no strong enemy opposition in front of the troops, they had hauled up at Eighth Street (also called "Radio Road" because of the Jap radio station) and had spread rolls of barbed wire along the street.

Just behind this Garapan line there were four knocked-out tanks, one of which was still burning. Surrounding the tanks were scattered dead Japs who were already covered with thousands of flies. The spilt blood of some had not yet dried. Some tanks still contained their crews, who had been fried inside. One tankman's crisp, upraised hands stuck out of his turret, as if in supplication to a power beyond his reach. Of those who lay on the ground, most wore the usual split-toed shoes and wrap-around leggings; their officers wore black rubber boots. Their shoulder patches were emblazoned with the Navy anchor insignia.

Near one pile of Japs a corpsman from B Medical Company was explaining the infiltration the Japs had attempted early in the morning: "The 37's knocked out the tanks. Then a bunch tried to slip through on foot. A Marine with a tommy gun challenged them. They ducked. He challenged them again. Then he cut loose."

A sacred park was on the south side of "Radio Road." A cast-iron Buddha, set on a pedestal, had suffered considerably from shell fragments, having been perforated in the chest and behind the right ear. The park must have been pretty before war wrecked it. There were fragrant, purple flowers near the concrete fences which surrounded various shafts. A small plaster vault had been only slightly wrecked. Inside the vault there were perhaps two dozen square boxes tied with white cheese cloth. These boxes contained the ashes of the dead.

One small incident of the morning seemed to typify a feature of the war against the burrowing Japs. Three of us had sat down in the sacred park, and had opened some K ration breakfast. We had hardly opened the cans of pork and egg yolk when a bullet whizzed overhead. It was close enough to cause us to "hit the dirt" (the "deck," in Marine parlance), just inside the concrete fence. A nearby Marine yelled: "I saw him. He jumped into a cave over there in the rock quarry." Several Marines ran toward the quarry, a hole in the ground perhaps 50 feet across and ten feet deep. Caves in the side of these scooped-out quarries were favorite hiding places for Japs.

The familiar game of "flush the sniper" began. A Marine sergeant took charge of the dozen or more men participating. First, he handed a Marine a grenade. This man jumped into the quarry, and began to edge around the rim toward the cave while a pal covered him with a Garand rifle. If a Jap should jump out of the cave brandishing a sword or a bayonet, as Japs often do, the man with the rifle would shoot him. The grenade was tossed into the cave. It exploded with a muffled thud.

In a movie version of killing Japs, the incident might have ended at this point. But the Marines had long since learned that one grenade did not always finish off a Jap in a trenched and compartmented cave—and very often it turned out that there were five to 20 Japs in whatever hole might be expected to contain one.

One of the Marines who fancied himself a linguist—he had been studying the posters on ship labeled "combat language"—took over:

"High de koy," was what it sounded like, as he yelled to the mouth of the cave. One of the other Marines explained to me: "That means, 'Come out'." The linguist said again, "High de koy," holding his rifle at the ready. But the occupant or occupants of the cave remained unmoved by his efforts.

"Shippee shenoddy," said the linguist, trying a new tack. I asked him what he was saying now. "That means, 'Don't be afraid'," he replied. That seemed a loose choice of encouraging words; there were at least twenty Marines surrounding the cave by now, with Garands and Browning automatic rifles (BAR's) poised. But after the linguist had made a couple more tries, it was obvious that whatever he said made little difference.

"Somebody go get a four-block charge of TNT," said the sergeant, who hadn't put much faith in the linguist, anyway.

At this point an armored bulldozer rumbled through the

underbrush. The sergeant explained the situation to him, and the bulldozer pilot drove his blade into the earth and started pushing dirt from the ground level into the quarry; it fell across the mouth of the cave. But there was hard coral rock only six inches under the surface, and the bulldozer driver didn't shovel much dirt.

Then the TNT arrived. The sergeant, who was quite angry by this time, snatched it savagely and said to the spectators watching the excavation proceedings: "A lot of crap is going to fly, so all of you stand back. Here, one of you riflemen, stay here and cover the hole. No telling how many bastards may pour out of there."

One of the Marines kept talking about coaxing the Jap or Japs out of the cave. He said, somewhat wistfully: "I wish we had somebody that knew enough Japanese to fetch him out." He said this in a low voice, so the sergeant did not hear him. Another private first-class observed that he didn't believe the Emperor himself knew enough Japanese to coax anybody out of that hole.

The TNT blew black dust high into the air. It made a terrific noise. Big waves of black smoke and some debris billowed out of the cave. But this was a well-constructed hole which went deep into the earth. How far back it went we never knew. About all that came to the surface that we saw when the smoke had cleared was the wooden framing of two-inch planks and a cheap suitcase filled with shirts and silk underwear and a cloth pocket-book that contained no money.

The bulldozer driver eyed the result, first with disappointment, and then with determination. "Hell, I'll fix him!" he said, as he swung his snorting machine around. He went to another side of the cave and dipped his blade savagely into the earth. This time he found soft dirt, and he scooped bladeful after bladeful over the mouth of the cave, until it was blocked with at least a five-foot thickness of earth.

We never found out what was in the hole, whether there were any Japs or many Japs. But I thought many questions in fighting the mysterious little Japs must forever go unanswered. After the war, I reflected, there would be enough material in many caves across the Pacific to keep archaeological expeditions busy a long time.

That part of Garapan which we held was a mass of rubble—tin roofs, broken concrete, burned timbers. Two red frame buildings which were fairly intact the Marines called "geisha houses," but plainly these were simple whorehouses whose occupants had long since been evacuated. Scattered about the floor, along the narrow hallways and inside the narrower cribs, were dozens of gayly colored kimonos and obis which fascinated Sergeant Bill Young, the Army photographer. He stuffed a dozen of them in his pack. There were also thousands of packages of venereal prophylaxis, and much cheap perfume which the Marines delighted to pour on each other's grimy dungarees. A dead cow was in the back yard.

The men in the line at Garapan were from K Company (Captain James Wendell Crain) and L Company (Captain Robert "Obie" O'Brien) of the Third Battalion, 2d Marines. Crain had had six men killed, 12 wounded, yesterday, in advancing into Garapan. Another casualty was reported as we talked to him. A Marine walked up to the company CP and said: "Captain, there was a man fooling around out there 200 yards in front of the barbed wire. A sniper hit him. Can we send for him?"

Crain said, "Is he walking? The runner said, "No, sir, he's either dead or wounded; he's lying out there." Crain said, "Well, get a corpsman and a minimum stretcher party; was he from K Company?" "No, sir, from the Scout and Sniper platoon." The last I heard of the incident the stretcher party had been fired upon, and had not yet reached the fallen souvenir hunter.

That was the way it was during these days of semi-idleness for the Second Division—a few men killed, others wounded, here or there. But when I climbed Hill Baker, where there was a knocked-out 5.5-inch Jap gun. I saw Captain John Schwabe, 2d Marine Regiment intelligence officer, and learned that some of these casualties had been costly indeed.

Night before last Lieut. Colonel Ralph E. Forsyth, the executive officer of the 10th (Artillery) Marines had been killed, and three artillery captains had also been wounded by the Jap shells which had found the range of our guns. This morning Jim Riseley's executive officer, Lieut. Colonel Ken McLeod, had been killed by a sniper while inspecting the Sixth Marines' front line at Tipo Pale (Hill 1190). On several mornings I had accompanied McLeod on these inspection trips. He held the Japs in high disdain; he usually refused to wear a helmet.

A combat correspondent said Lieut. Colonel Evans Carlson, the famed old Marine raider who was now war-plans officer of the Fourth Division, had also been wounded yesterday. Carlson had been on "The Rock," next to Mount Tapotchau, with Lieut. Colonel Justice Marion Chambers of 3/25 when a sniper began firing at them. Carlson grabbed a carbine, and said, "Snipers never bothered me much, but this one is pretty close." Then the sniper found him with several bullets; one arm was quite badly shot up; one leg drilled. The combat correspondent said Carlson smoked his underslung pipe as he was being carried down the hill on the stretcher, dictating a memo on the new site for a command post. He also said: "Last time I was wounded was in the first World War. If I can keep 'em that far apart I'll be all right."

The 8th Marines and the First Battalion, 29th Marines, finally took Mount Tapotchau, but suffered considerable losses in the process. Now the highest ground on the island belonged to us, and it was only a matter of time before the battle would end, and the Guam and Tinian battles start.

But nobody believed we would finish Saipan until nearly every Jap had been killed and until we had suffered the casualties we always had to take in wiping out the Japs. "Howlin' Mad" Smith told me: "The Japs are being smart, so far. I don't see the makings of a *banzai* attack yet. They are fighting a delaying action, and killing as many of us as possible in the meantime."

June 26

During my frequent visits to the First Battalion, 6th Marines, I came to know many of its officers and men quite well. By now they had moved forward about 1,000 yards, until they were on a line east and slightly south of Garapan. The 139 casualties the battalion suffered in the landing and in the big fight with the tanks had been followed by days and nights of comparative idleness, in patrolling and advancing against minor opposition. In the past eight days there had been only 48 casualties, and 22 of them (three killed, 19 wounded) had occurred last night when some infiltrating Japs had raised merry hell before they had been slaughtered.

There had been minor actions every day, and on only one day (June 20) had the battalion gone without a single casualty. Night before last twelve Japs had tried to filter through and knock out the 37-mm. guns. Jones's men waited in their holes, then sprang upon the Japs with their knives. They killed all the Japs, but had one man killed and four wounded.

"You left the other day just at the right time," said Colonel Jones, "right afterward Ken (Lieutenant Kenneth H. Crone) and I went back to hear Father Gallagher say Mass. While we were gone, a Jap mortar landed smack in the CP. Killed one man and wounded seven. By the way, we turned over the sacramental paraphernalia in that little cabin to Father Gallagher."

The battalion's three infantry companies had been built

up to a strength of about 160 men each. Some of the slightly wounded returned nearly every day, and 50 replacements, including two officers, had been sent up yesterday. Now a new captain had shown up, to take over A Company. He was husky, blue-eyed Bill Schwerin, "a damn good combat officer," in Jones's estimation. Schwerin, the son of a Marine, had busted out of Annapolis, had enlisted in the Marines and had gone to Guadalcanal, where he won a Navy Cross. Somehow, he had been assigned as a transport quartermaster, so he had been wandering around the ocean when the transports pulled out during the Philippine Sea battle.

Jones himself was an interesting character. He came from a well-to-do Missouri family which was able, when he graduated in 1937 from the University of Kansas, to help to set him up (with some classmate partners) in a small-homes-construction business. After some initial setbacks, the business had begun to prosper. But Bill Jones had a yen for the military life and he had a deep sense of patriotism. ("I still get a lump in my throat when they play the *Star Spangled Banner*.") At college, in the pacifistic '30s, they used to kid him about being a Boy Scout; he liked the ROTC. When his application for a commission in the Marine Corps was accepted, Bill had picked out his career.

Jones had spent all his military career in the same outfit, the First Battalion, 6th Regiment. Seven months before Pearl Harbor, as a second lieutenant, he went to Iceland with the old 6th. Upon returning to the United States in early 1942, he became a first lieutenant. Three weeks later he was a captain and executive officer to the battalion commander, John Easley. In this capacity he went to Guadalcanal, but the 6th was the last Marine regiment to reach Guadalcanal, only six weeks before the Marines were withdrawn to New Zealand. That was long enough for 600 men of 1/6 to come down with malaria (other casualties, 27 killed, about 50 wounded).

In September, 1943, when Easley moved to a division liaison job, Jones, not yet 27 but already recognized as an exceptional officer, took command of the battalion. The 2nd and 8th Marines were the assault battalions on Tarawa, but Bill Jones's battalion of the 6th which landed on the western beach (the crown of the bird-shaped island's head) on the second afternoon, played a big part in the battle. His fresh troops jumped off at dawn on the third morning and marched with tanks along the heavily fortified southern shore, burning and blasting Japs out of pillboxes as they marched. That night 1/6 stood off a Jap *banzai* attack, and Tarawa was all but secured. The battle cost Jones 201 casualties, including nine officers.

For his leadership on Tarawa, Bill Jones got a spot promotion to lieutenant colonel—and the Marines were very cautious about passing out spot promotions.

What made Jones a superior officer? I decided that many things caused him to stand out, even in the Marines, where officer caliber is generally high. In the first place, he knew his business. He was always prepared when the order came to attack. He had the "feel" of his companies, and even of his patrols—he could plug them in as though he were pressing a button. He knew terrain and he knew maps, which is not easy in strange country—and we fought all the way across the Pacific in country we knew little better than we knew the moon. He thought fast, and he gave his men every break. He never asked a man to do something he could not and would not do himself.

Jones's officers and men respected him, though he was far from being a martinet. He had a sense of humor which appealed to them all. He could josh his men without breeding any sort of the familiarity which lowers the bars of discipline. One day a grizzled sergeant, Dean Squires, of Taloga, Oklahoma, came in to make a report; Jones looked up and said, "Talk about old men; there's Squires; I've

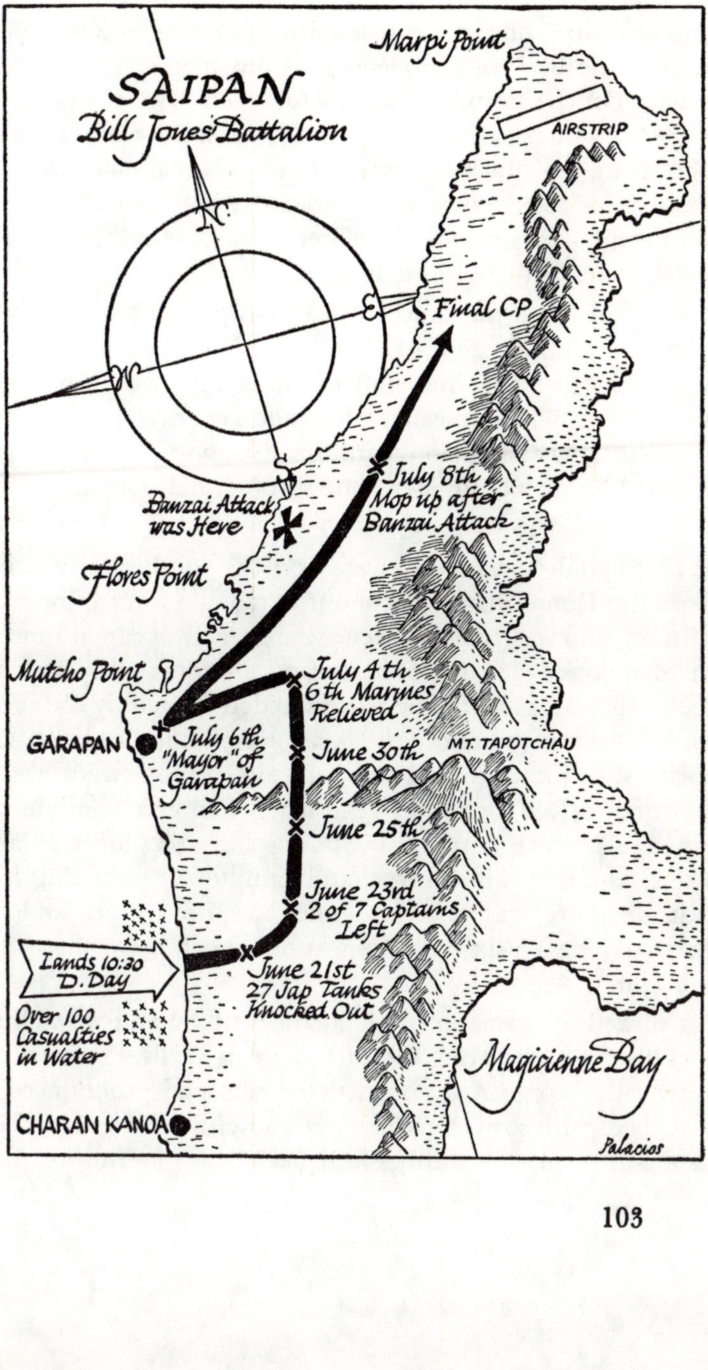
SAIPAN
Bill Jones' Battalion
Marpi Point
AIRSTRIP
Final CP
July 8th
Mop up after
Banzai Attack
Banzai Attack
was Here
Flores Point
Mutcho Point
July 4th
6th Marines
Relieved
GARAPAN
July 6th
"Mayor" of
Garapan
June 30th
MT. TAPOTCHAU
June 25th
June 23rd
2 of 7 Captains
Left
Lands 10:30
D. Day
June 21st
27 Jap Tanks
Knocked Out
Over 100
Casualties
in Water
Magicienne Bay
CHARAN KANOA
Palacios

been trying to get rid of him ever since we were in Iceland together, but he won't go away." Jones believed in his noncommissioned officers with a faith they reciprocated (and what is the basis of morale if it is not men's faith in each other?) On the transport he had told me: "I've got gunnery sergeants who have been in 19 or 20 years; those are the men who make the Marine Corps. Those old men take pride in making an officer. One of them said when I was a second lieutenant, 'I'll make an officer out of him if it kills me'." Jones added: "And it almost did."

Bill Jones had the touch of leadership which is not given to many men. Because of this, his colonel and his general relied heavily upon him. But the men who knew him best, his orderly, Tony Toscano; his headquarters company's first sergeant, Lewis Michelony; and his battalion sergeant major, Howard Lyon, would have gone through hell for him.

The battalion CP was located on the south side of a big rock. Jim Donovan, the Dartmouth graduate from Winnetka, Illinois, who was Jones's executive officer, walked with me to an abandoned Japanese aid station in some rock crevices about 300 yards away. The natural ledge formed by the rocks made it almost bombproof; it had an opening only on the north side. Scattered about this aid station were shoes, headnets, a Red Cross flag (the first I had ever seen among Jap equipment), rations, including big sacks of rice and beans, anti-mosquito gloves, and bundles of new clothing. Outside there was one Jap, who had been dead so long (perhaps five or six days) he was not much more than skin and bones.

I picked up a small can of Japanese ration and we walked back to the CP, hitting the dirt twice as shells screamed far overhead. George Azud opened the can, and pronounced it roast beef with soy-bean sauce. "It's a delicacy," he said. The taste was good; the thinly-sliced beef had a fine flavor. But

Ken Crone said, "In North China they used to can cat meat"—and nobody ate any more.

But a few minutes later, about dark, there was some use for the can's contents. A five-foot Jap prisoner was brought in. After he insisted on getting down on his knees, bowing and putting together his hands in a prayerful clasp, the Jap was handed the can of "roast beef." He ate it greedily, for he was obviously very hungry. Then he drank a can full of water, and started talking and hissing as Jap prisoners almost always did. He made sweeping motions with his arms, as if he were wielding a scythe, then he shook his head as he held his arms up and squinted down an imaginary rifle sight. We judged he was trying to tell us he was a farmer, not a soldier. He wore only shorts, so he might have been either.

When the tall, blonde language officer arrived, he asked the prisoner a few questions, and reported that the Jap was indeed trying to say he was a farmer. (Next day we learned he was lying.) Then the Jap pulled out a wallet made of dirty canvas. It was stuffed with 10-yen notes; he probably had over 1,000 yen. He gesticulated and hissed wildly, and pointed toward the rocks where he had been captured (in the far recesses of the aid station). The interpreter reported: "He says there is lots more money where this came from. He was with a group of 300 Japs, and he thinks less than 30 of them are still alive; artillery got most of them. The bastard has apparently been robbing corpses." Nobody was interested in uncovering the Jap's hoard, so he was led away to regimental intelligence.

Captain Schwerin reported in. Jones told him to send out patrols at 0600 in the morning and to have them return by 0730—jumping-off time. Then we turned in, in the lee of the rocks, and listened to the 105's whistle overhead all night. If artillery could defeat the Japs on Saipan, we were giving it every chance.

June 27

The Japs did little firing during the night. One mortar

shell hit about 50 yards back of us. There were two red alerts during the night, and we learned later that enemy bombs had killed three men on Aslito Field, and Japs had also infiltrated from Nafutan Point and burned one P-47. About 0400 three Japs had crept through the lines and dropped a grenade off the cliff to the east of Jones's CP. At 0600 there was intense rifle and machine-gun fire over there (in the 3/6 area), and after a while we learned that 60 Japs were killed. After the fire ceased, Jones sent his patrols out.

They had not been gone long when B Company phoned in and asked for four stretchers to be sent up to them, plus a demolition squad to seal a cave. Two men on patrol had been killed and one wounded. The Japs were becoming more active all around. In mid-morning they threw three mortar shells within 100 yards of the battalion CP, hitting nobody. Then they threw another far over our heads, squarely on a road leading up to Mount Tapotchau, and, apparently, squarely on the trucks. The drivers of the trucks jumped out into a ditch. When the smoke cleared away we could see that the trucks, instead of being smashed to pieces, were not even hit. The drivers got back into their seats and scurried up the mountain road.

I started walking the half mile back to the regimental command post, but caught a ride halfway up the mountain road. The regimental surgeon, Doctor English, said Major Monk Rentsch's battalion had had quite a bit of fighting on his mountain slope yesterday. Forty-six casualties had been evacuated through English's small tented hospital, but the total that came through including 8th Marine regimental casualties, ran to 104, plus 28 cases of combat fatigue. The wounds were some of the nastiest the doctor had seen: "Nine shell fragment cases for each bullet wound."

I drove to Charan-Kanoa with Lieut. Colonel Easley, who had come out of the hospital anxious to get his battalion back from Rentsch. Colonel Riseley promised he could have it in a few days. Easley did take it back toward the end of the battle, and he led it on to Tinian late in July, but fate, never kind to Easley, played her last trump against him on Tinian. On Guadalcanal she had given him a severe case of malaria; she let him go through Tarawa all right, but he was wounded the first day on Saipan; on Tinian a sniper shot him through the heart. I was glad later that I had been able, when we reached the correspondents' shack, to gratify his expressed wish for "one good, stiff drink of bourbon." No man could have given his last drink to a finer or unluckier officer than John Easley.

When Easley and I arrived at Charan-Kanoa I learned that I had lost another friend. Colonel Carl D. Silverthorne, the genial, pink-skinned, white-haired Army officer whom I had met at Eniwetok, had been killed by a sniper who shot him from a cave near Agingan Point.

June 28

With several other correspondents, I drove down to Aslito Field, where our own planes had been operating for several days. Last night our "Black Widow" night fighters shot down their first Jap plane, about 30 miles off Rota. P-47's from the 19th and 73rd Squadrons were parked around the airstrip, and nearby were a couple of TBF's, off carriers, which had made emergency landings. In any island operation, rapid success depended heavily on early capture of a serviceable airfield, and Aslito was in excellent condition.

Lieut. Colonel Louis Sanders, the tall young commander of the 73rd Squadron, was full of the story of the Jap attack on the airfield night before last. He said about 200 Japs broke out of Nafutan Point around ten o'clock, lobbed hand grenades into the 105th Infantry CP, stole some BAR's. About 20 of the Japs reached the southeast corner of the field and started sniping at plane crews and engineers. They tossed a bottle of gasoline and a grenade into a P-47 cockpit and set it afire. Others jabbed tires and belly tanks with bayonets.

The ground crews killed four Japs, and the rest withdrew into a pocket, or scattered around the field. Even now, a day and a half later, snipers occasionally fired at pilots while they were warming up their engines. Ground crewmen who had been infantrymen were scouting holes around the airfield.

The highlight of the wild evening, Colonel Sanders thought, came when an officer from the 804th Engineer Battalion spied two Japs as he was driving a jeep. He fired only one shot before his carbine jammed. Then he ran over one of the Japs and killed him. Colonel Sanders swore the story was true.

This evening the new air-raid siren sounded about 2100. Soon afterward, four bombs exploded somewhere near the airfield, about a mile from the correspondents' house. Then our anti-aircraft began to twinkle at about 15,000 feet. One of the first bursts apparently caught the Jap squarely. His flaming plane wafted slowly earthward, to the cheers of thousands of men. At 500 feet, the plane flared brilliantly and disappeared over the eastern side of Saipan.

The unusual feature of this anti-aircraft work was this: The 751st AA Battalion had been in the Pacific for about two years but had never before fired at an enemy plane.

Such shooting was almost as extraordinary as the manner in which a Jap torpedo plane had been brought down a few nights ago. The Jap went down so low over the water that he flew into the boom of a cargo ship. The ship's captain promptly demanded, and received, credit for one Jap plane.

June 29

The Saipan battle had progressed so far that there was now a mess set up for corps personnel—but the front-line troops would not get such luxury until the battle had ended. The kitchen and screened mess tables were set up three dusty blocks from corps headquarters. Breakfast was powdered eggs (cold and lumpy), apricots, coffee, and C-ration biscuits—but it seemed like a breath of civilization.

The correspondents even had an intelligence officer by now, to brief them on the day's events. After breakfast the officer, amiable young Steve McCormick, an Army major from Washington, D. C., told us that Nafutan Point had at last been cleaned out, after nearly a whole battalion of Japs had been dug out by the 105th's soldiers. Yesterday 17 Japs were killed down there, and 120 civilians came out of the caves to surrender. The 2/105 troops had gone into reserve.

But there was yet another stumbling block, Hell's Pocket, in the center of the line opposite Kagman Point. The Japs were holed up in coral caves similar to Nafutan Point's.

Correspondents and officers coming ashore from Admiral Turner's flagship reported that the number of casualties was still climbing. Even the flagship's corridors were lined with wounded waiting for treatment, and some small boats evacuating the wounded wandered from one transport to another, trying to find a place to park their burden. Casualties, they said, were nearing 9,000, divided approximately as follows: Second Division, 200 officers and 3,000 men; Fourth Division, 200 and 4,000; Twenty-seventh Division, 70 and 1,100.

This afternoon several of us set out to visit all three division command posts. We succeeded, but it was no easy task. The divisions were spread across the island, and twice we deserted our jeep for the ditches when the Japs began laying mortar fire along the connecting roads.

General Schmidt's Fourth Division CP was in a hillside gully below Mount Tapotchau. The Fourth had made excellent progress, but casualties were mounting high enough to threaten combat efficiency. "Lots of good stories over here, though," said Captain McCahill, the division public relations officer, as he displayed the file produced by his combat correspondents. These newsmen had turned in no less than 402 separate stories.

The Twenty-seventh's CP was about half a mile east of the Fourth. It was still under occasional mortar fire. The new division commander, Maj. General George W. Griner, Jr., of Whitesburg, Georgia, had taken over from General Jarman, who had commanded the division between Ralph Smith's departure and Griner's arrival. An infantry officer since 1917, General Griner had been a supply officer in Europe, and had most recently commanded the Ninety-eighth Division in Hawaii. General Griner greeted us briefly, and continued writing a V-mail letter. His assistant division commander, Brig. General Ogden J. Ross, a lawyer from Troy, New York, pointed out the division's line on the map.

The Twenty-seventh had been dogged by hard luck. Colonel Kelley of the 165th Regiment had been wounded and evacuated. Yesterday one of the most promising battalion commanders in the division, Lieut. Colonel Harold I. Mizony, of Spokane, Washington, a candidate for regimental command, had been killed, with two of his radio operators, beyond Hell's Pocket. Several days earlier Colonel Harold G. Browne, of Binghamton, New York, and Major John M. Nichols had been killed. Lieut. Colonel J. F. McDonough, battalion commander of 2/165, had been wounded, as had Major Brusso, who succeeded him. In one 72-hour period, said General Ross, the division had lost seven field officers.

We drove about a mile north, along a dusty, truck-jammed road, and stopped at a groove of scrub trees. There the Third Battalion, 106th Infantry, was resting after having been pulled out of the battle for Hell's Pocket. Major Francis Fisher of Parkersburg, West Virginia, who had taken command of the battalion after Colonel Mizony's death, said his whole outfit was exhausted, after many days of fighting. His battalion strength, he said was down to 432 after 292 had been killed or wounded (the dead included four officers,

30 men). Thirty-three sick had been evacuated. "I don't know how we have stood as much as we have," he said. Then he added: "The Marines work differently. We push forward on one side, then on the other. They push straight forward and knock out what's in front of them."

Farther forward, we stopped on the crest of a small hill, overlooking a rolling valley below. About 1,000 yards forward, several Army tanks were advancing against the Japs in the woods ahead, firing their machine guns as they rumbled onward. From the high coral ridge on the left, Japs fired from caves. One of the soldiers manning a 37-mm. anti-tank gun said: "Better not try to go down where the tanks are. The Japs have got machine guns trained on the whole valley down there." The valley floor was spotted with knocked-out tanks, eight Jap, two American.

On the way back we stopped again to see Major Fisher. He looked toward Hell's Pocket and said, in a tired voice: "They have put I don't know how much mortar and artillery fire on those caves. But it takes men with rifles and machine guns . . . " (How many times I heard that refrain during the war against the Japs! Everybody concurred, but nobody seemed able to do much about it . . . unless the atomic bomb was the instrument that finally could do the trick.)

We crawled back into the jeep, and started toward the front on the eastern side of the island, cutting back through Chau Chau village. Then we drove about a mile north, into the Fourth Division's front lines. C Company of the 24th Marines had pulled up near a farm house, near which lay the first dead goat I had seen on Saipan—artillery and bombs killed hundreds of cows, but goats seemed to know how to take cover. We stayed there only a little while; Jap mortar shells began falling around us, and the ditch near the dead goat was much too shallow. I suggested we had seen enough of the eastern side of the island. The others, Mac R. Johnson of the U. P., Frank Kelley, and Captain Stan McClure, the Army public relations officer, agreed.

We swung back across the island, then northward beyond the Charan-Kanoa airstrip, which was used as a highway only. At Second Division headquarters we heard that it was now possible to drive all the way to the top of Tapotchau, where a good view of the battle below could be had. It was nearly dark by now, and we put off the ascent until tomorrow.

At corps headquarters, old "Howlin' Mad" Smith was in a better mood. We now had more than half the island, and, although only about 4,000 Japs had been counted dead (less than half of our own casualties), we had undoubtedly killed many more who had been dragged back of their own lines. Our tactical position was good; the end of the Saipan battle was in sight. The only uncertainty was its total cost.

"That 165th Infantry did a good job today," said Smith, "and the 105th and 106th gained a couple of thousand yards." Fighting in the Second and Fourth Division areas had almost ceased until the Twenty-seventh caught up along the eastern slopes of Tapotchau.

June 30

The steep and narrow road which wound to the top of Tapotchau was no highway, but to ascend it was possible. There were times when it seemed that the jeep would explode from overheating. The road curved upward through semi-jungle, over big rocks, past the unmistakable smell of the dead (we saw none along the road). Trucks and jeeps were puffing up the mountain regularly now, and we met four ambulance jeeps coming down with wounded.

The view from the peak of Tapotchau was remarkable. It was simple to see the south end of the island, where Isely Field (renamed today) was like a beehive, then to look northward and see Marpi Point at the tip of the island. The battle did not look nearly so complicated, nor the island so large. One had a feeling that this could not last much longer; it seemed almost possible to jump to the end of the island —and the battle.

On a ledge just below the crest a mortar squad from 2/8 was firing shells into the woods forward and below. A rifleman, ("the best shot in the company") was taking deliberate aim through a telescopic sight attached to his Springfield—a better sniping rifle than the newer Garand. Once in a while he squeezed the trigger, but I could see no Japs down below —not even with glasses.

I walked down the incline forward of Tapotchau. Our troops were already on the reverse slopes and in the little valleys between slopes. There were five dead Japs along the path. They had evidently been killed by artillery days earlier. I started to pick up a Jap knee mortar which lay near them, but there were wires attached to it, and I had long since become booby-trap conscious. Farther along there were about 20 more dead Japs scattered along the path. In the midst of a circle of five of them lay a woman in blue and white slacks. Her face was calm in death. I thought she was prettier than any live Jap woman I had seen in the civilian compounds. She and her companions apparently had been killed by artillery; there was no evidence of suicide.

The forward OP (observation post) of the First Battalion, 29th Marines, which had taken the crest of Tapotchau, was perched back of some rocks on a sheer, 500-foot cliff. From there we could see the fight below. Incessant mortar and artillery fire burst in the woods and fields immediately ahead of the OP. There was rifle fire and machine-gun fire to the right, but not a Jap in evidence, as usual.

Lieut. Colonel "Tommy" Tompkins (whose leadership of 1/29 won him a Navy Cross) was haggard and dirty and pale. "Well, I've got 284 men left in my battalion," he said, "less than 90 men to each infantry company." Three days later Tompkins himself was a casualty, shot through the leg by a Jap machine gunner.

General Edson, who made daily inspections of the three regimental front lines of the Second Division, offered me a ride down the mountain. "It's a tough battle," he said, "and it's drawn out—more like Guadalcanal than Tarawa. I wouldn't be surprised if it took three more days to get to the 0-6 line, and seven more after that to clean it up."

One of our own TBF's was hit by anti-aircraft fire this morning. The pilot bailed out at 400 feet and landed safely behind our own lines. But the radioman and an Army artillery observer crashed with the plane, which landed in Lieut. Colonel "Woody" Kyle's area and wounded eight of his men. The same Jap anti-aircraft gun (at Tanapag Harbor) yesterday shot down another TBF, from which nobody escaped.

The Second Division Hospital was set up in the old Jap radio station, about 400 yards from where I had landed on D Day. Commander Eugene R. Hering had a total of 19 surgical tables, on the lower floor of the burned-out radio station and in big black-out tents. Cases were being admitted at a rate of about 180 a day, and there were altogether 680 in the hospital, half of them ambulatory. Six died yesterday. Eighty-nine were evacuated, 13 of them by air evacuation which had started functioning recently, the rest by DUKWS (amphibious trucks, pronounced "ducks") to transports and hospital ships.

Doctors tend to be philosophers about war. "Doc" Bruner said at supper: "The thing that impresses me is this—these Japs know they can't win. They have nothing left except some small arms and a few mortars, and we've got a world of everything. But the Japs fight on and on and on, and we're going to lose 10,000 men before we win this damned little island."

CHAPTER SEVEN

THE SEMI-FINALS

July 1

WE COULD NOT WRITE MUCH ABOUT CASUALTIES UNTIL THE report had been released in Admiral Nimitz' communique. Today's communique listed 9,752 casualties as of June 28: Killed in action, Marines 1,289, Army 185; wounded in action, Marines 6,377, Army 1,023; missing in action, Marines 827, Army 61; totals, 1,474 killed, 7,400 wounded, 878 missing.

July 2

Several war correspondents went aboard a submarine at the suggestion of Commander Waldo Drake, CINCPAC public relations officer, who said, "You might not get the story released right away, but they will let down the bars some day." (They did—about a year later.) Because I had never been aboard a submarine, I was interested in going along. Everybody agreed enthusiastically that the submarines had done a great job in the war against Japan, but the Navy made a fetish of secrecy about their actions, and not much about them was printed beyond the announcement: "Our submarines have sunk 17 more Japanese ships in Far Eastern waters."

The submarine we visited was the *Cavalla*, named for a South Seas fighting fish. The *Cavalla*, launched in November, 1943, commissioned three months later, was now on her first cruise. Her hull was already a splotched, dirty gray, but on the inside she was spick-and-span as a cocktail lounge. She was air-conditioned, and her wardroom had green leather cushions. About the whole ship there was evidence of efficiency and of the high morale which invariably goes hand-in-hand with the most dangerous jobs.

The crew wore shorts and sandals, as did her captain, Commander Herman J. Kossler of Portsmouth, Virginia, a 32-year-old Naval Academy graduate. Captain Kossler had a big nose, a black moustache, close-cropped black hair which was already turning gray, and dark blue eyes. He looked not unlike Mike Romanoff, the Hollywood restaurateur. He had been executive officer aboard Commander Burt Klakring's *Guardfish,* the submarine which was off the coast of Japan in 1942 and allegedly attended the horse races. That story, said Kossler, was somewhat garbled. Actually, the *Guardfish* had spotted what looked like an excursion train puffing along the coast of Japan. Somebody said, "There goes a crowd to the racetrack." The *Guardfish* was tempted to fire a torpedo at a trestle over which the train had to pass, but it was impossible to calculate the speed of the train so that the torpedo would hit the stanchion as the train crossed. So the *Guardfish* allowed the train to proceed to the horse races—or wherever it was going.

The *Cavalla's* first combat cruise had been eventful. Early in the evening of June 17 she had been patrolling somewhere in the Philippine Sea when the Jap fleet—or a large portion of it—was picked up at 15 miles, heading directly for Saipan. "It scared hell out of me," said Captain Kossler.

"We were patrolling surface, and we picked up the ships astern. We put in to investigate. So, we were making 19 knots toward them and they were making about the same toward us. We turned tail. Then we began tracking the ships at 15,000 yards. It was fairly dark, but I could make out one of the ships as a carrier. It looked like the Empire State Building," said Kossler.

"We could see seven ships, a carrier, and two columns of ships I thought were battleships and cruisers but couldn't be sure. We submerged directly ahead. They closed in to 10,000 yards and we picked up other ships—at least fifteen.

"We had a perfect set-up on the carrier; I'm sure I could have hit it. But I hadn't seen any report of that task force, and I figured my primary mission was to get word out that there was a task force headed for Saipan.

"Their destroyers could have held me down five or six hours, so I decided to let them go. I went down 100 feet. We tried to count the screws—we were about 300 yards from the nearest—but there were so many of them. It took half an hour for the ships to pass. I figured my estimate of 15 ships was low.

"Two destroyers began weaving back and forth. [Here Kossler gestured with both hands like a fighter pilot explaining his tactics.] But they did not pick us up, and I finally decided to surface. I sent out my contact report and it got through.

"We dove at 2018, and were down about two hours. We came up and started chasing the ships. At 0500 we still had not regained contact. I sent another report, negative this time.

"I chased 'em on four engines, and never did sight them all day. I decided to head over to my area. About 0300 on the morning of the 19th I was driven down by a plane. We surfaced, but were driven down again about 0700, and again about 1000. This last time we came up in about 15 minutes. When he did we sighted four planes on the starboard bow. We kept watching. Then we saw the mast of a ship and recognized it as a destroyer. We came to the right, speeded up and took another look. It was a carrier taking planes. There were four planes to go, and 30 or 40 already on board. She was making 15 knots on an easterly course."

Kossler remembered every detail because he was coming to the climax: "We headed in. I took three observations. Meantime, we had a destroyer on our beam. It was 1100.

I was afraid these ships might be our own outfit. I let the executive officer (Lieutenant Thomas B. Denegre) and the gunnery officer (Lieutenant (j.g.) A. G. Rand) take a look. We were pretty sure it was a *Shokaku* class carrier of 20,000 tons, but I couldn't make out what kind of flag I saw. I took a last look and—God damn! there was the rising sun, big as hell. The exec and gunnery officer saw it, too.

"This destroyer hadn't sighted us as we headed in. I put the periscope up. We were at 1,000 yards. I got ready to fire six torpedoes in such a way that if our dope was good at least four would hit. After I had fired the fourth torpedo I looked over at the destroyer and he was still on my neck. I fired the fifth and sixth on the way down. I know the first three hit.

"The destroyer must have seen my torpedoes. Shortly afterward the depth charges started coming. We counted 105, and minor explosions which must have been bombs from the fourth plane; three of those planes had landed but the fourth hadn't. We had seen two heavy cruisers and just this destroyer on our port bow, but evidently there were lots more. Two more destroyers were working on us, too. The first two hours they worked in earnest, but in the last hour they dropped between me and the point of attack. I figured they left only one destroyer in the last hour.

"I never saw the carrier afterward. I figured the two extra destroyers went back to the scene of the attack and left this one for nuisance value. Two and one-half hours later our sound gear picked up very loud water noises. I said to myself, 'That damn thing is sinking.' We went down deep because we had some leaks. After a while I decided to come up to look. As we started up we heard four explosions a couple of seconds apart, very loud. I've been bombed and depth charged, but I never heard noises like that before. After those explosions there was no more depth charging, either."

As she returned to Saipan yesterday the *Cavalla* ran into some more fireworks. "I figured we were close enough in to surface," said Captain Kossler; "we got within about three miles. There came a plane, a friendly plane. The exec was topside with me. 'Hey, he's shooting,' said the exec. We pulled the plug and went down again. All I could think of was the old crack, 'That friendly son-of-a-bitch dropped a stick of bombs'."

I had never been on a hospital ship, either. But a correspondent must produce stories and, although I had found the submarine an interesting ship, I knew the story of the *Cavalla* would make no copy for next week's issue. So, late in the afternoon I caught a ride in an LCVP to the *Solace*, several hundred yards north of Admiral Turner's flagship.

The *Solace* was one of four hospital ships evacuating the wounded from Saipan. The others were *Relief, Samaritan* and *Bountiful*. The hospital ships' names sounded like funeral wreaths, but, actually, they were the most cheerful ships in the Pacific, and only about one per cent of the patients died before reaching a rear-area hospital. The *Solace* had already made one Saipan run when I went aboard her. She had arrived on D plus 3, had been loaded by D plus 5, and during the trip to Guadalcanal she had lost only six patients out of five hundred and eighty-three.

Hospitals ships are incongruous in the midst of heavy artillery, continuous machine-gun fire, and blackouts. They were painted spotless white, with a broad green stripe around the ship on which a large red cross superimposed. They sailed through the Pacific brilliantly illuminated, although they blacked out to protect other ships when they were in harbor, and they even showed movies at night. Hospital ships were so far removed from military operations that, by international law, they could not carry any kind of combat supplies, not even mail for the troops ashore.

The hospital ship's sailors and the medical personnel,

doctors, nurses, enlisted corpsmen, wore spotless white, in contrast to other ships' blue-dungareed men. Everything about the ship was intended to make the wounded man forget about mud and foxholes, the blackout, and the whine of artillery shells. Most soldiers, if asked to name their chief impression of battle, would probably point to the mud and dust, the dirt and the filth. That was one reason for every effort made aboard the *Solace* and her sister ships to keep everything white. Likewise, men who had spent many days eating cold canned rations appreciated hot, well prepared food. The trouble with the hospital ships was that there were not enough of them. At Saipan, not more than twenty per cent of the wounded could be taken aboard these marvelous ships. The rest, except for a trickling evacuated by planes, sweated it out on the crowded bunks of transports.

The *Solace* in peacetime had been the Clyde Line's *Iroquois*, which plied the tourist trade on the New York-Miami run. Her decks were spacious. She had beds for 480 wounded men. In emergencies, as at Saipan, she could add cots and sofas, and her ship's personnel could be routed out of their bunks onto the decks, thereby making room for another hundred.

Doctor Howard K. Gray, the famed Mayo Clinic surgeon who served aboard the *Solace* with the rank of navy captain, kept statistics on the casualties his ship carried. Sixty-five per cent of all casualties at recent battles, Tarawa, Kwajalein, New Guinea, Saipan, had been wounded in the arms or legs[2] ("extremities," in medical language). One fourth of all patients had more than one wound. One to two per cent had gas infection, and, despite penicillin, mortality for gas was one-half. At Tarawa, Doctor Gray noted, 57 per cent of the *Solace* cases had been bullet wounds; at Saipan, only 25 per cent (65 per cent of the Saipan wounds were caused by mortars and artillery). Because there were more counter-

[2] But not at Iwo Jima, eight months later. See Chapter Thirteen.

attacks at Saipan, 6.6 per cent of the wounds were caused by bayonets and knives, five times as many as Tarawa.

A battle that is drawn out, as Saipan was, naturally produced a higher percentage of combat-fatigue cases. During the two days when it first anchored at Saipan, the *Solace* had taken aboard about 150 cases. With one or two days' rest, all but 48 returned to shore and to combat. These 48 probably would never be fit for combat again, Doctor Gray thought.

Besides its senior surgeon, Doctor (Captain) John T. Bennett, a Navy regular for nearly 30 years, who acted as medical supervisor, the *Solace* had 17 doctors (including a dentist and an oral surgeon), a chief nurse and twelve other nurses, 175 medical corpsmen. The ship's crew of several hundred men was captained by a grizzled, soft-voiced Navy regular, Commander Earl C. Peterson. Until long after the Saipan battle, the Central Pacific campaign was a womanless war except for the nurses aboard the hospital ships. They were a source of curiosity for men who had not seen a woman in months or years. Aboard the *Solace* the women had their own wardroom and their own secluded quarters on one of the decks. They came out for special occasions into the male officers' wardroom. (I ate Christmas dinner, 1944, on the *Solace* in Ulithi anchorage; it was a special occasion.)

Doctor Gray took me on a tour of the ship, six double-bunked wards, a three-tiered convalescent ward, five operating tables, x-ray room, pharmacy, and all the furnishings of a first-class hospital. "The most amazing thing," Doctor Gray said, as we walked, "is the way these healthy young kids bounce back. Good food, plenty of fluids, and some rest do wonders for them. What they get is the best of attention, with a salt-air luxury-cruise thrown in. The equipment and the doctors aboard here are as good—or better—than they could get back home. We pull out with nearly 600 bedridden patients. By the time we reach Guadalcanal, about half of them are walking. Every night more and more of them appear at movies topside."

Another thing that impressed Doctor Gray was the courage and sense of humor of the American fighting man. "Coming out of Tarawa we had to amputate a young Marine's leg. He cried a little bit when we told him we had to do it. But next morning, when I asked him how he felt, he said, 'Okay, doc; there's not so much of me to hurt now.' There was another kid *in extremis* when we brought him aboard. He had been shot from only a few feet away, and he had a big hunk of his chest gone. But he pulled out of it, somehow. When we got to talking to him, we found that his first thought was one of complete disgust for Jap marksmanship. He said, 'If that had been a Marine, at that range he would have shot me square through the forehead.'"

Hospital ships got first priority on everything. Some shore hospital doctors were likely to growl when the hospital ships came around, because of this priority. Likewise, doctors who had to give primary treatment under fire—battalion aid men and sometimes division hospital men, often referred to hospital ships as "sissies." There was nothing clean about the work at the front.

About 1900 the *Solace* began receiving wounded. The amphtracs and the amphibious ducks came alongside. White-clad stretcher bearers waited at the specially wide gangway, lifted the dirty, bloody men gingerly, and took them up to the "lobby" where they were set down for classification. An embarkation officer, Doctor Richmond Beck, of Huntington, New York, examined the red-bordered casualty tag on each man and also looked at his wound, which, of course, had already been dressed ashore. Doctor Beck was a psychiatrist by specialization, but this evening it was his job to diagnose the cases and send the men to the proper ward.

The first patient brought up the gangway was a soldier who had been wounded in the side and the arm by mortar fragments. Doctor Beck looked at his tag and pried under his bandages, "Put him on Surgical One, lower," he said. The stretcher bearers picked up their man and took him to the ward and lower berth indicated.

As Doctor Beck examined each man and spoke briefly, the procedure became almost mechanical: "Medical One"; "Medical Two"; "Orthopedic." A Marine assigned to one of the wards had been shot through the throat. Doctor Albert F. Clements, of Evansville, Indiana, came back in a few minutes and said quietly to Doctor Beck: "He got it through the larynx, and he is spitting some blood. But there's no paralysis. He can even talk. God is good."

After examining one particularly bloody case, Doctor Beck said: "There's a delicate one. Looks like he got a hand grenade between his legs. But I think we can save one testicle."[3] A Marine who had a shattered kneecap was set down. Someone asked whether he would walk normally. "Sure, he'll be good as new," said Beck.

Then came a man who had been shot through the thigh, another who had at least five wounds around his neck, chest, and right arm, another with a shattered chest to whom Beck said solicitously, "What's the matter with you, son?" The boy said a mortar had got him about noon. "Keep him level," said the doctor, who turned and said, "Apparently, he isn't suffering, but it might have gone through his lung."

Each man was further tagged with a piece of white cardboard from a compartmented box. "When we run out of tags we know we've got a shipload," Doctor Gray explained. The clothes of each wounded man were cut off him and thrown overboard. The ship carried 2,000 pairs of fresh dungarees for those who could wear them when they were ready to go ashore at some distant base.

The *Solace's* atmosphere, its fine equipment, its skilled doctors and nurses, were all a part of the care the United

---

[3] Many months later Doctor Beck told me his prognosis was correct.

States showered on its fighting men. But to the Marine or soldier arriving from the filth and dust of Saipan, nothing else could compare with the food. Tonight for supper there were chicken a la king and strawberry ice cream—honest-to-God, cold ice cream.

July 3

This morning the brass held a press conference aboard Admiral Turner's flagship, *Rocky Mount*. Most of the men responsible for carrying on the Central Pacific campaign were there: Spruance, Turner, Holland Smith, Rear Admiral Marc A. Mitscher, Maj. General Roy Geiger, whose III Amphibious Corps was still waiting to land on Guam, and Rear Admiral Richard L. ("Close In") Conolly, who would have immediate control of the Guam landings under Turner.

Not much news came out of the conference, but it provided some sidelights on some of the brass. Admiral Spruance, who shied away from publicity as if it were a booby trap, opened the conference typically: "Gentlemen, I wish you'd hurry this up. We have men here who want to get back and get along with the war."

"Pete" Mitscher, the wizened little caricature of Popeye the Sailor whom naval airmen loved like a father, was asked if he had noticed any improvement in Japanese anti-aircraft. "You're damned right," he chirped; "they're getting better with their ship-based and shore-based guns." Then he added, cockily: "They're no match for our planes and pilots, though. The pilots came back the other night, you know [from the Philippine Sea battle] even if they had to land long after dark. Only 21 planes are missing, and that's good flying."

General Smith predicted that the Saipan battle would last about four more days. Then we could get on with the Guam and Tinian invasions. He was all for aggressive action: "Our casualties are actually lower when we push forward than when we stand still." He estimated that the total Jap forces on Saipan would be found to be 23,000 to 24,000, considerably higher than we had expected.[4]

For the first time today, Admiral Nimitz's communique identified the three divisions fighting on Saipan. This made it possible for war correspondents to mention officers of field rank in their stories, without having to resort to phrases like "a certain regimental commander," or "a high-ranking officer."

July 4

When I rejoined the Second Division I found that most of Garapan was now in our hands, and the rest was being taken this morning against little opposition. Lieut. Colonel Arnold Johnston, who had returned to duty, had his 3/2 CP set up on 22d Street. His executive officer, Major Ben Owens, with whom I had gone ashore at Tarawa, walked around part of the rubble of the ex-city. We passed a newly dead Jap about 50 feet from the CP. "He tried to sneak through early this morning," said Owens. A Marine who was digging a deeper foxhole on the side of the street looked up and grinned: "I killed him."

Garapan was wrecked as thoroughly as any similar area I had ever seen. Many days of bombing and shelling had reduced its concrete and plaster buildings to piles of rubble three or four feet high. It seemed that no more than one wall was left of any building, and mostly there were no walls at all. Oddly, the paper-thin wooden houses stood up better. They were riddled by shell fragments, but they were upright.

Correspondent Keith Wheeler and I walked through Garapan together. Along the narrow, hard-surfaced streets the Marines following the mine detectors dug up kettle mines. Behind most of the houses there were dead cows, whose legs stuck out horizontally from their bloated bodies. We stopped

---

[4] Actually nearly 30,000 had been killed or captured even before the count was completed.

in what had been a small store. Its clapboard front had been bashed in, but otherwise it was in fair condition. Inside there was the inevitable Singer sewing machine. Many phonograph records were strewn about the wreckage, Columbia records made by the Nipponphone Co. Ltd., of Kawasaki, Victor records by another Japanese company, plus other records by the Teitoku Gramophone Co. Ltd., Nara. The titles were in Japanese, so we couldn't read them.

From one store a naked dress dummy had been blown into the street. She was a strictly occidental, yellow-haired blonde who wore only brown composition shoes. In a neat, wooden house across the street there were many photograph albums which apparently had belonged to a well-to-do Jap family. Some pictures showed Japanese women in formal evening gowns and men in full dress. But the wedding pictures were as oriental as the *obis* the women wore. There were pictures of Japanese baseball teams and of groups of expressionless school children. A box full of books also contained maps of various atolls. Scattered around the rooms were wooden shoes and western-style leather shoes. An empty can of Morinoya's Superior Wafers lay upon the floor.

The house next door contained three phonographs, two of them still in operating condition, but the records were all weird, monotonous oriental chants which made tiresome listening. Some Marines nearby had found many albums of Wagner, Beethoven, and Bach, which they played on an expensive machine at the street corner, while waiting to move up front. Near the music lovers there was a storehouse containing dozens of bags of rice, hundreds of the omnipresent paper-wrapped kits with toothbrushes, soap, and toilet paper, all stamped with the Jap Army star.

Half a mile north, about 30th Street, at Mutcho Point, Captain "Obie" O'Brien had set up his company CP. O'Brien said he hadn't killed 30 Japs since leaving 8th Street. The Japs had pulled out of Garapan, leaving only a few snipers who took their toll—18 men yesterday, four this morning. At 25th Street O'Brien had run into a machine-gun outpost, but the Japs managed to pull back with their weapon. At another point six Japs manning a machine gun had been shelled with 37-mm. canister. They waved a white flag. The Marines ceased firing. Then five of the Japs ran to the rear, leaving one sniper to cover their retreat. Only the sniper was killed.

O'Brien's set-up was near a concrete blockhouse which had been a Japanese CP. The Japs had left behind several cases of crabmeat, "packed for the Evers Company, Hamburg." The crabmeat was excellent, but before a can could be opened, approximately 500 flies were hovering to pounce upon it.

We took a different route back to the heart of Garapan. The Mutcho Point naval supply base indicated the importance of Saipan to the Japanese. Lying on the ground were many hundreds of rolls of barbed wire, and no less than 30 guns, about 90-mm., still uncrated. There were also about 20 big searchlights, of the kind which fighter pilots delight to shoot out. Two big buses and 20 burned-out trucks in the motor pool bore the naval insignia. The big gasoline dump had been only partly exploded. The Japs must have known we would come to Saipan. Why, then, had they been unable to uncrate those big guns, which could have added considerably to the hell we were catching? Somebody was too late with too little—and it was not the Americans.

In mid-afternoon I arrived at the 6th Marines' CP, which was set up on the reverse slope of a hill a mile northeast of Garapan. The 6th was now being pulled out of the line and sent into corps reserve, and Bill Jones was preparing to move into the town as "Mayor of Garapan." Somebody remembered that today was the Fourth of July, and that the Second Division had spent the previous Independence Day in New Zealand. Riseley's new executive officer, Lieut.

Colonel Russell ("Whitey") Lloyd, fished out some photographs taken near Wellington. It was not a very happy reminder; many of the handsome, laughing officers now lay in graves on Tarawa and Saipan. As "Whitey" showed the pictures, I noticed a bag under the corner of the tarpaulin. The name stencilled on it was "Lieut. Colonel Kenneth McLeod."

The 6th Regiment's casualties by now amounted to 71 officers and 1,392 men, leaving the regiment with 2,225, including shore party reinforcements. Of these casualties 1/6 had suffered 419, 2/6 had 471 and 3/6 had 476; the remaining 97 were distributed among headquarters and weapons company. Bill Jones's outfit had incurred slightly fewer casualties than the other two battalions, but it had run into some stiff opposition as its line advanced beyond the outskirts of Garapan, along the western and northern slopes of Tapotchau. In the past two days the battalion had suffered 92 casualties in cleaning out Jap caves. Lieutenant Thomas George Roscoe, the tall young artillery observer, was killed yesterday by a sniper. Schwerin's A Company had lost 34 men in one day, and was down again to 119 men. The company had killed 62 Japs in one cave, and had fetched 142 civilians out of another. It had witnessed one rare scene; a Jap officer in a well had committed traditional hara-kiri by disemboweling himself in full view of his would-be captors. On the other hand, a lieutenant had surrendered to Marines of 3/6. He maintained stoutly that Japan would win the war despite American firepower. He granted that he could see why the Americans thought they might win, with all that firepower. But, he simply refused to let any such thought enter his Japanese mind.

Among Schwerin's casualties was Gunnery Sergeant Howard D. Self, of Cullman, Alabama, one of the indispensable old-line non coms. Mention of his death reminded Schwerin of another heroic character. "Colonel," he said to

Riseley, "I've got a lanky boy from Louisiana, a p.f.c. named Watson, who ought to get every medal there is. He was Durfee's runner; now he's mine. He is the first to volunteer for every patrol. He's always going around asking if there's to to be a night patrol, because he wants to go along. He goes out front and brings back the wounded when it looks like he hasn't got a chance to come back alive."

I recalled that I had found many men who seemed to be drawn to the spots where the danger was greatest. It wasn't that many men *like* to fight. I knew some Marines and some soldiers who relished combat; I think Bill Jones really liked to fight. Most men would have preferred to stay out of it. But I had seen dozens of characters, particularly in the Marine Corps, who seemed always to turn up where the chances of getting killed were highest. Perhaps they could not forget the motto they read before they enlisted: "First to Fight." And I never saw a Marine who had been promised, even by implication, that he would not be called upon to face danger in large doses.

Riseley remembered an incident a few days earlier: "They brought an old man, a Marine sergeant about 30, through here. He had been wounded in the shoulder and in the hand. He stopped and said to me, 'Colonel, there's an 18-year-old corpsman out there that's the bravest man I've ever seen. He always goes after the wounded, regardless of what's happening, and regardless of how much stuff the Japs are throwing at us. Jesus, I hope you won't forget him! His name is Lake, I think.'"

July 5

There was a report that the Japs were still working feverishly on the Marpi Point Airfield. "We shell it as soon as they get a little work done on it," said General Smith; "General Saito is not going to get away in an airplane if we can help it."

By this time we controlled at least two-thirds of Saipan,

including most of the high ground south of Marpi Point. The Fourth Division had advanced rapidly on the eastern side of the island and, since the line was much narrower now, the Second Division had been pulled into reserve and the Twenty-Seventh assigned to the western half of the line. The Twenty-Seventh had run into some pillboxes on the western coast—the slits in the pillboxes had pointed seaward, but the Japs cut slits in the other sides and pointed their guns toward the advancing soldiers. Generally, progress was rapid everywhere. Smith gave the Japs two more days, but he had revised the estimate of Jap troops up to 30,000. Smith's chief of staff, Brig. General Graves B. Erskine, thought it would take a few days longer.

July 6

Major Steve McCormick's morning G-2 report said the Twenty-Seventh Division was being held up by fairly heavy resistance on the left flank, going north of Garapan; the Fourth was advancing swiftly on the right flank. The Army division had kicked off at 0700 and the Marines were starting forward at 0900. Yesterday Jap mines and bangalore torpedoes had destroyed one of our tanks and knocked the treads off four more.

This morning I saw the first newspaper since I left Honolulu more than a month ago. The San Francisco *Chronicle* for June 29 was full of political news, and I reflected that I had not heard politics mentioned twice since we landed. I doubted that one man in ten on Saipan had even heard that Dewey and Bricker had been nominated by the Republicans. There was one story about Saipan; a reporter in Pearl Harbor had interviewed men wounded on the beach the first day, and had faithfully recorded their views on Japanese strategy and tactics on Saipan.

Several correspondents got into a jeep and started for the Twenty-Seventh Division CP, now located northwest of Garapan, about half a mile off the road which lined the western shore of the island. On the way we stopped at the Second Division cemetery, where Captain Todd reported that 870 were now buried. Counting about 100 bodies in scattered graves, the Second's dead were near 1,000, about the same as at Tarawa. The wounded were many more.

When we reached General Griner's CP we started toward his tent, but turned back when we found that he and General Smith were in conference there. We went over to the G-1 tent and talked to Lieut. Colonel M. Oakley Bidwell, of Orlando, Florida. Colonel Bidwell guessed that the battle would take five to seven days longer. "Of course, it looks a lot easier, back at corps headquarters; you just move a blue pencil mark forward on a map." The colonel had his division's figures efficiently compartmented and easily available. He gave them to us: Killed, 31 officers, 331 men; wounded, 104 and 1,665; missing 2 and 41 (the two missing officers were liaison men in planes which crashed). Total, 2,174.

A breakdown of the Twenty-Seventh's figures, nearly as complete as the overall count, showed that officer casualties were high, one officer for each 9.8 enlisted men killed, and one for each 13.1 wounded. The 6th Marine Regiment had suffered two-thirds as many casualties as the entire Army division, but its officers' casualty ratio was 1 to 20, not 1 to 12. The killed included one colonel, one lieutenant colonel, one major, six captains, ten first lieutenants, and eleven second lieutenants; among the wounded were a colonel, two lieutenant colonels, three majors, 16 captains, 31 first lieutenants and 43 second lieutenants.

The infantry regiments' 2,096 casualties three days before the end of the battle were divided as follows:

	105th		*106th*		*165th*	
	off.	*enl.*	*off.*	*enl.*	*off.*	*enl.*
KIA	4	80	14	135	10	104
WIA	23	433	40	634	30	548
MIA	0	19	0	18	0	4

Since the War Department's final figures showed Army casualties on Saipan as 941 killed, 2,696 wounded, 118 missing (total 3,755), and since most of the remaining casualties were incurred in the July 7 break-through, it appeared that the Twenty-Seventh lost over 1,000 men in the break-through, perhaps as many as 1,500. One unofficial figure released by corps headquarters on July 12 put the break-through casualties of 1/105 and 2/105 as 409 killed, 650 **wounded.**

CHAPTER EIGHT

BATTLE'S END BANZAI

July 7

AT CORPS HEADQUARTERS IN CHARAN-KANOA THERE WAS SMALL indication that all hell had broken loose early this morning. At 0830 Major McCormick walked across the street from the G-2 house, and held his morning briefing for correspondents. Night fighters piloted by Lieutenant A. B. Hanson, of Minnesota, and Lieutenant Francis Eaton, of Roanoke, Virginia, had each shot down a Betty (twin-engined bomber), one near Rota, the other near Guam. The Japs had fired shells from Tinian, probably 120-mm., which had caused three casualties on Isely Field, and corps artillery and destroyers had retaliated, with results unknown. It had been decided to retain the Twenty-Seventh Division at its present position on the west side of the island above Garapan, to clean up the pocket of Japs there, and to pass the Fourth Division (with the 2d Marine Regiment attached) through to wipe up whatever opposition remained in the northern fifth of Saipan.

McCormick read more from his notes: Two hundred civilians had surrendered yesterday who said they had had enough of our artillery. Then the major said: "We've got a report that at 0510 this morning two Jap tanks and two companies of infantry broke through, and overran one of our gun positions in the 10th Marines' area. There were considerable casualties. At last report the 106th Infantry had got 15 tanks and a battalion up to recapture the battery."

The major was deceived as badly as the correspondents. Nobody paid particular attention to another *banzai* attack; they were common enough. I went off to gather material for a story on Negro Marines, who were being used in combat for the first time on Saipan—the 800 colored men in the three field depot companies, the 18th, 19th and 20th, and in an ammunition company, the 3d. They had made an excellent showing in their first time under fire. Three had been killed, five wounded. They had unloaded mountains of supplies and ammunition, and had evacuated hundreds of wounded.

It was nearly noon before I got into a jeep and started for the front to see what had happened. On top of a hill overlooking the sea, about a mile north of Tanapag Harbor, I stopped at a little shed. Inside there were four dead Marines from G Battery of the Third Battalion, 10th Marines. This was the farthest point of the Jap advance, and only a handful had got this far.

From the hillside I could see the tanks of the 106th Infantry edging into the canefields, 500 yards below, alongside a narrow-gauge railroad. The tanks were firing thousands of rounds from their machine guns, and occasionally they let go a blast from their 75's. The recovery from the most savage counterattack of the Pacific war had begun, although it was not yet possible—and never was possible, exactly—to estimate how heavy was the desperate attack the Japanese had staged a few hours earlier.

"It started about 0430 this morning," said Marine R. J. Patrick, "when the Japs broke through the Army lines. They just kept coming until they hit this artillery battalion—G, H and I batteries and H & S battery. H Battery is still surrounded. Major Crouch, the battalion commander, was killed. I guess the best men in the battalion were killed."

There were two knocked-out Jap tanks in the canefield below. Pfc. Edmund O. Sargis, of New Britain, Connecticut, swore he knocked out one of them with a 50-caliber machine gun. "The bazooka men tried to get at it, but it was too far. The Nips would follow the tank, then get under a tree and fire. They were thicker than fleas in the canefield. We swept the cornfield and killed many of them."

I drove a couple of hundred yards farther, then I got out of the jeep and walked the rest of the way to join the infantrymen who were following the tanks. The men were from the Second Battalion, 106th Infantry. We walked up the east side of the railroad, through an open field, about 30 yards behind the tanks whose machine guns were now chattering incessantly, sweeping every inch of the fields ahead of them and on either side of them. When we came to a small culvert under the railroad track somebody yelled "Engineers!" The cry was repeated, and finally some engineers came and planted a mighty charge in the culvert which must have blown up whatever Japs were in it, if there were any. On our unplanted side of the field there was scattered twelve dead Japs, and I recalled how few Japs I had seen on Saipan who were killed in the open. Up to now Saipan had been largely cave warfare.

On the other side of the railroad embankment there were at least 40 dead Japs, also killed above ground. But there was a little house nearby, and there were more Japs underneath it; I counted six and there may have been a dozen. All that I saw had committed suicide—right hand gone, chest or head blasted open by their own grenades. The house sat no more than two feet off the ground, but these men had chosen to squirm under it before taking their own lives.

Beyond a line of small trees there was an open field which extended to the water's edge. On the edge of this field H&S Battery of the Third Battalion, 10th Marines, had set up its fire direction center. Here the Japs had struck in full force, had passed through as far as G Battery which I had recently left on top of the hill. Several dead Marines lay nearby, their rifles still clutched in their hands. Most of the dead had been covered with ponchos.

I talked to Pfc. Bailey Naber, of Los Angeles, California, who had weathered the attack in a foxhole until recently rescued. He said. "And to think I wrote home yesterday afternoon and told my folks the island was secured!" Naber was firing a BAR as about 30 Japs descended on his foxhole. He said he had killed some of them but he didn't know how many.

Corporal Anthony B. Kouma, of Dwight, Nebraska, had been corporal of the Marines' guard. He said: "You can imagine our surprise when the Japs started coming through 'way back here behind the lines. We stayed in our foxholes and shot it out with them, but we didn't have many weapons or much ammunition. A couple of hours ago my buddy and I decided one of us ought to go for help. I went. He covered my withdrawal, but they got him." Kouma pointed to a dead Marine.

Kouma took me and Frank Kelley for a tour of the open field. There were three tents, one each for headquarters, fire direction and medical aid. A parked jeep was in front of one of the tents. "Staff Sergeant Lea Bell, an ex-Raider was under that jeep," said Kouma, "he lay there wounded until an hour ago. When they got to him he was still squeezing the trigger of his rifle. It fired two shots."

There were nine dead Japs in a ditch. One of them had carried as his *banzai* weapon a bayonet tied to a stick. He had been shot through the head. Near the ditch, beside a burning jeep, lay a dead Marine. "That is Lieutenant Stewart [Hoyt Stewart, of Iowa Park, Texas]. I was with him when he was wounded, and he begged me to shoot him, because he never wanted the Japs to get him, but I told him he would be all right. He died in a few minutes, though."

Seven dead Japs were in another ditch, and another was just outside it. Three of them had committed suicide. Near the center of the field lay a dead Marine private. Beyond him Kouma stopped and cried, with a half sob: "My God, there's the major! I thought he got out all right. There's a man they'll never replace." Major William L. Crouch of Lawrenceburg, Indiana, commander of the battalion, had evidently been shot through the side, some 20 feet from where he finally fell—his helmet and carbine were that far from his body. Beside his hand were two V-mail letters, which he may have tried to read as the life ebbed out of him.

Not far from the major there were two more dead Americans. One had the name "Clauson" stenciled on his uniform. The other was a medical corpsman whose aid kit was still unopened.

Among the trees immediately north of the field where Major Crouch lay there were Japs stacked in tiers. In an area no more than 100 yards square I saw between 300 and 400. Most of them wore the Navy anchor on their caps, but some wore helmets mounted with the Army star. I counted in a ditch no more than 15 feet long and three feet deep, 31 bodies, sometimes stacked three high. Three light machine guns, two motorcycles with sidecars, and several uncrated airplane engines stood beside this ditch full of carnage. One Jap in four, I estimated, had taken his own life.

Wandering through the woods and up the narrow dirt road, I noticed that the Japs lay in bunches of three to ten. It was remarkable that Japs rarely seemed to die alone. The same thing was true at Attu, and it was true at Tarawa.

I had seen enough for the day. Back at corps headquarters, estimates of the number of Japs in the suicide attack varied from 500 to 2,000. From what I had seen of only a portion of the attack I thought the latter figure probably came closer to being accurate. Our own casualties were still going up. They stood at 12,700, not including very heavy losses today.

General Smith said he would pass the Second Division through the Twenty-Seventh tomorrow, and let them clean up what was left of the Japs in the *banzai* area.

July 8

To the morning briefing, Major McCormick brought three survivors of the Jap suicide charge. They were a naval gunfire liaison officer attached to the 105th Infantry, Lieutenant (j.g.) Charles J. Blank of Dayton, Ohio, and two enlisted soldiers, Technical Sergeant Frederick W. Stilz, 29 years old, of Brooklyn, sergeant major of the First Battalion, and Corporal Joseph A. Ferrer, 23 years old, of Syracuse, an artillery observer of the Second Battalion. Blank said: "It was about 0450 when all hell broke loose around us and on top of us. I think there must have been between 2,000 and 3,000 Japs charging down on us at once."

Stilz said: "The First Battalion was ordered up the afternoon before, to fill a gap between the Second and Third. The Second was on the left [the beach] and the First was next inland. The Japs were on a hill, and we were in an open field. The First and Second had a five-hundred-yard front, and the Japs hit both battalions. We were working so close to the Japs we didn't need to have any patrols out.

"When they hit us there were so many of them we couldn't shoot fast enough. Some of them came down the beach and others came through the woods and along the railroad track. They had clubs and swords and bayonets. The second bunch that came through were killing our wounded. Any of our men hit up above are sure dead.

"The Second established a perimeter down by the beach. They had us surrounded. We were shooting them at 15 or 20 yards. The pocket was about 50 yards deep and 100 yards across. Artillery was breaking them up some, but some of the artillery fell short and hit among us. We must have killed 300 or 400 Japs; they were piled up around us. About nine o'clock we got some red cloth and tried to put panels up for artillery observation planes to see.

"When the artillery fell short, the Japs started using mortars on us. We made our first break-through about 11 o'clock to try to get some help. Sergeant 'Lefty' LeFay of B Company led the break-through. When the break-through started, some men backed out into the water, then started swimming."

Ferrer, the red-headed corporal, said: "I don't know how many men were killed. Lieut. Colonel William J. O'Brien of Troy, New York, commander of the other battalion, was one of them. There were about 100 men who broke through the Japs to the rear with Sergeant LeFay. I think the Japs had been drinking *sake* and it was beginning to wear off. We were mowing them down as we went through. The Japs blew up two medical cars that tried to get the wounded out. About 0600 or 0630 some LVT's had come in and taken out some wounded.

"This perimeter was about half-way between the front line, where the Japs first broke through, and the artillery battery. The Jap mortar fire was what was taking a terrific toll. It was unobserved fire, but it hit a lot of men. All I could think of was the 'Lost Battalion' in the last war."

McCormick added some data that had been compiled at corps headquarters. He said: "The Japs overran the First and Second Battalions and drove through about 1,200 to 1,500 yards. The battalions' front had been about 500 yards." In answer to a question, he said he did not know whether there was a gap between the two battalions, as had been reported.

The major went on: "The Japs partly overran 12 guns of the 10th Marines. All guns have been recaptured, and ten are back in commission. The artillery battalion fired their 105's at point-blank range, with fuses cut to four-tenths of a second, before the Japs overran them. There is some discrepancy in the number of Japs who broke through. The G-2 of the 27th Division says there were 2,000.

"Most of the strength in the break-through was Jap Navy personnel, led by an Army colonel. The attack showed a good degree of organization. The Japs came in with grenades, sticks with bayonets on them, and rifles, many of which were rusty. There was a good deal of fighting at the 105th CP.

"Light naval vessels picked up the men who had swum

out to the reef. There were about 135 of them. Some of the wounded are still on the beach up there; they were still cut off at 0630 this morning. The Second Division this morning will move up through the Twenty-Seventh or what's left of it. The 165th will remain on the left flank of the Fourth Division.

"At 0530 this morning the Second Division reported a small counterattack of 50 to 100 Japs. Nine or ten Marines were killed. The First Battalion, 106th, reported a fairly heavy counterattack at 0520 by Japs with knives on sticks. There was little organization to the attack."

Regarding the night's air raids, McCormick said: "Isely Field was strafed, and a few of our planes were lightly damaged. The plane was brought down by automatic weapons. One of our night fighters shot down a Jap near Rota. Another plane was reported by three radar stations, which said it apparently blew up down south in mid-air. Twelve bombs were dropped on target square 248 N-Q. There was no damage.

"We have now fired more than 10,000 rounds of Jap 81-mm. mortar shells back at them."

With Correspondents Kelley and Wheeler, I drove again to the scene of the counterattack. It was possible now to cover most of the ground. The carnage proved to be denser than it had seemed yesterday. There were at least 1,000 dead Japs in an area 300 by 500 yards. Strewn along the beach there were at least 50; we were told that others had swum out and drowned themselves. In trenches near the beach, just north and west of Major Crouch's open field, there were at least 150. The canefield west of the railroad track, which the 106th Infantry's tanks had raked so thoroughly, contained about 200, as did the field on the other side of the track. Along the track and right-of-way there were approximately 150. The whole area seemed to be a mass of stinking bodies, spilled guts and brains. I wrote in my notebook, "They are thicker here than at Tarawa."

I encountered the first man I had seen from H Battery, a private first class named Buggey. He said the battery had 15 killed, ten missing, 39 wounded, before it was rescued late yesterday. "But we must have killed a thousand Japs," he said proudly, pointing to the scene about him. "The Japs came at us four abreast. We fired the 105's into the ground 50 feet in front of us."

But the mop-up was by no means complete. It was possible that more Japs were killed today than yesterday. Major Leroy Hunt's Second Battalion, 6th Marines, were unrolling the left flank, going north along the beach, as far as 400 yards inland. We joined E Company which was working northward from the vicinity of the railroad. Lying in the ditch of the railroad right-of-way, we watched four Japs dash across the tracks about 300 yards ahead. A Marine beside us had been waiting for just such a move. He fired several times, but we saw no Japs fall. After a minute a Jap sniper began shooting at us from the woods. We got down low, and the bullets fluttered overhead.

A Marine ran along the bank. He shouted, "Jesus Christ, Captain Bradley got hit!" He fetched some stretcher bearers, and after a few minutes they returned from the woods, bearing the bespectacled captain who lay face down on the stretcher. His back had been bandaged, and blood had soaked through the gauze.

We moved over nearer the beach, walking through the carcass-ridden canefield to the G Company area. In a small creek and on its banks we noticed piles of dead Japs, perhaps 150 in all. I counted 14 dead Americans, about half of them soldiers, half Marines. (The Marines' helmets were covered with camouflage cloth; the soldiers' were not.) An Army tank, No. 57, had been knocked out near the wooden bridge crossing the creek. Beside it lay a soldier whose upturned dogtag identified him as John T. Slavik.

On one side of the road lay a brown-haired Marine who

had been killed only a few minutes before. Someone stooped over to pick up the Jap officer's sword next to the dead man. "Leave that sword alone!" shouted a short Marine. "That man just got killed fetching it."

I went over and spoke to the little Marine. He was Captain Thomas Wheeler, of Kansas City. "He was souvenir hunting," said Wheeler, "and a sniper shot him. Least we can do is send the sword home to his folks."

Tanks and half-tracks rumbled over the little bridge and started north along the narrow road through the woods. At this point we were about 100 yards north of Major Crouch's field, and about 75 yards inland from the beach. We were now beginning to roll back the Japs in the area where they had streamed through, yesterday morning.

The infantrymen formed a line from the beach inland, abreast of the tanks and half-tracks, each man about ten feet from the man next to him. The whole line, about 400 yards long, began moving forward. It was an impressive spectacle, this long, thin line of men moving forward through the sparse woods. Nobody sought cover; the whole line stood straight up and walked slowly forward, like so many men sweeping the woods with brooms.

Actually, there was little opposition, almost none. Once in a while a sniper's bullet "pinged" through the trees, but the Marines paid no attention. Again, a Marine would stop occasionally and pump five or six shots into a hole. When we looked into the hole there would be one or more dead Japs.

The fight was gone out of the Japs. They simply waited in their holes for death. "It's just like killing rats now," said Captain Wheeler—and, indeed, he was right.

The tank we were following stopped and blasted a little farmhouse with its 75. On the other side of the road there was a small crib. A gangling, left-handed Marine looked cautiously under the crib, then like a cat he pounced into it, over rice bags. Then he fired his BAR four or five times.

Another Marine climbed over the rice bags and came out with an officer's sword. I asked the left-handed man why he didn't get the sword for himself.

"I let my buddy have it," he said; "I can't carry any more." He pointed to his pack, which he had dropped on the ground before jumping into the crib. The pack had three *samurai* swords hung on it.

I looked inside the crib. The Japs had fashioned a foxhole of rice bags. Inside the hole were two Japs the left-handed BAR man had just killed. A widening circle of blood centered on the shirt of one of them, and the color of the shirt caused the blood to turn purple as it soaked through. On the face of the other, who had been shot twice through the head, the blood ran crimson. Unlike many other Japs. these men had not brought themselves to commit suicide. They had waited stoically to be killed.

In a hole on the east side of the road the Marines found a soldier who miraculously had escaped death. As the Japs poured through his area yesterday morning, the soldier, a cook from B Company, 105th Infantry, had been trapped and encircled. Somehow, the Japs had not killed him, and somehow the Marines had distinguished him as one of our men before they fired into the hole. The man could hardly talk. He munched a cracker from a C ration, and said slowly: "Don't know where my outfit is; guess I'm the only one left."

Captain Wheeler's company alone killed between 300 and 400 Japs during the afternoon. Besides the souvenir-hunting Marine, he lost only one other man, who tossed a grenade and tripped on his own rifle as he tried to get away.

July 9

Saipan was declared secure today. Organized resistance had ceased, but there would be mopping up for over a year, as more and more Japs came out of caves. The number killed in caves by explosives and the number who starved will probably never be known.

A Jesuit priest, his assistant, and six nuns were brought in yesterday. The priest, a Spaniard, had been on Saipan 13 years, his assistant 26 years. The priest said that Japanese military police had been left behind to guard them, even during the final attack.

Today Admiral Turner held a press conference aboard his flagship. He told the correspondents D Day for Guam would be July 21, for Tinian July 24 (east longitude dates). The admiral also said he had held up stories (already passed by censors) about the Japanese counterattack because reporters had named the units whose lines the Japs had broken through. There were no inaccuracies in the stories, he said, and they could be rewritten and passed by censors, but he felt that as a matter of policy it was inadvisable to list the infantry and artillery units involved. No question of security was involved, he added.

July 11

Major McCormick said the mopping up was still yielding high returns. Between 2,100 and 2,300 Japs were killed yesterday, 508 by the Second Division, 84 by the Twenty-Seventh, and between 1,561 and 1,711 (reports disagreed) by the Fourth, which had pushed up to the north end of the island. Civilian deaths totaled 780 to 800, and there were now 86 prisoners of war. The Fourth was now concentrating on caves at Inagasa Point, at the northeast corner of the island, and the 165th Infantry (which was never relieved during the entire battle) was still digging Japs out of a ravine southeast of Mecunshah Point.

By July 11 the island had been "secured" for two days, and all that remained was the mopping up of a few snipers at the extreme northern end of Saipan. Late that afternoon two correspondents, Keith Wheeler of the Chicago *Times* and Frank Kelley of the New York *Herald Tribune,* and photographer Peter Stackpole of *Life* returned to press headquarters on "C" Street in the village of Charan-Kanoa with a story almost too fantastic. It told how on Marpi Point (the northern tip), whole families of civilians were wading out to sea and drowning themselves rather than surrender; fathers were throwing their children off the cliffs; seven-year-old children were throwing hand grenades, and some families were clustered together, pulling the pins out of grenades—all in an orgy of self-destruction.

Next morning I got into a jeep and drove the twelve miles to Marpi Point. Just beyond the small Marpi Airfield I stood on a 200-foot cliff and watched the sea, 300 yards away. On the edge of the slippery, tide-washed rocks a Japanese boy of perhaps 15, attired in knee-length black trousers, walked back and forth. He would pause in meditation, then he would walk on, swinging his arms. He sat on the edge of the rocks; then he got up. He sat down again, waiting.

When a high wave washed the rock, the boy let it sweep him into the sea. At first he lay face down, inert on the surface of the water. Then his arms flailed frantically, as if an instinct stronger than his will power bade him live. Then he was quiet. He was dead.

I watched his body rock back and forth on the waves until it was perhaps fifty yards offshore. Then I could see it no more. There were nine men (from the Third Battalion, 24th Marines) on the cliff, trying with ropes to recover the bodies of two of their men who had been shot the previous day on the rocks below. They paid scant attention to the Jap who had just drowned himself. "You should have been here yesterday," said one of them.

Platoon Sergeant Charles B. Rogers of Mount Clemens, Michigan, said: "There are lots of kids with their heads off in the pockets of those rocks below. Men from I, K and L Companies who were mopping up here yesterday said the kids' own parents did it, then jumped off themselves."

The story became more and more incredible as I heard its details from various men who had observed the wholesale self-slaughter.

Japanese soldiers scattered throughout the rocky Marpi Point area not only would go to any extreme to avoid surrender, but also tried to keep civilians from surrendering. The Marines had tried to dislodge a Jap sniper from a cave just below the cliff where we stood. For a Jap, he was an exceptional marksman; he had killed two Marines (one at 700 yards) and wounded a third. The Marines used rifles, bangalore torpedoes, and TNT, in a 45-minute effort to force him out. Meanwhile, the Jap had other business.

He had spotted a Japanese group, apparently father, mother and four children, out on the rocks, preparing to drown themselves, but evidently weakening in their decision. The Jap sniper took aim. He drilled the man from behind, dropping him off the rocks into the sea. The second bullet hit the woman. She dragged herself about thirty feet along the rocks. Then she floated out in a stain of blood. The sniper would have shot the children, but a Japanese woman ran across and carried them out of range. The sniper walked defiantly out of his cave, and crumpled under a hundred American bullets.

Some of the Jap civilians went through considerable ceremony before snuffing out their lives. In one instance Marines watched in astonishment as three women sat on the rocks leisurely, deliberately combing their long, black hair —much after the fashion of Leonidas and his Spartans before their last stand at Thermopylae. Finally, the women joined hands and walked slowly out into the sea.

But the most ceremonious, by all odds, were 100 Japs on the rocks who bowed to the Marines watching from the cliff. Then they stripped off their clothes and bathed in the sea. Thus refreshed, they put on new clothes and spread a huge Jap flag on a smooth rock. Then the leader distributed hand grenades. One by one, as the pins were pulled, the Japs blew their insides out.

The Marines had observed a circle of about 50 Japanese, including several small children, solemnly tossing grenades to each other, just as baseball players do in warming up before a game. Suddenly six Japanese soldiers dashed from a cave, from which they had been sniping at Marines. The soldiers posed arrogantly in front of the civilians, then blew themselves to kingdom come; thus shamed, the civilians did likewise.

Two hundred yards offshore I saw another floating body in what looked like a red print dress. Then other bobbed up nearer the coastline. Almost directly in front of us, from behind the nearest rocks, a five-year-old child's body, attired only in a white shirt, floated by. It was followed by that of a woman, then of a man. Around the tip of the cliff, to the right, four more bodies eddied in a slow, gruesome march. Keith Wheeler had said, "There's a procession of the dead up there," and he was right. An hour after the boy in black pants had killed himself I turned and walked back to the jeep.

Lieutenant Emery Cleaves, on the minesweeper *Chief*, had as good a view as anybody. Said Cleaves: "Part of the area is so congested with floating bodies we simply can't avoid running them down. I remember one woman in khaki trousers and a white, polka-dot blouse, with her black hair streaming in the water. I'm afraid every time I see that kind of blouse, I'll think of that girl. There was another one, nude, who had drowned herself while giving birth to a baby. The baby's head had entered this world, but that was all of him. A small boy of four or five had drowned with his arm firmly clenched around the neck of a Jap soldier; the two bodies rocked crazily in the waves. I've seen literally hundreds in the water."

When I got back to Corps headquarters I heard the story of Lieutenant Kenneth J. Hensley of the Second Battalion, 6th Marines. Some Jap soldiers had fled to the reef, several hundred yards offshore. Hensley had taken a detachment of amphibious tractors to fetch them. As the amphtracs approached, one of the Japs, apparently an officer, drew his sword. The six men with him knelt on the coral rocks, and the officer started methodically to slice off their heads. Four heads had rolled into the sea before the amphtracs closed in. Then the officer, sword in hand, charged the amphtracs. Hensley's men turned their machine guns on him and the two remaining men.

What did all this self-destruction mean? Did it mean that the Japanese on Saipan believed their own propaganda which told them that American beasts would murder them all? Many a Jap civilian did beg our people to put him to death immediately rather than put him to torture. But many of those who chose suicide could see other civilians, who had surrendered, walking unmolested in the internment camps. During the day the Marines saw most of the suicides at Marpi Point, there were loudspeakers set up on the cliff. The surrendered civilians pleaded with the others to give themselves up, assuring them that they would be well treated. But that did not stop the suicides. Among many Japanese there seemed to be a pressing compulsion to die, regardless of everything. The attitude of these civilians seemed comparable to that of Jap soldiers on Peleliu who lettered a sign before they died: "We will build a barrier across the Pacific with our bodies."

What would the really fanatical citizens have done if our armies had invaded Japan, considering that the second-class Japanese on Saipan killed themselves in fairly large numbers? Radio Tokyo asserted again and again that women and children would be armed, too, and 100,000,000 Japanese stood ready to repulse the invaders, and thus "ease the mind of His

Imperial Majesty, the Emperor." Thousands, perhaps millions, undoubtedly would have been killed, or would have killed themselves if the Emperor had not ordered the war stopped before the invasion.

On Saipan and, nine months later, on Okinawa, we found some evidence of women and children attempting to fight. One soldier on Saipan said his squad had encountered a woman wildly firing a rifle; the squad's sharpshooter took careful aim, shot the woman through the leg, then took her to the hospital. What we found was what we probably would have found had we invaded the home islands: a certain percentage of civilians attempting to kill us, a higher percentage willing to kill themselves. In Japan, as on Saipan, some Americans probably would have been killed trying to save the Japanese from themselves.

Before I left Saipan I paid one more visit to Bill Jones and his 1/6 outfit. Bill had barely settled down as "Mayor of Garapan" when he and his battalion were routed out and sent to the front to help to roll back the counterattacking Japs. To his outfit had been assigned the ridge which ran down the northern end of Saipan like a spine. On Jones's left in the final line was 1/8, then 3/6, then Hunt's 2/6 on the western beach area. Jones's outfit had not killed nearly as many Japs in the final roll-back as Roy Hunt's had, but numerous small parties and stragglers in caves had been destroyed, and a few captured.

Between July 6, when there were no casualties, and July 11, Jones had had seven men killed and eight wounded. This brought his total casualties for the battle to 440, distributed as follows:

	KIA	WIA	MIA	Total
Officers	4	16	0	20
Enlisted men	79	316	25	420
	83	332	25	440

Jones had started the battle with 880 (33 officers, 805 men, two doctors, 40 corpsmen), so his casualties, as applied to the starting figure (*i.e.*, not counting replacements) amounted to exactly 50 per cent. This was slightly less than either of the other two battalions of the 6th Marines suffered, but it seemed pretty high.

About 50 per cent of Jones's wounded had returned to duty during the battle. Some, like Lieutenant Donald Seibert, who returned only to receive a more serious second wound, became twice casualties.

I stayed on Saipan until July 13. The invasions of Gaum and Tinian were about to take place, but I had been ordered back to my New York office, and I was not sorry. When I arrived in New York July 20 I had been gone less than two months, but it seemed like two years. Saipan was war at its grimmest, and its scenes were seared into my brain.

The Japanese knew Saipan's importance; the Tojo Government fell because of Saipan. I never read a story of the B-29's and their raids on Japan without remembering the 15,000 soldiers and Marines who were killed or wounded in the acquisition of the first B-29 base in the Central Pacific.

CHAPTER NINE

WE LEAVE FOR IWO

CONCERNING THE CAPTURE OF IWO JIMA WE WERE CERTAIN OF two things: (1) we had to have it; (2) it would be costly. The necessity of Iwo Jima was clear to us in the far Pacific, if not to everybody back home. The chief reason went back to our heavy bombardment program for Japan.

The B-29's began operating from Chinese bases, coincident with the invasion of Saipan in June, 1944. But it was obvious from the beginning that China and India bases were too far from Japanese industrial targets in the Tokyo-Osaka area, and it was obvious that enough supplies could not be delivered to the bases by air. The capture of Saipan, Tinian, and Guam gave us B-29 bases closer to Tokyo. The bases could be supplied by tankers and cargo ships. In November, four months after Saipan, the B-29's began bombing Japan from the Marianas.

These raids made big headlines in American newspapers. But they were not as effective as they sounded. In June, 1945, the B-29 public-relations chief, Lieut. Colonel St. Clair McKelway, writing in *The New Yorker,* quoted realistic Maj. General Curtis LeMay as saying, on March 6: "This outfit has been getting a lot of publicity without really having accomplished a hell of a lot in bombing results." That was only three days before LeMay began the really effective, low-level fire bomb raids on Japan—his decision to bring the big planes down to low levels was, incidentally, one of the most courageous acts of the war.

There had been several reasons for the stalling—failure to gain momentum—of the B-29 program. One was the weather over Japan, which was as violent as the nature of the Japanese people. At 30,000 feet, the wind frequently blew 200 miles an hour. This meant that a plane flying into the wind was traveling at only 50 or 100 miles per hour, and was in great danger from anti-aircraft fire or from Japanese fighter planes. But planes going downwind, as nearly all of them did, had to drop their bombs at somewhere around 500 miles an hour. One B-29 pilot told me in February: "The navigator must be awfully good, the bombardier must be awfully good—and, even, then, the ballistic error is too great for accuracy."

These early B-29 raids met with determined resistance. As in all pioneering, great heroism on the part of the airmen was required. Japanese anti-aircraft fire, even at great altitudes, was intense and often accurate. Japanese fighter planes rose in great numbers to meet the raiders. If the Japs could not shoot down the big planes, they frequently rammed them.

When I saw the B-29 flyers in February, they were at low ebb. "We feel it has been worthwhile; we have to believe that," one of them said, "but the cost has been high. We've lost a lot of good men, especially key men like group and squadron commanders." Out of a flight of 36 planes, nine had just been lost.

The flyers could see their losses mounting, and they could see no immediate hope of relief; no policy had been set regarding the number of missions a man was to fly before he went home. To flyers, who kept an eye cocked at the percentage tables, this was important. A man needed something to look forward to—something besides an increasing chance that he would not come back from the next raid.

Damaged planes had a good expectancy of rescue if they could make more than half the distance on the return from Tokyo to Saipan. If they were ditched between Iwo Jima and Saipan, Dumbo planes could probably rescue the flyers. But planes which were damaged so badly they could make it only a few score or a couple of hundred miles out of Tokyo—

these planes were nearly always lost. With Iwo in our hands, rescue planes could fly to the very shores of Japan.

"If we can have Iwo Jima to land on, we'll save a lot of men who haven't got a chance as things are," said one of the pilots. Before the war's end he was proved right far beyond his own expectations—more than 2,000 B-29's pulled up at Iwo on the way back from Japan. Not all these planes would have been lost, because many pilots stopped at Iwo rather than take the outside chance. But the B-29's could afford to carry much greater bomb loads—seven tons as against two tons—and much less gasoline, if they knew they could rely on Iwo.

To the Marines, Iwo looked like the ugliest place on earth, but B-29 pilots who made emergency landings months later called it the most beautiful. One pilot flew eleven missions in the three months following the island's capture, and landed on it five times. Another said, "Whenever I land on this island, I thank God and the men who fought for it."

But Iwo had other advantages beyond serving as a lifesaving station for B-29's. Iwo-based Jap planes had been raiding Saipan, where they destroyed some B-29's. Their threat tied up protecting fighter planes and anti-aircraft crews who might be used elsewhere, and Iwo-based radar warned the Japanese home islands of the approaching B-29's, giving the Japs a chance to get their fighters into the air.

In our hands Iwo could be used as a base for long-range fighters. These P-51's could escort the B-29's into Japan and could make their own strafing and bombing runs on enemy airfields which had hitherto been accessible only to fighters based on carriers. They also could pin down Japanese planes in the home islands.

Iwo Jima was only eight square miles, so nearly everybody assumed that it could be captured in a relatively short time. Some said five days; Maj. General Harry Schmidt, "the stolid Dutchman" who commanded the V Amphibious Corps, thought ten days. Nobody imagined that it would take 26 days.

But everybody did know we would lose a lot of men. We knew the underground defenses of this little island were as nearly impregnable as man could devise, and that 74 straight days of bombing had not knocked them out. "Iwo Jima is as well defended as any other fixed position in the world today," said Vice Admiral Kelly Turner at a press conference aboard his flagship off Saipan on February 16, three days before D Day. "Gibraltar would be a set-up in comparison," said another officer.

Lieut. General Holland Smith told me he feared 15,000 casualties. Vice Admiral Charles H. ("Soc") McMorris, the bald, Mississippi-born chief of staff to Admiral Nimitz, thought they might run as high as 20,000. (The actual figures for Marines alone proved to be about 19,200, Navy, Army, and Coast Guard casualties probably added 1,000 more). As usual, we underestimated the number of Jap defenders. We expected about 15,000; there were probably 20,000—more if our estimates of the dead in caves were accepted.

The press conference aboard Turner's flagship was a rather emotional affair—there was the sort of pit-of-the-stomach emotion one feels when he knows that many men who love life are about to die. Kelly Turner, peering over his spectacles and looking like Grant Wood's "American Gothic" farmer, ran the conference. He had a surprise; the Secretary of the Navy, James V. Forrestal, was aboard, and would accompany the invasion fleet.

"The primary objective," said Turner, "is to capture Iwo Jima for fighters which can accompany the B-29's in their raids on Japan. Today, D minus 3, our carrier raids on Honshu begin, and the ships' bombardment of Iwo itself begins. A few minutes ago I had word of a red alert in the bombardment force."

Turner, who would command the invasion, was charged with censorship of press copy, which would be sent chiefly by ships' radio, as against the old, bungling system whereby the copy had to be flown back to Pearl Harbor for belated transmission. (Much more was sent by radio from Iwo than had been thought possible.)

To the press, Turner said: "We feel that photographers are not evil. Correspondents we also have the highest regard for; they take the same chances we do. We expect facts in stories to be verified. The opinions correspondents express are their own; that's between them and the American people. Censorship will be liberal, except for highly secret technical information.

"We request that you refrain from forecasting future operations. In the past we have been very successful in keeping the enemy in the dark. We will make every effort to get your stories out promptly. We cannot send all stories by radio, but we'll send as much as we can. There will be some difficulty in getting stories out by seaplane. The water will probably be rough and the schedules uncertain. The planes will fly your stories back to Guam for transmission; the copy will be dropped on airfields at Guam to public relations officers. But we need airfields on Iwo; I cannot be too optimistic about the seaplanes, which will have no protected anchorage.

"The stories must be within the scope of the CINCPAC communique, as you know. The ships you are embarked on are new to these operations[1] but the communique will be radioed each day to the ships, and you can insist upon seeing it."

Turner mentioned several secret weapons which could not be mentioned yet (among them: fire bombs, or napalm). Then he went on: "We expect losses, of ships, and of troops. They will be considerable. We are taking steps to keep them

[1] More than 75 per cent of the transports used at Iwo were brand-new.

as low as possible. We are going to have losses. But we expect to take the position.

"The weather is an important factor. Iwo is in the center of a disturbed area. There is no haven where we can land. We expect to land on the southeast beaches, but we shall have great difficulty in getting boats on the beaches. We hope for two or three days of reasonably calm weather, so we can get the troops and supplies ashore. We have made arrangements for planes from carriers and land-based planes from Saipan to drop supplies, if necessary."

After Turner had finished, Army Colonel Thomas Yancey, the V Corps intelligence officer, spoke: "Iwo is 625 miles north of Saipan and 660 miles south of the Japanese empire. It is of the greatest importance to the enemy. It is small; five miles long and two and one-half miles wide at its widest point. Mount Suribachi on the southern tip is a volcano, 554 feet high. About one-third of the island is airfields and revetments, one-third is canefields and scrub growth, one-third is barren. The beaches we will land on are volcanic ash, the northern two-thirds of the island is a plateau whose height goes up to about 350 feet."

Colonel Edward A. Craig, a Marine who was operations officer on Schmidt's staff, spoke of the plan for maneuver: The Fourth Marine Division would land on the right of the southeast beaches, the Fifth Marine Division on the left. The two divisions would aim for the bigger airfield, Motoyama No. 1, which lay just ahead of the landing beaches. The Fourth would then swing and go up the right flank toward the northern end of the island. The Fifth, except for one regiment (the 28th), which would wheel southward and capture Mount Suribachi, would head north up the left flank. The Third Marine Division had been loaded into transports and would remain offshore in reserve until, and if, it were needed. One regiment of the Third would be available D Day, the other two by D plus 1.

The command set-up for the Iwo operation was explained by Admiral Turner, whose command was called the Joint Expeditionary Force. Rear Admiral Harry Hill was his deputy who commanded the transports and control vessels. The expeditionary troops were commanded by Lieut. General Holland Smith, and the V Corps, which included all three divisions, as fast as they were released by Smith, was headed by Harry Schmidt; the support force, which was already bombing Iwo, included gunfire support, escort carriers, minesweepers and underwater demolition teams—all commanded by Rear Admiral W. H. P. Blandy, who delegated the gunfire to Rear Admiral Bertram J. Rodgers, including old battleships, cruisers, and destroyers, plus the *Washington* and *North Carolina* and some cruisers which would be detached from Task Force 58. Among the old battleships would be four from the European theater, *New York, Texas, Nevada, Arkansas.*

The transport squadrons (one for each division) were commanded by veteran amphibious Commodores Henry C. Flanagan, Donald W. Loomis and John McGovern. The three Marine divisions would be withdrawn from Iwo after the island's capture, and troops of the 147th Infantry would come from Noumea to garrison it. The post-battle island commander would be Major General James E. Chaney.

The Joint Expeditionary Force was a part of the Fifth Fleet of Admiral Spruance. The Fast Carrier Task Force, another part, would be available for Iwo support after the carrier bombardment of Tokyo; one group would be available by D Day. "We expect attacks from Japan, although it's a one-way trip for Jap fighter planes. We shall need plenty of fighter cover."

Land-based aircraft from the Seventh Air Force would assist in the Iwo bombing, and would bomb Chichi Jima and other islands between Iwo and Japan. Submarines were associated in the Iwo operation, and would have a special deployment. Planes from the Southwest Pacific air forces would hit China, Formosa, and Miyako Jima. Planes from India were attacking other airfields which might feed planes toward Iwo. Part of Task Force 58 would hit the Nansei Shoto (Okinawa).

The transports would arrive in operating areas early on D Day, about eight miles out, with the LST's stationed closer in. The transports would move in closer as soon as Jap gunfire from the beach had been eliminated.

Admiral Turner casually mentioned at the end of his explanation that he expected to leave the scene of operations after a few days because he had to prepare for future operations (Okinawa, of course). Admiral Hill would assume command of the Force when Turner left. On that hot morning aboard Turner's flag ship nobody could realize that Turner himself would not be able to leave Iwo Jima until D plus 18. Iwo Jima took a long time; it was to seem like centuries before it was over.

Holland Smith was choked up when he got up to talk: "There is very little I can say. The stage is set. Everything has been done that can be done. There has been a tremendous amount of work by a large number of officers and men.

"This is no set-up. Anybody who indulges in such wild flights of fancy has had no experience against these Japs. Every cook and baker will be on the beach with some kind of weapon. We will be ready for an early counterattack in one of three places. We welcome a counterattack. That is generally when we break their backs.

"The aerial photographs show that the number of pillboxes has increased since last October, and especially since last December. The Japs have no barracks above ground on Iwo. We have got to dig them out. There is no maneuver ground. This is a frontal attack. The proper way is to do it as quickly as possible. We are not accustomed to defensive positions. There is nothing more detrimental to morale than to be stabilized.

"Almost every weapon the Japs have got can reach us on the beaches. We may have to take high casualties on the beaches—maybe 40 per cent of the assault troops. We have taken such losses before, and if we have to we can do it again. The Navy brought us out here, and we have never yet had to swim ashore. The Navy has never let us suffer from lack of food, water, or ammunition. Sometimes it has been close.

"The Third and Fourth Marine Divisions are experienced troops. The Fifth is new, but we believe it will do its stuff. In Admiral Turner we have full confidence—we would rather go to sea with him in command than any other admiral under whom we have served."

The gruff old man was misty-eyed as he concluded: "We have never failed, and I don't believe we shall fail here. It's a tough proposition. That's the reason we are here."

Granite-faced Harry Schmidt clearly was not accustomed to making speeches. His stage-fright was as obvious as his speech was short: "The landing force is ready for combat. We are not sending any boys to do a man's job. We expect to get on their tails and keep on their tails until we chop them off."

Admiral Turner, as master of ceremonies, added a few more bits of information for the correspondents before he introduced the Secretary of the Navy: Real unity of thought and of command had been achieved for his operation, between the Army,[2] Navy, Marines, and Coast Guard, and even the Coast and Geodetic Survey, which had a few men along.

[2] Although no Army infantry was involved in the assault on Iwo, some Army units participated before the battle ended: the 471st, 473rd, 476th Amphibian Truck Companies, 138th AAA Group, signalmen of the 7th Fighter Command and 49th Signal Construction Battalion, a Bomb Disposal Squad, some port units and, of course, the P-51 fighter squadrons which landed as soon as airfields were ready.

Jim Forrestal exposed himself to the dangers of warfare as no other United States official of his rank did in World War II. He wanted to know what went on in his Navy, and he knew he was not choosing a minor affair when he set out for Iwo Jima. On this morning he wore khaki, as did everybody else, but he wore no insignia, because he was entitled to none. He addressed himself to the 70-odd correspondents in the flagship's wardroom:

"It has been said here this morning that you are honored to have me present on this operation. Quite the reverse is true. It is a high privilege for me to see in action the quality of leadership America has produced. I have seen Admiral Turner before, under less auspicious circumstances, when I was Under Secretary of the Navy. That was in the summer of 1942. His job then was to invade and take Guadalcanal with the Marines. It was a tough job, a very tough job. But that was his mission, and he did it. The American people still do not realize the narrow margin of that pivot of the Pacific war.

"I am impressed with the great amount of material we have accumulated since then, things with which to fight. I am also impressed by the meticulous precision that goes into these operations, the amount and extent of planning that is required.

"This is a different kind of war that must be fought out here. These assaults on limited land areas present a tough task. This next target, Iwo Jima, like Tarawa, leaves very little choice except to take it by force of arms, by character and courage.

"You news correspondents have a responsibility somewhat like my own—to the public. The tremendous scale and scope of this war can best be conveyed to the people by the press. Only to the extent that the people get the military and logistics problem will we be able to keep the peace in the future. Back home there is a great tendency to count the victory as already won, to have the turkey on the table before it is shot. The people should understand that we are fighting a fanatical enemy who can be beaten only by death.

"Last summer, after I came back from France, I was asked what impressions I brought back. I drew up a set of four conclusions: First, the extent to which the working of seapower is vital to our country; seapower enables us to land on enemy shores instead of his landing on ours; second, airpower alone would not win a war; third, nobody in his right mind would undertake the mission of winning without airpower; fourth, the guy with the rifle and machine gun is the man who wins the war in the last analysis—and pays the penalty to preserve our liberty.

"My hat is off to the Marines. I think my feeling about them is best expressed by Maj. General Julian Smith, in a letter written to his wife after Tarawa. He said: 'I can never again see a United States Marine without experiencing a feeling of reverence.'"

It was only two and one-half days from Saipan to Iwo Jima. The transport I rode was the Coast Guard vessel *Bayfield,* Captain Walter R. Richards. Many of my old friends were on the *Bayfield.* It was to be expected that I would see more and more familiar faces after three years of the Pacific war, but somehow I was always surprised to find an acquaintance or two aboard every ship or in every battalion.

Until I went aboard the ship I did not know that Commodore Henry C. Flanagan, commander of Transport Squadron 15 (24 ships), had his flag aboard. He had been Captain Flanagan of Transport Division 28 on the *Bolivar* when we went into Saipan. With him were several officers I had known: Lieutenant Robert L. Hyder of Missouri, a Justice Department lawyer in Washington before the war; Lieut. Commander Lester A. Wheeler, the squadron boat-control officer, and his assistant, Lieutenant Laton A. Jaton.

I also found on Flanagan's staff Lieutenant Samuel M. Shimer, who seemed to bob up everywhere I went in the Pacific. He was on the *Tennessee* when I rode her from Pearl Harbor to Efate (New Hebrides) before the Tarawa landing. Later he appeared on the AK (cargo-transport) *Virgo* off Tarawa when I went out there to write a story the third night.

I had known that the commanding officer of the Fourth Marine Division, Maj. General Clifton B. Cates, would be aboard the *Bayfield*. He had taken command of the division between the Saipan and Tinian operations, when Maj. General Harry Schmidt took over the V Amphibious Corps job. I had visited the Fourth Division at its Hawaiian base in November, and I had asked to be assigned to it for the next operation because I knew many people in the outfit. Such previous acquaintanceship simplified the correspondent's job. However, I was surprised to find the Fourth's 24th Regiment commander, Colonel Walter Irvine Jordan, also aboard the *Bayfield*. He had been an observer at Tarawa who suddenly had to take over the battalion I waded in with, after Lieut. Colonel Herbert Amey had been killed. There was no quicker way to become acquainted with a man than in a foxhole on the beach at Tarawa.

The Fourth Division was a seasoned, cocky outfit which had recently been awarded the Presidential Unit citation for its Saipan and Tinian record. Iwo Jima was its fourth amphibious operation in 13 months (it had taken Roi and Namur Islands in the Kwajalein atoll in early February, 1944). One of its colonels, Franklin A. Hart, had been made a brigadier general and was now assistant division commander. Another, Louis Jones, had also become a general, and was chief of staff of the corps. The third infantry colonel, Merton J. Batchelder, was now chief of staff and was also aboard the *Bayfield*. Most of the battalion commanders had been seasoned in the division's previous amphibious landings, and if anybody knew how to take one of these small, heavily defended islands, they and their veteran troops did.

To the Fourth Division had been assigned the northern strip of beachhead, Beaches Blue and Yellow. The Fifth Division would land below them on Beaches Red and Green. Nobody in his right mind could look at the maps and conclude that either assignment would be easy. When the message came through on the night before D Day saying that naval gunfire had been unsatisfactory—*i.e.*, it had failed to flush out the underground fortifications—we knew we were in for some trying times.

In the divisional area the 25th Marines under Colonel J. R. ("Pat") Lanigan would land on the right, the 23d Marines under Colonel Walter W. Wensinger on the left. The 24th Regiment, with which I would go into the beach, was in reserve; it might be committed at any time General Cates decided. The more I thought about the situation, the more I was satisfied that I would not hit the beach with the early waves.

The 25th Regiment had what looked like the toughest job. It would land almost directly under a heavily fortified hill below a rock quarry, on the extreme right of all the American troops, next to the massed defenders of Iwo. It seemed to us impossible that bombing and naval gunfire could destroy the fortifications we knew the Japs would have built into that steep hill—and we were right.

The Third Battalion landed on the right of the 25th's area, the First Battalion on the left (the Second Battalion was regimental reserve, which meant it would not land for an hour or two after H Hour). We knew 3/25 could expect the most intense fire. Said General Cates: "If I knew the name of the man on the extreme right of the right-hand squad of the right-hand company of 3/25, I'd recommend him for a medal before we go in." (Two months later he told me he had never been able to learn the man's name.)

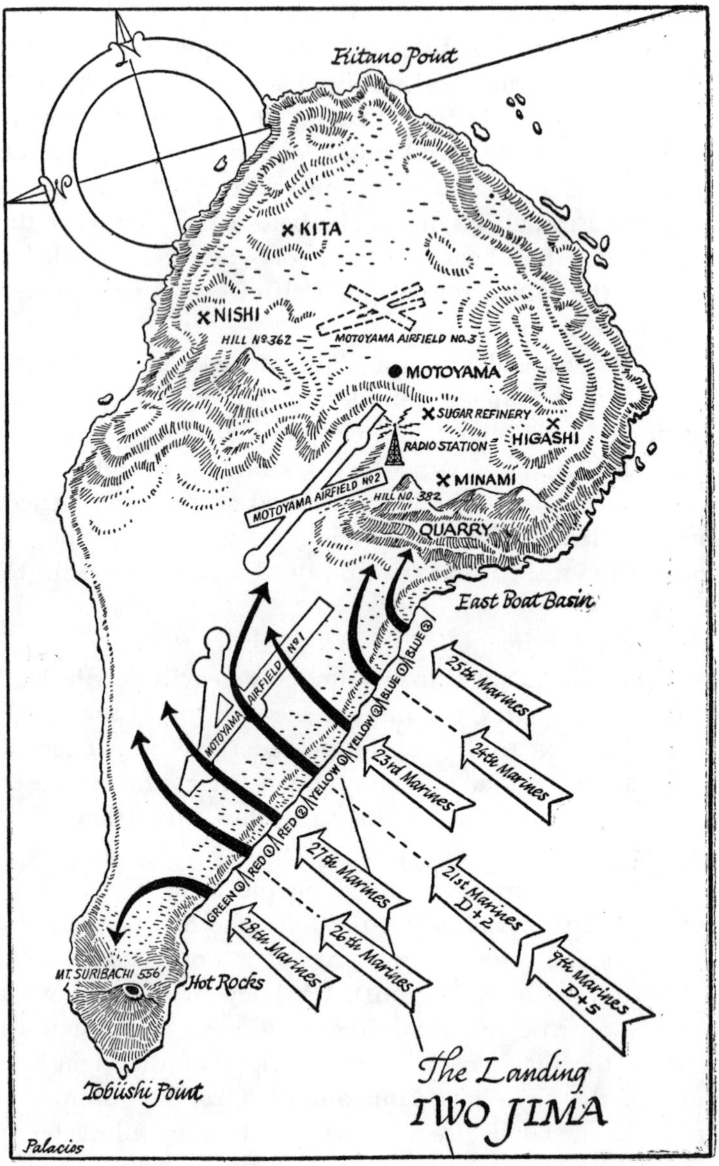
Kitano Point
KITA
NISHI
HILL No. 362
MOTOYAMA AIRFIELD NO. 3
MOTOYAMA
SUGAR REFINERY
HIGASHI
RADIO STATION
MINAMI
MOTOYAMA AIRFIELD No 2
HILL NO. 382
QUARRY
East Boat Basin
MOTOYAMA AIRFIELD No 1
GREEN 1
RED 1
RED 2
YELLOW 1
YELLOW 2
BLUE 1
BLUE 2
25th Marines
24th Marines
23rd Marines
27th Marines
21st Marines D+2
9th Marines D+5
28th Marines
26th Marines
MT. SURIBACHI 556'
Hot Rocks
Tobiishi Point
The Landing
IWO JIMA
Palacios

The men of 3/25, who had had some tough landings before, had a song about themselves. It represented the cynical bitterness of men who got the assignments to die. It is sung to the tune of Chopin's *Funeral March:*

> We are the ghouls of the Third Battalion,
>   One thousand men and one Italian.[3]
> We waded through the swamps;
>   The earth we learned to hug.
> And all we got was a goddam dizzy bug,
>   But ten thousand dollars went home to the folks.
> But won't they be happy, won't they be surprised,
>   When ten thousand dollars go home to the folks!
> We landed on Kwajalein like a bunch of Spars,
>   When we got back *some* were issued Silver Stars.
> Our next landing will be our hoax,
>   And ten thousand dollars go home to the folks.
> Happy, happy we will be, when we board the LST,
>   Busy little tractors heading for the shore,
> Everybody looking for a clean gook whore,
>   And ten thousand dollars go home to the folks!"

The author of the song had no $10,000 sent home to his folks. He was only seriously wounded. And 3/25, though it had the toughest initial job, had fewer total casualties than some other battalions, only 684 out of approximately 900, if the number who died of wounds is subtracted from the total wounded, and if replacements added to the battalion are not counted.

Despite their lugubrious song, and their cynicism, the Marines were essentially an optimistic crowd. They had to be. One of them said on the *Bayfield:* "I figure I'll get wounded four or five times before I get killed. Look at the law of averages."

One of the more optimistic people on the *Bayfield* was Major Frederic O. Wolf of Atlanta, Georgia, the division

---

[3] A tribute of distinction to a popular Italian officer.

language officer. Born in Georgia, he had spent most of his life in Japan and he spoke English with a distinctly British accent; he spoke Japanese as well as the enemy. Like all language officers, Major Wolf hoped we would get a lot of prisoners. I bet him ten dollars to one we would not get 1,000 prisoners, five to one we would not get 700. I never was able to learn definitely who had won, but I knew that when I left Iwo, on D plus 18, a week before the battle ended, we had about 80 prisoners.

Major Wolf came, on D minus 1, into the room I shared with the transport squadron quartermaster, Major Tom Alexander. He had some definite ideas about the Japanese, whom he had known not only in Japan but on Guadalcanal, where he was also a language officer. "They will surrender whenever the emperor tells them to," he said (correctly, it turned out), "and the politicians in Japan will become impressed when they receive fingers in the mail and accompanying notes, 'Here is the evidence of the honesty of my intention if you do not bring peace'—meaning, 'Next time it will be your head, not my finger, that comes off.' " Major Wolf had other assorted bits of information—the word "iwo" meant sulphur, "jima" and "shima" (we all knew they meant island) were interchangeable, depending on alliteration.

I asked him why the Japs cut off their prisoners' heads. "That's old stuff," Wolf said; "they behead each other, and consider it an honorable way to die."

On D minus 1 I was assigned to the boat I would ride to the beach. The boat captain was a big, bespectacled lieutenant from Ironton, Minnesota, named Sam Dobervich, who was always smiling, and the senior officer was Lieut. Colonel Austin R. Brunelli, now executive officer of the 24th. Popular Sam Dobervich was killed on D plus 3, and Colonel Brunelli had his face nicked by a mortar fragment on D plus 1, but the rest of us came through without a scratch. I doubt that the occupants of any other single boat which hit the beach on D Day had so few casualties. The names of the lucky others in the boat were: Major Milton G. Cokin, of Pawtucket, Rhode Island; Captain Thomas M. Kerr, Jr., of Sidney, Montana; Sergeants James Ross, of Crawfordsville, Indiana; Edward C. Bengston, of Glendale, California; Randall B. Mason, of Mayfield, Kentucky, and Lynn J. Peterson, of La Moure, North Dakota; Corporals Luverne E. Overlid, of Minneapolis, Minnesota; Donald W. Mahn, of Bonduel, Wisconsin, and William F. Sullivan, of Salem, Massachusetts; Privates First Class Joseph M. Yeager, of Altoona, Pennsylvania; Peter P. Sandoval, of Lukachukai, Arizona, and Bobby R. Swinson, of Isabel, Kansas; and Private Donald R. Treber, of Marion, Indiana.

CHAPTER TEN

BEACHHEAD IN HELL

IN THE DAWN OF D DAY, IWO JIMA LOOKED LIKE A FAIRLY HIGH plateau—even the landing beaches seemed much steeper than the aerial photographs had indicated. At the foot was Mount Suribachi, which resembled an inverted, slightly melted scoop of ice cream. The shells from the battleships, cruisers, and destroyers were the same arching red balls of fire I had seen on previous landings. Oncoming daylight changed their color to a fading yellow and, finally, to invisibility.

What was discouraging about watching the shells (total pre-invasion bombardment 7,500 tons) was this: they seemed to set nothing afire. They burst on the beaches, the northern plateau, and the sides of the mountain with a fierce twinkle, but no flames arose in their wake. We could see very early that the Japs were deep underground on Iwo. After watching the terrific hail of steel for two hours General Cates turned to me and said: "By this time ten or 15 per cent. of the bastards *must* have been killed by all this shelling and bombing." But I could tell he feared not.

There was one beautiful thing about D Day: the weather was fine. We had picked the right day for the landings and, as it turned out, the only day for a long time when we could get ashore easily in small boats. The four days after D Day were miserably rough and amphtracs and LCVP's nearly always got badly battered or sunk if they even tried to negotiate the surf.

At 0720 the sun was about five degrees above the horizon, and the B-24's from Saipan arrived. They circled slowly for their bombing runs, then their bombs walked down the island like twinkling Christmas lights. A lot of smoke and dust arose from the ground, but no fire blazed. The battleships and the cruisers took up their shelling again—one cruiser seemed to be no more than 500 yards from shore—and at 0805 the dive bombers came in with more tons of bombs. Soon the island was covered by a pall of smoke and dust, and only the topmost peak of Suribachi was visible.

This pounding of the island went on for a long time. Some planes dropped fire bombs which spurted a terrific plume of flame when they burst—one plume continued burning at the base of Suribachi a long time after it had been started, and it seemed that maybe something was inflammable on Iwo, after all. The F4U's flew low over the island, strafing, and the F6F's let loose barrage after barrage of rockets. The destroyers began firing air bursts; their shells exploded in black puffs a couple of hundred feet above ground, raking the island with hot steel. The bombardment of Iwo, I thought, was more terrifying than any other similar spectacle I had ever seen.

I wrote in my notebook: "Though I've seen this many times, I can't help thinking, 'nobody can live through this.' But I know better."

The first waves of amphtracs were lining up for the final charge toward the beach at 0840. It was 20 minutes before H Hour. The bouncing craft left an irregular white wake as they set out for that long, long ride before the sand crunched under their bottoms.

At 0850 General Cates said: "The first wave is getting rather bad fire from Suribachi, probably 40-mm. or 57-mm. But the smoke and dust are being blown inland; this northeast wind is a blessing. We certainly could not have asked for a better day." At 0855 the delayed radio report came in: "Seven hundred yards to go." Then the fighters, lined up overhead, awaiting their turn, began strafing the beaches; thousands of rounds of 50-caliber bullets poured in ahead of the first landing craft, to make sure that no Jap on the beaches stayed above ground to fire at the Americans who were about to hit his shores.

But the Japs farther north and inland seemed to be able to fire. A control boat between our transport and the beach got a direct hit as we watched the first waves of boats churning through the surf. Other heavy mortar or artillery shells splashed in the water around the landing craft, but from our distance I saw none hit.

About 0905 I saw four flares go up from the beaches. A minute later a fifth arched through the sky. An ensign beside me said: "Well, somebody got ashore alive, anyway." A few minutes later one of our planes caught an anti-aircraft burst and went flaming into the ocean.

The actual landing on Iwo was not so tough as we had expected. At 0930 our first waves were reported 100 to 200 yards inland, and other waves were landing behind them in good order. Some mortar shells splashed on the beach, but remarkably few in those first two hours. What reports got through—and they were not many and not always quite accurate—indicated no great enemy activity: "1/23 is receiving light machine gun and mortar fire." "Light opposition on the beach." "We appear to be getting no concentrated machine-gun or mortar fire." "Air observer reports entire line 200 to 300 yards inland." "Only sporadic bursts of mortar fire." A captain in Radio 4 said: "It must be our rolling barrage of naval gunfire is working;" for this operation the Navy was not ceasing fire as the troops worked inland: the guns merely lifted their fire ahead of the troops.

The *Bayfield* was still about six miles offshore, but we could see the amphtracs and tanks waddling up the beaches like so many black bugs. The new Fifth Division troops were going inland quite rapidly. Heaviest opposition, as expected, was reported on the Fourth Division's right flank; the ghouls of 3/25 were catching it early.

At 1040 heavy mortar fire was reported on the right and

left flanks. The boats of the later waves going into Blue Beaches also sent word that they were receiving heavy fire. I could count 14 tanks on the uphill beaches which seemed to be moving not at all—whether they had been knocked out or whether they had stalled in the volcanic ash, I did not know. At 1045 General Cates observed: "We've averaged about 150 yards an hour so far; that's not enough. We've got to get that airfield and get that right flank anchored before night . . ." We could not know then that 150 yards per hour would seem like a lot of mileage before the day was over.

At 1100 Colonel Lanigan reported that his 25th Marines were 200 yards inland, about half way to the airfield, but resistance was increasing and casualties were considerable. If any other reminder of casualties were needed, the ship's loudspeaker provided it: "Prepare to receive casualties at No. 3 hatch on the starboard side." A boom was lowered, and our first casualty—a psychiatric case, for which the *Bayfield* was a designated ship—was lifted out of an LCVP. His stretcher was set down through the uncovered hatch, into the sick bay. The Marine seemed to be asleep, but he twitched every few seconds. The other cases in the LCVP— three Marines and a sailor—had bloody wounds. They were carried on to another ship.

By general consensus, 11 o'clock is called the turning point on Iwo's D Day. Until that time, progress had not been easy, but the first two hours were a picnic compared to what followed. From the north and from Suribachi on the south the hidden Japs poured artillery and huge mortar shells onto the Marines struggling up the beachhead. Many tanks churned helplessly and became easy marks for Jap artillery. Machine guns poured bullets into the men on the right flank. Before noon, casualty estimates indicated the cost: 20 per cent on both Yellow beaches and on Blue 1, 25 per cent on the Blue 2 beach of the 25th Regiment. Colonel

Louis G. DeHaven, the division artillery officer, recommended that his guns not be landed until after the reserve battalions had gone in; there was hardly any space to put them in, yet. And that artillery had to get in before dark.

At 1315 General Cates said, worriedly: "I wish we had six more hours of daylight than we are going to have, or even four more. Hell, I'd compromise for two! I'll have to shoot the artillery in pretty soon, anyway." A few minutes later Colonel Wensinger reported by radio that his 23d Marines needed more air support, "mortar and artillery fire are increasing." He added: "The gunfire spotters have got to get down low and locate these mortars. We can't see them. They are buried in six-foot-deep holes." Cates observed: "You can lick machine guns with infantry, but mortars are tougher."

The results of the mortar fire could be seen more easily as we moved in closer. They were being aimed at the boats heading for the shore, and water splashed 100 feet high when the big "ash cans" exploded. "Must be 150-mm.," someone guessed. (Actually, they were as large at 320-mm., we learned later.) We could see some wrecked boats on the beaches where mortar shells crashed into the frail craft. "Look at that God-damned murderous fire on our Yellow beaches," said Cates; "there goes another hit square on a tank—burned him up." He thought a minute, and said: "I swear I hate to send in the artillery when there is no cover for it, but I've got to do it." He ordered in the First and Second Battalions of the 14th (artillery) Marines.

At 1430 the First Battalion, 24th Marines, was ordered to the Blue Beach 1 area, and the Second Battalion to the Blue 2 area. Another casualty report came in: Fifth Division, ten per cent, the 3/25 ghouls reported 30 per cent, and 2/25, the regimental reserve, had pushed through them. One tank was reported to have reached the much-desired airfield, but it had to retire.

At 1530 came word that my boat, No. X-2, was ready to

load at Station Blue 4, second cargo net on the portside. Suddenly, the *Bayfield* seemed like a nice haven, a precious place to be. On the beaches between the airfield and the water line I could see tremendous mortar shells exploding one after another, sending debris high into the air. Knowing that those beaches were crowded with Marines, I knew that hundreds must be dead by now. An LCVP carrying the Red Cross casualty flag came alongside with three more psychiatric cases, one of them screaming at the top of his voice and twisting violently in his stretcher. No man can look at a severe psychiatric case without thinking, "There is war at its worst."

Five enemy shells suddenly splashed into the water near the *Bayfield's* bow, cracking loudly in the water as they exploded. They were quickly followed by eight more. Now the Japs were really fighting back. LSM No. 70 passed to the retirement area, with two gaping holes in her side. The small boats had been taking it for three days already; twelve LCI's had been hit during the preliminary rocket bombardment.

It was 1705 before Boat X-2, 16 men and a communications jeep, was ready to head for the beach. Climbing down the cargo net, I felt that I had no business there. I had climbed down cargo nets several times before, and I had seen tough beachheads before—and the law of averages seemed to jump up and stare me in the face after a while. But when I turned and asked a Marine in the boat, "What do you think?" he said, "I believe the worst is over now." He knew better, and I knew better, but it made me feel good to hear the lie.

The boat bounced through the water toward the PC control boat, where we went for instructions before we were formed in a wave and told where to land. The afternoon was wearing fast, and it was getting chilly. I consoled myself by remembering that I had brought a blanket which would feel good in a foxhole tonight, provided I got ashore all right and got a foxhole dug.

I hopped aboard the PC boat with Colonel Brunelli to find out what the score was. The first person I saw was Keith Wheeler, the Chicago *Times* man who had already been ashore in one of the earlier waves, and had returned to write his D Day story. His news was even more alarming than I had imagined: "There's more hell in there than I've seen in the rest of this war put together. The Nips have got the beaches blanketed with mortars. There are dead Marines scattered from one end to the other, and it looks like nearly every boat is getting smashed before it can pull out."

The colonels of both the 24th and 25th Regiments, Jordan and Lanigan, were also aboard the PC, awaiting directions for landing their headquarters. Their faces were grave; there was no doubt that the situation on the beach was very serious. The small boats continued to mill around the PC, like angry bees.

"I wouldn't go in there if I were you," said Wheeler, "it's plain foolishness. The Nips are going to open up with everything they've got tonight." I was almost convinced that no purpose would be served by my going ashore now. I took off my pack, canteen belt, and combat jacket, and laid them on the PC deck. After all, this business of taking long chances could be carried too far.

After we had been on the PC boat about an hour, it was nearly dark and the beach, though it was only a few hundred yards away, looked more like shadow than substance, except when the thunderous crash of a Jap mortar shell shook it and the splashing fire of the explosion lit it up. Then our small boat, containing Dobervich and Cokin and Bengston and Sandoval and the others, came alongside.

I looked down into the faces of the men in the boat, and I saw written on them the same fear that gripped at my guts. I knew these men could not stay on the PC, where it would be warm, and there would be coffee, and there would not be much danger. They had to go in. When I looked at these faces and realized these things, I knew I could not stay aboard the PC. I had cast my lot with these men when we set out for the shore, and this was no time to desert. I put on my jacket, buckled on my belt, and shouldered my pack. Colonel Brunelli appeared and said, "Ready to go?" I said "sure," very bravely, though I was mighty scared.

Later I attempted to analyze the reasons men endure the great dangers that war entails. I never heard a satisfactory explanation, so I tried to set down the reasons for my own little venture into the fearful unknown which was the Iwo beachhead that twilight of February 19. Ordinarily, the war correspondent took only a fraction of the risks a combat infantryman had to take; the writer had to knock out no pillboxes and their flanking machine guns. On this particular occasion my own risk happened to be as great as that of the men in the boat I was riding in. My only protection on a barren beach would be, like theirs, a foxhole in the volcanic ash. If the Japs succeeded in tonight's counterattack, then I would get killed along with the others.

Then, why did I go instead of staying aboard the PC? (Remember, this is a *post facto* analysis—I reacted automatically at the time.) The first reason was pride; these men in the boat knew me, and I didn't want them to know me as one who was afraid to face something they had to face. The second reason was sympathy; the fear I saw in their faces certainly met a sympathetic response in what I felt in my stomach. Besides, these men knew I had made several rugged landings; what would they think of this one they were facing or of me if they saw me back down now? The third reason was probably duty; I could write a more authentic story of the Iwo landing and the first night's counterattack if I got in there on D Day. The fourth reason was self-defense; some of us, notably Wheeler and I, had been critical of "communiqué commandos" who wrote about battles from rear areas, without knowing what gunpowder actually smelled like.

In all these reasons behind this minor venture there was none which might have been called lofty, but I believed they were approximately the same reasons combat infantrymen endured their hell. Men in combat rarely considered that they were fighting for liberty, or democracy, or for any of the nobilities so often attributed to fighting men. They fought because of pride, sympathy, duty—and in self-defense. The most important of these was pride—personal pride, pride of unit, and pride of country (the latter seemed quite remote, it had to be added).

The LCVP chugged toward the beach with the headquarters wave of the 24th Marines. Having made my decision, I felt almost no fear—there was now nothing I could do about going or not going into the hell of Iwo Jima. "Everybody get down," Colonel Brunelli said. I knelt beside the radio jeep in our boat. Three mortar shells cracked on the water, but they were far beyond us.

It was only a few minutes before the boat grounded on the coarse, black sand of Iwo. The ramp went down. As directed, we dashed a couple of hundred yards inland through the semi-darkness. As I ran, shovel in hand, I noticed scattered dark forms on the loose earth—perhaps 20 dead Marines between the water line and the 200-yard line. The smell of death was wafted lightly through the cool evening air.

Digging a foxhole in that foul earth was exasperating, even if the Japs had let up momentarily in their shelling of the beachhead. Whenever I scooped up a shovelful, three-quarters of a shovelful rolled back into the hole. The grains of volcanic ash were as loose as so many buckshot, and just as big. "God damn!" said a nearby voice. "It's like diggin' a hole in a barrel of wheat." But by the time dark had settled over the island I had managed to excavate a hole in the enemy earth, two feet deep and six feet long. I wrapped my khaki blanket about me, for the weather had become colder, and nestled into the hole. "Who are you?" said a voice in the two-man foxhole about ten feet farther up the slope. I said, "War correspondent," half apologetically, as though I were trespassing. "Okay; just wanted to make sure I knew what was next t'me," the voice replied.

When dark came, the ships offshore began to fire star shells, which lit up the front line (and most of the rest of the island) all night long. The brilliant yellow lights would burst high in the air, then float to earth slowly on their silk parachutes. The Japs could not move secretly during the night, because we had brought our daylight with us. The ships' guns, 5-, 6-, and 8-inchers, also kept a fairly steady tattoo of high explosives on the northern end of the island. And we had managed to get some land-based artillery into action—the Fifth Division had landed nearly two battalions, the Fourth somewhat less—whose shells whistled softly overhead, then burst in the Jap area.

During this first night we held somewhat less than ten per cent of the island's land area. Our line curved from the northernmost end of Motoyama Airfield No. 1, along the lower bank (the east bank) of the field, until the southern end of the airfield was reached. Below this southern end, the Fifth Division had cut across the island's neck, had actually occupied the southernmost tip of the field, and had isolated Mount Suribachi from the rest of Iwo. In other words, we had a T-bone and the Japs had the rest.

All night long we expected a counterattack. Somehow, I never doubted that we could stop the attack, though the Japs had advantages of land mass and terrain. Perhaps it was because I knew how intently our troops had been drilled against such enemy outbursts; perhaps it was because the sergeant in the next foxhole said to his companion, "Well, they counterattacked the first night on Tinian, and we slaughtered 'em; let 'em come." Actually, the Japs did attempt one attack on the Fifth Division flank, but it was small; only about 100 men; and the Fifth's men beat it off. I believe our guns and star shells kept the Japs from forming a big attack.

Once in a while the Japs threw their giant mortar shells at us. I could hear them crash on the beach 200 yards to the east, or in the front line 200 yards to the west. We in the middle seemed to have chosen the best possible spot to dig in. From where I lay, the first half of the night seemed relatively quiet, and the bitterly cold weather seemed nearer than the mortar shells. I managed to get a couple of hours' sleep.

It was slightly after four o'clock in the morning that my illusions and my sense of security were shattered. The Japs apparently decided to shift to the center of the beachhead. The first big mortar shell hit only a few yards from my foxhole, and it sounded like the break of doom. I foolishly had my head a few inches above my foxhole at the time, and I was lucky not to lose it. The blinding red light of the explosion was exceeded in ferocity only by the unholy detonation. Ash particles fell on my blanket for a full minute afterward.

Then the rain of steel began. The heavy shells burst around my foxhole every few seconds in a furious tattoo. Once I timed the explosions, and there were 20 (within 50 yards, I guessed) in one minute. In the midst of this thunder and lightning there was a thud in the bank of my foxhole, next to my left arm. I reached over and dug out a piece of hot steel that must have weighed a half pound.

After a while, the Navy's guns and rocket ships and the Marines' 75's and 105's opened up with a concentrated barrage that outdid everything else that night. They fired continuously for a long time, until it seemed that they had returned a hundred times what the Japs had loosed on us.

Whether or not the Japs' firing had given away their own artillery and mortar positions I did not know. But the Japs did not fire again for about an hour after that pasting.

Daylight seemed colder than the night, but it was welcome. As I rose from the foxhole (which had caved in until I was almost covered) I drank a two-ounce bottle of medicinal brandy a doctor had stuck in my pocket, and looked around. Next to the foxhole were two unexploded Jap mines. In a big shell hole ten yards away there were eight dead Marines who had evidently received a direct hit the day before; their position indicated they had sought cover in the hole.

I walked over to the 24th CP. This regiment, on the basis of early reports, had fared well during the night: one man killed in headquarters, ten in 2/24, one in 1/24. Everybody talked about the narrow escapes during the night. One runner who took off for the front line swore his hair had been parted by a mortar fragment; he had his halved helmet to show for it. "There must have been fifty hits within ten yards of our shellhole," said Colonel Jordan; certainly, the pock-marked area around his CP tended to prove his assertion. As he spoke, the Japs opened up again. The heavy shells began falling on all sides of us; those which fell in front made no noise until they exploded; the overs whistled loudly just before they burst.

Even as the shells were bursting, corpsman bearing two stretchers came by. Doctor Charles H. Conley, Jr., the regimental surgeon, popped out to examine the wounded, then sent them on to the evacuation station on the beach.

As soon as the Japs let up, I started walking to the water line. It was a dismal sight; battered tanks and amphtracs littered the area around the CP. And along the beach, to the left and to the right, there were many of our dead, some of whom, apparently, were killed advancing uphill after landing, others killed by direct hits in the holes where they sought cover. Two men lay dead under an amphtrac. In one shell hole there were 12 dead, in another eight, in another seven. Four corpsmen, their stretcher beside them, had perished not far from the water line.

At the airfield edge I stopped and talked to Major Horace C. Parks, executive officer of 1/24, and Captain Frederic A. Stott, battalion liaison officer. Two dead Marines lay on the embankment just ahead of us. The major said, "You know, I saw only one dead Jap on the beach yesterday." Near the beach I saw Major John B. Edgar of 1/14, who had set up his 75-mm. artillery CP in a shattered blockhouse. He had had twelve men killed or wounded by mortars during the night.

I walked south and uphill again, ducking occasionally into a foxhole whenever the snipers hiding under the wrecked Jap planes began firing. (They were still shooting four days later, long after we took the airfield.) The sloping sands were spotted with American dead. Here and there were dead Japs, but it was apparent that the enemy had not defended his island from the beach. He depended mostly on his mortars, artillery, and hillside machine guns. Whether the dead were Japs or Americans, they had one thing in common; they had died with the greatest possible violence. Nowhere in the Pacific war had I seen such badly mangled bodies. Many were cut squarely in half. Legs and arms lay fifty feet away from any body. In one spot on the sand, far from the nearest cluster of dead, I saw a string of guts 15 feet long. Only legs were easy to identify; they were Jap if wrapped in khaki puttees, American if covered by canvas leggings. The smell of burning flesh was heavy in some areas.

After the long climb through the coarse ash—I wondered how men had ever negotiated the climb under heavy fire— I stopped at the edge of one of the airfield turntables. There I found some men from the 23d Marines: Gunnery Sergeant N. P. Mills, Platoon Sergeant Angus MacCorquodale, and a corpsman, Pharmacist's Mate First Class Bernard Maloney. The First Battalion had suffered heavily during the night. Lieut. Colonel Ralph Haas had been killed, also his operations officer, Captain Fred C. Eberhardt, and his communications officer, Lieutenant Francis W. Lowry. The personnel officer, Lieutenant Charles J. Maxey, had been wounded. B Company had been hardest hit by casualties. Captain James E. Tobin had been wounded and his executive officer, Lieutenant Stanley Gordon, was dead. So was Lieutenant Karl Davis, Jr., a platoon leader, who yesterday had received a bullet through his thigh which exploded a phosphorous grenade in his pocket. Out of the 28 medical corpsmen in Maloney's outfit, five had been killed, 12 others wounded.

It was the same everywhere I went. The toll of the first 24 hours on Iwo was very high. "Jumping Joe" Chambers' ghouls of 3/25 were reported to have over 40 per cent casualties during their inhuman uphill assignment facing the rock quarry. The Fifth Division had fewer casualties than the Fourth, but had already lost more than a thousand men.

The Fifth was a new division, but it had many veterans as its core. One of these was Gunnery Sergeant John Basilone, one of the Marine Corps' top heroes. He finished parochial school in Raritan, N. J., at 15; then he started driving a laundry truck. At 18 he joined the Army and in due time was shipped off to the Philippines. After a three-year hitch he quit, but in 1940 he joined the Marines. One night in October, 1942, on Guadalcanal he became famous: with a handful of survivors he wiped out 38 Japs, helped save Henderson Field. For this he got the Medal of Honor. Soon he tired of being a hero; after a round of war bond tours and public adulation he asked for more overseas duty.

"Manila John" fought well on Iwo Jima, too. He hit the beach in the first wave, led his men up the steep slope, personally knocked out a blockhouse from the top with grenades and demolition charges, then directed a tank through a minefield despite intense mortar and artillery fire. About noon, as he reached the southern end of the airfield, he was killed. I never met Basilone, but two weeks after his death I saw three Fifth Division men standing in front of Grave No. 41, Row 3, of the cemetery. One of them read Basilone's name on the white cross and said, "There was a man." That was all.

Another of the Fifth Division casualties was Captain Robert L. McCahill, whom I had known since he was a Second Lieutenant in a Marine parachute battalion. A handsome, husky youngster, he had been noted as a football player at Marquette University. He met his fate about 2200 of D Day when a huge Jap mortar shell crashed into his foxhole near the airfield. Captain Ralph Hall, commanding officer of H Company, 27th Marines, was killed with him.

It was nearly dark of D plus 1 when I walked to the beach to catch a boat to the *Bayfield,* so I could write my story. By now the ocean was rough; the boats were having a hard time evacuating the wounded who littered the beach. Doctors and corpsmen were trying frantically to provide some sandbag protection for the long rows of wounded, as Jap shells occasionally crashed nearby, compounding the misery of the bloody soil. There were too many wounded waiting for what boat space could be provided; I turned back to spend another night on Iwo Jima.

CHAPTER ELEVEN

JAPS ARE HARD TO BUDGE

BY THE TIME NIGHT FELL ON D PLUS 1 WE WERE ANCHORED MORE securely. Motoyama Airfield No. 1 was ours, and the line across the island just north of the airfield was fairly well straightened out. Casualties on the second day again had been high, but not as high as D Day's. The Jap counterattack no longer was the fearsome thing it was the first night. Our line was stronger, and we had much more artillery and more serviceable tanks.

Nonetheless, the Jap mortar and artillery fire was still heavy. At Colonel Jordan's CP, where about eight of us dug individual foxholes within a big shell hole, the fire was particularly severe early in the evening. The Japs began using phosphorus shells, and some men near the CP were badly burned. But the firing let up about midnight, and sleep was possible. By now the weather had turned bitterly cold. I shivered all night because now I had only a poncho; I had given away my blanket when I thought I was returning to ship.

During the night this fantastic island seemed more weird than ever. The earth trembled beneath us; the sound was not unlike someone banging on the radiator in the apartment below. Everybody surmised that the tremors were Iwo's own manifestations of an earthquake, but nobody laughed when a sergeant in the shell hole sighed and said, "Oh, my God, the Japs are digging underneath us now; I guess they're going to blow up the damn island." (Later in the battle an official investigation was actually undertaken to find out if the Japs really were digging under us.)

183

February 21

The Fourth Division burial officer was scheduled to arrive at 0900. When this news came, someone said, "There's a lot of work for him to do."

Colonel Lanigan's 25th Regiment CP was no more than a hundred yards from Jordan's 24th, and I went over there soon after daylight. There I learned that Keith Wheeler of the Chicago *Times* had been wounded yesterday afternoon by a sniper who shot him probably from the wreckage of Jap planes on the airfield's edge. The regimental surgeon, Lieut. Commander Herbert Eccleston, said: "He got it right through the neck when he stood up in the shell hole. He was lucky at that. He might have bled to death if he had been off by himself somewhere. But he fell into the arms of two doctors, less than ten feet from a box of plasma." I rescued Wheeler's typewriter and, as his souvenir, the plasma tube which had succored him. It seemed little enough to do for a man who had shared Attu, Tarawa, Saipan, Iwo, and several naval strikes with me. (The gesture was just that, instead of sending the typewriter from the *Bayfield* to Wheeler's hospital ship, a shipboard gremlin sent it back to the beach.)

At Colonel Lanigan's CP I learned something of the terrific odds against the 25th Regiment. Landing under the Japs' heavily fortified cliffs—from where we stood we could see some of the concrete gun emplacements in the hillside— the 25th's battalions had been subjected to simple murder. The Japs were dug deep into the cliffs and, although many of their bigger guns had been knocked out by naval gunfire, their machine guns and mortars only had to fire a few yards downhill at the Marines. "Jumpin' Joe" Chambers' ghouls had done a magnificent job on the right flank, and Lanigan thought Chambers's leadership of his men up the cliff on D Day was one of the most inspiring feats he had ever known.

Lieut. Colonel Lewis C. Hudson, commanding 2/25, had seized the high ground next to the airfield on D Day; but had been wounded yesterday. Also wounded (by a mortar shell in the CP) were Hudson's executive officer, Major William P. Kaempfer, and his operations officer, Major Donald K. Ellis. So, Chambers's executive officer, Lieut. Colonel James Taul, was sent to take over Hudson's battalion.

Chambers himself was not wounded until D plus 3, when his battalion had lost all but ten of its 36 officers. Ordinarily his command would have passed to another lieutenant colonel or to a major, but it had to go to a 6-foot-2-inch captain named James G. Headley, a reserve officer well past 30. Captain Headley led the 3/25 ghouls with such distinction throughout the rest of the Iwo battle that he was awarded a Silver Star and a second Navy Cross to add to the one he had won on Saipan.

The regiment's first battalion had a wider front than the other two, and it was hit fully as hard. Its executive officer, Major Henry D. Strunk, was one of the first members of the battalion wounded on D Day. The commanding officer, Lieut. Colonel Hollis U. Mustain, who had distinguished himself at Saipan and Tinian, was killed today (D plus 2) by a 47-mm. shell.

Mustain, Hudson, and Chambers were an exceptional trio of battalion commanders; a lot of searching would have failed to uncover three better men. Yet the Iwo battle was hardly three days old when all had been killed or wounded. The 25th probably took heavier casualties in these first days than any other regiment on the island, but the battalions fought on, under Major Fenton Mee, Lieut. Colonel Taul and Captain Headley.

The near-impossible conditions faced initially by the 25th required superior leadership, and superior, battle-disciplined troops who had to be prepared for great shock. These troops knew somebody had to take Iwo Jima, and they knew somebody had to make that right flank stick in spite of all the mortar shells and machine-gun fire that make up the infantryman's hell. In the first two days this flank next to the Japs was the key to the whole battle. In thinking it over later, I could suggest no better preparation for the shock than Chambers's men's cynical *Funeral March* ditty. It left little room for disillusion. Not many of our men died in World War II with a song on their lips. They usually died grimly, without a murmur.

At 0830 we turned loose the greatest concentration of fire I had ever seen. Dozens of planes circled overhead and came in by twos and fours, dropping hundreds of bombs and rockets. The Navy guns fired salvos of 5-inch to 14-inch shells; it seemed as fast as typewriter keys beating against a sheet of paper. The land-based 75's and 105's and 155's kept their shells bursting over the entire northern two-thirds of the island. Yet we knew that when the multiple barrage ceased the little men would pop up in their holes to wait for our infantry's charge. Then their mortar shells would begin flying into our end of the island.

The trip to the *Bayfield*, where I had to go to write my story of the landing, was no easy task. The surf was rough, and only occasional LCVP's could get in to take out the casualties. Ensign Gardner was taking out four stretcher cases whenever he could get them aboard, and I went along with him in one of the LCVP's flying the red "X" of the casualty boats. It was a good time to leave. We were no more than 200 yards offshore when a huge mortar shell splashed near the beach evacuation station. Another blew up an ammunition dump nearby.

The casualty boat went first to a new type of ship we had designated Hospital LST. The LST was a workhorse of a ship, and we could never have fought an amphibious war so well without it, but its designers probably never dreamed it would see service as a hospital ship, too. In daytime the LST —the initials meant "Landing Ship, Tanks"—served mostly as a clearing station for the wounded. The small boats, chiefly LCVP's, came alongside, and the doctors indicated which transport the wounded should be sent to. At night the LST usually took aboard the wounded who were brought alongside, and kept them until morning in the big, converted sick bay.

There was a flat barge alongside the LST Hospital Ship No. 930 (one of three at Iwo). Doctor Joe Bailey stood on this barge, directing the shifting of the wounded to the proper boats going to the proper transports. He had little sleep in the past three days, what with great numbers of casualties and rough weather. He could not say enough for the courage of the wounded: "One Marine came alongside a while ago with his leg blown off. He smiled and said, "Doc, I think I'm going to be all right if I get enough blood.' I said, 'Son, we got all the blood anybody needs.'"

Doc Bailey continued: "There was one who had third-degree burns all over, and one foot blown off. You know what he said? He said: 'Don't mind about me. Look after my buddy. He's over there.'"

As we were talking, another LCVP came alongside the rocking barge, and the coxswain said one of his cases had died since he left the shore. "Put him aboard the barge," said Dr. Bailey; "we'll send him ashore for burial when we can get a boat."

After a while an LCVP arrived which was going in the direction of the *Bayfield* after it called at two other transports and discharged its eight wounded, of whom only three were stretcher cases. This boat had a crew of three: Coxswain I. W. Rice, of Houston, S1/c Virgil Tormberg, of Tucson, and MM3/c James Brooks of San Diego. They had taken some Seabees ashore in the fourth wave on D Day—the Seabees went in very early at Iwo—and they had learned that 29 of the 36 had been hit, said Brooks. Since D Day the boat had been evacuating wounded whenever the weather permitted it to get ashore. Like so many Navy small boatmen, these three had not left their craft. They ate K rations and slept, if at all, on the bloody, corrugated open deck.

It was well past noon when I reached the *Bayfield*. The ship had long since become more than a psychiatric specialist. The number of wounded had increased so sharply that the sick bay held more than 200 (only about 20 were combat fatigue cases). One of the doctors commented: "I was on this ship in the Normandy invasion, and not more than five per cent of our cases required major surgery; here, I swear I believe it will run 90 per cent. I never saw such nasty wounds." Seven men had died, including one who was dead upon arrival. Supplies had to come first, so the men received a sea burial over the side.

Since the *Bayfield* was a Coast Guard ship and the Coast Guard had no medical service of its own, most doctors aboard were United States Public Health Service men. I walked through the sick bay, and the Coast Guardsmen's quarters which had been cheerfully turned over to accommodate the accumulation of wounded, with one of these USPH men, Doctor Richard K. Winston of Athens, Georgia. The wounded were indeed pitiable sights. A first sergeant had an eye shot out, and I was told that his brother was dying in the next room. Many men had lost limbs. The tables in the crew's messing compartment had been turned into operating tables.

Most of the men were quiet, but one big Coast Guardsman stopped Winston and said, almost hysterically, "Doc, don't fool me; tell me how I'm getting along." Winston told him he was all right. After we had passed him, Winston said: "There's a real sissy for you. He's got a little bullet through his hip and he thinks he's going to die."

At 1730 the gong began its hammering sound, and the warning over the loudspeaker immediately followed, "Man your battle stations!" I put on my helmet and went topside.

Before the smokepots could cast their murky pall over the ship I saw the destroyers' anti-aircraft open up. Then a Jap plane caught fire and fell into the sea a mile or two aft. "Splashed one Betty," said the radioman. Other planes were reported at ten, 20, 30 and 45 miles, but none others got into the transport area up to 1910, when I went below again. But not all the Japs were shot down, I soon learned. The *Saratoga*, about 50 miles from Iwo, had been hit by two suicide planes, according to the first report. Four planes, said the second. (Months later the announcement gave the correct figure, seven suiciders.) A later report said 200 had been killed on the venerable *Sara*. (The correct figure: 123 killed, 192 wounded.) The escort carrier *Bismarck Sea* was sunk tonight by a suicide plane, with 312 killed, 93 wounded.

Later in the evening I saw General Cates. According to his latest figures, the Fourth Division had as casualties 70 officers, 1950 men. The 21st Marines of the Third Division had landed, and had been placed in corps reserve. (So, I thought, the Third Division, which had feared three weeks earlier it would not be called upon, was going to get into the Iwo fight, after all.) Casualties in the Fourth Division were somewhat smaller today. (Fifth Division casualties in the first three days, I learned later, were consecutively 904, 582, and 571.) The line had been established north of Motoyama Airfield Number One, but no progress had yet been made in the center assualt on Number Two.

Among other information I picked up on the ship was the following: Of the Fourth's regiments, the 23d had by now surpassed the others in total casualties—1,160. The 25th had lost 980, and the 24th, the reserve regiment, only 186. Dr. Kenneth J. Murray, the popular battalion surgeon of 3/25, had lost both legs when he was hit by a mortar shell; he died later of his wounds. One of the Seabees' doctors was reported killed. My friend Lieutenant Pete Zurlinden, who had been commissioned a Fifth Division public relations officer after serving as a combat correspondent at Tarawa, had been badly wounded in the leg. (Said AP correspondent Jim Lindsley: "There I was in the casualty boat with Pete, whose leg looked like it was going to fall off. He looked up and said, 'You look shaky, Jim. Have some medicinal brandy.'")

February 22

During the night the Japs blew up a Blue Beach ammunition dump consisting of nearly all the Fourth Division's 81-mm. mortar shells, plus some gasoline and flamethrower fuel. The report on tanks was also discouraging: The Fourth Division had 28 inoperative out of its 56; the Fifth Division tank situation was said to be equally bad.

The Fourth Division borrowed mortar ammunition from the Third; the ordnancemen set to work on the tanks. The battle went on.

At this point we held about one-fourth of Iwo Jima. Our total casualties were estimated at about 4,200. Despite our losses in men and material I wrote: "It is possible to say after three days that the Japs will lose Iwo Jima and we will have airfields within 750 miles of Tokyo. One reason for this is sheer power, including naval and air supremacy which mounted for the attack some 800 ships and made available a total of perhaps 1,200 planes. But there comes a time when power alone has reached its limits . . . that is when men on foot must pay for yardage with their lives . . ."

But I was overoptimistic. I was trying to figure Iwo on the basis of previous battles; I did not then know the real underground strength of Iwo, nor the capabilities of its defenders (who turned out to be more numerous than we knew in advance). I wrote: "It seems certain that we will take Iwo Jima at a smaller cost than Saipan's 15,000, though Iwo's defenses are much stronger . . . Probably no large number of the Jap defenders have yet been killed, but henceforth Jap casualties will rise sharply while ours decline."

What made Iwo different from previous battles was the failure of the Japs to crack. Our casualties did not decline. Even late in the battle they stayed high. The Japs did not waste themselves on a *banzai* attack. They stayed in their holes, and they fought better than they had ever fought before. That is why our losses per division per day were higher than in any other except the three-day Tarawa battle. That is why battalions like Major Amadeo Rea's 2/26 (which was not sent into the line until D plus 3 incurred 99 per cent casualties—see p. 213). Knowing Jap tenacity as we did, we were still surprised by their ability to hold out on Iwo. We put about 40,000 tons of high explosives on the eight square miles of Iwo Jima—and the Japs, bomb-happy or not, kept shooting at us.

In the afternoon I rode in a small boat, through the fog, to Admiral Turner's flagship. In the operations room I saw Secretary Forrestal. He was studying an aerial photograph of Iwo, which was pockmarked from stem to stern, and he was shaking his head. "The planes just can't do it on an island like this," he said.

Forrestal was eager to get on the beach and see what it was like. Lieut. General Holland Smith said No, it was too risky. A couple of days later Forrestal got ashore anyway.

February 23

Today the weather was again choppy and stormy. The smaller LCVP's failed to make the beach at all, and we were forced to depend on LSM's and LCT's. General Cates was anxious to get ashore with his headquarters, and, finally, an LSM (203 feet long) was ordered alongside the *Bayfield*.

As we approached the beach about 11 o'clock somebody yelled, "Look, they've got the flag up on Mount Suribachi!"[2] It was a dramatic moment. It seemed that we could do any-

[2] This was not the flag whose raising was photographed and widely reprinted. That one was substituted for the original (and photographed) later in the day.

thing if we could capture that vertical monstrosity at the south end of Iwo. Tears welled in the eyes of several Marines as they watched the little flag fluttering in the breeze.

After we landed I walked south on the beach to a sandbagged dug-out where Maj. General Keller E. Rockey, the hefty commander of the Fifth Division, had set up his command post. He and his assistant division commander. Brig. General Leo D. Hermle, were studying a map laid on a wooden box. A young officer walked in; it was Lieut. Colonel Robert H. Williams, executive officer of the 28th Marines. The generals congratulated Williams on his regiment's capture of Suribachi.

Williams said: "There wasn't a great deal of opposition after we got past the guns at the base of the mountain. We figured we've killed about 800 Japs down there, but we'd have a hard time finding 100. We must have blown up 50 caves." The 28th, he said, had had about 115 killed, about 500 wounded, but casualties among key noncommissioned officers and platoon leaders had been high. Rockey's division casualties were put at 150 officers and 2,000 enlisted men (Cates' Fourth now reported 130 officers and 2778 enlisted men as casualties).

Another visitor to the Fifth CP was the corps commander, Maj. General Harry Schmidt. I asked him how long he figured to take Iwo. His reply: "Five more days after today. I said last week it would take ten days, and I haven't changed my mind."

In spite of continuous efforts to clean the Japs from under the wrecked planes on the field above us, a sniper's bullet still whistled overhead once in a while. Somehow, the Japs managed to sneak back into the wreckage during the night. Later, several Japs were flushed out of the wreckage and out of nearby caves; they wore Marine uniforms which they apparently had removed from our dead.

The big problem in advancing northward on Iwo was

still the center of the line at Airfield Number Two, an area which had been assigned to the fresh troops of the 21st Marines. Said General Rockey: "About all we are doing now is taking casualties. We've got to hit that center with everything we've got, and blast our way through there. We've got to have that high ground beyond Airfield Number Two."

With several other correspondents I started in the afternoon to walk south through the Fifth Division area toward Mount Suribachi. On the way we stopped at one of the blockhouses the Japs had built (and carefully concealed) in the sand of the sloping beach. This pillbox had been knocked out by Fifth Division men on D Day. A nearby officer looked at it in awe: "You wouldn't think it possible to knock the Nips out of this thing."

And no wonder. This blockhouse was more cunningly contrived than any other even on Tarawa. The outer walls were 40 inches of steel-reinforced concrete. The vent opened, not directly toward the sea, but slantwise toward the upper beaches. Thus the 120-mm. gun inside the blockhouse opening could fire on the beaches and on some of our ships, but could not be hit except from a sharp angle. Our naval gunfire simply could not reach inside. There was no indication that the blockhouse had been hit by anything except a passing flamethrower.

Inside the partially sunken blockhouse, which was perhaps ten by twenty feet and five feet high, there were three rooms separated by 12-inch walls of concrete. Openings between the rooms were narrow; a demolition charge tossed into the vent would have no effect on occupants of rooms to the rear. The crowning touch to the blockhouse was a pillbox which sat atop it and contained a heavy machine gun. Next to this piggy-back pillbox was an excellent artillery range-finder. The whole affair was covered by eight to ten feet of sand so carefully smoothed over as to make it look like just another sand dune. There was a trap-door exit in

193

the rear. Nearby lay the bodies of eight Marines whose assignment apparently had been the knocking out of this redoubtable structure.

Near the foot of Suribachi we found the 28th's tall gaunt regimental commander, Colonel Harry ("The Horse") Liversedge, a one-time Raider Battalion c.o. He was talking to Lieut. Colonel Chandler Johnson of Highland Park, Illinois, who had seven days to live. Colonel Johnson's Second Battalion had scaled Suribachi and planted the flags there. Said Liversedge: "Prisoners are few and far between, but we give the Japs a chance in every case. We send an interpreter to the mouth. He yells in, telling them they'll be well treated if they surrender. They hardly ever do." Thus far the 28th had captured two prisoners, neither of whom could walk. The 28th was finishing off the Japs in Suribachi's caves; most with demolition charges which closed the caves, some with bulldozers which sealed the holes dug on the lower slopes.

Along the lower fringe of the volcano the Japs had placed rock-crushing machines for use in airfield construction. These had been thoroughly smashed by naval gunfire. Near the machines were nine dead Japs, including one with a bullet squarely through his forehead. "That's what you call good shooting," said an admiring Marine.

Fifty yards to the right, its reinforced-concrete roof demolished, was a long-barrelled 6-inch coast-defense gun whose turret indicated it might have been removed from a cruiser. Try as they did, the Japs could not hide this gun. Naval gunfire had blown its intricate mechanism to pieces, and had chipped the barrel itself in many places.

It was late in the afternoon, and the slopes of Mount Suribachi looked too steep for some war correspondents in their thirties to climb. We trudged through the volcanic sand back to Fifth Division CP. As darkness neared and the chill of the Iwo evening caused us to shiver despite coats, sweaters, and wool trousers, someone remarked: "I guess the warm weather in this war is over. Pretty soon the troops will be longing for the dear old steaming jungles and the sun-baked atolls." Another remarked, "Still the people back home talk about it as the 'South Pacific war.'"

Four of us spent the night in a hole near Lieut. Colonel George Roll's D-2 section. As usual, Jap planes raided Iwo soon after dark. They were met by the rain of tracer bullets and shells from the ships' anti-aircraft guns which seemed to throw a solid red blanket over the island. Unfortunately, no Jap planes were hit, but their bombs fell harmlessly near Suribachi. This performance was repeated twice during the night, with similar results as far as we could see.

But the Japs raised hell all night with mortars and rockets which they fired up and down our beaches by the hundreds. For one to two-hour periods the Japs on the northern end of the island would fill the air with their heavy missiles. After a long pause, they would start again. Actually, on this fifth night, the Jap mortar fire seemed almost as heavy as it had been on the first two nights.

February 24

At 0800 our heavy naval barrage signaled the beginning of a new offensive against the hard-to-crack center of the Jap line. The battleships joined the destroyers and cruisers, the 105's and 155's from the southern end of the island, the infantry mortars. Then the planes came in by the dozens, dropping bombs, strafing Jap positions, and firing their sizzling rockets. After an hour of this unrelenting fire the northern half of Iwo could be seen only through a haze of black smoke, billowing topsoil, and flying debris. On Iwo we really had the power.

General Cates, who managed to remain dapper and clean-shaven throughout the entire battle, removed his cigarette holder and said: "They are dug in up there, but I think we'll crack their center today. See the tanks moving up toward the second airfield." I asked him what would happen if we didn't crack their center. "Well," he said, "we'll keep on hitting them. They can't take it forever. We've got to keep pressing 'em until they break. Don't let up." Major Arthur B. ("Tim") Hanson, the popular, bantamweight R-2 of the 24th Marines, came by and said: "You know how big those damn mortars are? We've found some as big as 220-millimeter."

That was slightly larger than the eight-inch shells of our heavy cruisers, and far larger than any land-based missiles we had in the Pacific. It seemed odd that the miniature-loving Japs would suddenly come up with so prodigious a weapon. Their knee-mortar (about two inches)—also an effective weapon, in its way,—seemed more in character. A few days later we discovered they had other mortars ("spigot mortars") five feet long, twelve inches in diameter. We could see the huge explosives flying through the air—somebody called them "floating ash cans"—and we knew what a terrific explosion they made. But we were still surprised when we learned how large they actually were.

The Japs also had a nine-foot-long rocket, with a nine-inch diameter. From the ships we could see these leave the ground as they were fired. A constellation of sparks was left in their wake. These missiles apparently were hard to control. They usually chug-chugged through the air, far over Mount Suribachi, somewhere out to sea. Their nickname: "Bubbly-Wubblies."

If we needed any reminder that the Japs intended to keep on shooting, we got it as we watched the tanks advance. A Grumman Hellcat was caught by a burst of anti-aircraft fire about a mile ahead of us. The plane flared briefly and dived toward the ocean. The pilot seemed to jump or fall out just before his plane hit the water, but he never had a chance.

In mid-morning I started walking toward the front line

with Correspondent John Lardner. Three hundred yards beyond Airfield No. 1 we climbed the scrub covered cliffs which the 25th Regiment had taken at great cost. About 100 yards back of the front we stopped to talk to Captain William Ketcham of I Company, 24th Marines. As part of Lieut. Colonel Alexander Archer Vandegrift Jr.'s Third Battalion, I Company was waiting to attack on the right of center whenever the 21st Marines had made enough progress down the middle. Captain Ketcham had already been nicked in the arm and leg by snipers, and he wore two bloody bandages, but he was contemptuous of Jap marksmanship. "Shot at me twelve times and barely broke the skin with two bullets," he said.

One of Ketcham's sergeants spoke of the Jap infiltration attempt last night. He guffawed: "Some of the sons of bitches tried to get through K Company's barbed wire, but the Marines sprinkled grenades and bangalore torpedoes around so they would go off like booby traps. Blew hell out of the Japs."

The front line was atop a hill on the southern edge of a natural amphitheater. There we found Vandegrift (the Marine Corps commandant's son). He walked along the line of entrenched riflemen who awaited the word to attack, making certain that everybody was ready. "The front has been up here three days now," he said, "but we didn't relieve Chambers's battalion until yesterday. We spent four days in reserve down there on the beaches, and it made a lot of my men jittery. They wanted to get up to the front and start fighting instead of lying back there and getting pounded with mortars." Even so, Vandegrift's battalion had suffered about 100 casualties, including five officers, in its one day in the line—mostly from the fire of snipers, whose bullets still sang through the stunted trees once in a while. "Better keep down," said Vandegrift, "sniper fire gets pretty hot around here when you least expect it."

A leather-legginged Jap lieutenant lay dead in a foxhole on the front line. "He managed to sneak through the barbed wire last night," said Colonel Vandegrift. "He tossed a grenade into that next hole and killed two men, then he jumped into this hole and hacked another man with his sword. Then somebody shot him. We gave the sword to the man who got cut up." The Jap officer wore a blood-soaked bandage around his right wrist, indicating that he had been previously wounded. Whatever we felt about the Japs, we never doubted their courage—not even when it made no sense. Or, perhaps it did make sense for a lone officer to crawl through the front lines and kill two American enlisted men and wound another. It would have, if the Jap had had any chance of returning with an intelligence report, but this one had no chance of getting back, and he must have known it.

This amphitheater we faced was a notable landmark on Iwo. It was just in front of Hill 382, which we captured six times and lost back to the Japs five times. Into the side of the amphitheater were built ugly concrete pillboxes, facing in three directions according to the curve of the hill.

But the amphitheater seemed harmless enough on the afternoon of D plus five. The artillery opened up on the hill, splattering it with hundreds of rounds. This went on for about 20 minutes, accompanied by incessant mortar fire. Then Vandegrift's riflemen started moving out, running ten to twenty yards at a time before dropping into shellholes. All the while machine gunners from their frontline positions poured thousands of bullets into the caves. Flamethrower men followed, firing each hillside cave as they scaled the heights.

Not a man was hit in this advance across the bottom and up the sides of the amphitheater. It simply looked as through we had captured another hill without much trouble. (On our left we could see that G Company of Lieut. Colonel Richard Rothwell's battalion had some casualties in its advance).

Before we left young Vandegrift's observation post we inspected the deserted Jap mortar positions on a line with our front. These were holes about six feet deep, inlaid with cement. The cement walls had painted on them the degrees of the circle, for aiming. Each hole was half covered with a board or stone slab; soil had been heaped on the slabs, and flowers or bushes planted. It was no wonder the airplanes could not discover the mortar's positions! From the air such positions would only look like the rest of the scrubby land. But there was an opening large enough for the Japs to fire their 81-mm. mortars. There were boxes of shells in each hole, but the mortar tubes had been removed when the Japs withdrew.

We did not know it until later, but the Japs struck back savagely not more than ten minutes after Lardner and I left Vandegrift's OP. They started throwing mortar shells in the area in great profusion. Archie Vandegrift himself was wounded by a piece of mortar fragment through both legs, another man was wounded, and the four others in the shellhole we had shared with him had been killed by the direct hit. The fight for Hill 382, which seemed to be no fight at all when we watched, had only begun.

On the way back to the beach we counted 16 dead Marines who had not yet been removed for burial, and nine dead Japs whose bodies had not been retrieved by the enemy as we advanced. As we walked down the runway of Airfield No. 1, captured four days previously, we heard the old familiar whine of Jap sniper bullets, one whine per 15 steps. There was nothing to do except keep walking and hope we didn't get hit. I was about ten feet in front of Lardner when I heard him get hit—the thud sounded as though an ox had been hit on the head with an axe. Lardner writhed on the ground for a minute, then he managed to crawl a few feet into a shellhole. "That felt like no bullet; that felt like a rock," he said. The welt on his leg proved that it must have been a rock. The best he could figure was that a sniper's bullet had struck a rock, which ricocheted into Lardner. "That's what I get for writing that the Japs are suckers for a fast curve," said Sports Writer Lardner.

CHAPTER TWELVE

THE RAVINES OF IWO

THE MORE WE LEARNED ABOUT THE JAP'S UNDERGROUND DEfense system, the more we marveled at its intricate nature. They had simply put everything in caves and tunnels except the muzzles of their biggest guns; even their howitzers and machine guns (and, of course, their holed-up mortars) were susceptible to nothing except direct hits by the heaviest explosives. It was no wonder that 74 days of pre-invasion bombing had done little more than knock out the airplanes on the field. We had not expected that the bombs would kill many Japs—bombing never killed many people if the people stayed in holes—but we had hoped that guns and supplies had been destroyed. The Japs had stored them out of our reach.

Every hillside, every ravine, had its camouflaged cave or pillbox; some were so carefully hidden that men stepped on them before they were aware of them. One cave in the Fourth Division area, northeast of the first airfield, had a tunnel 800 yards long with 14 entrances. Each entrance was covered by a series of pillboxes containing machine guns. If the inmates of one pillbox were killed by bombs or artillery the Japs could easily send out replacements from another entrance. Japs would pop out of holes in the ground far behind our own lines.

Our chances of enfilading hillside cave entrances were not good. Our chances of knocking out all the hidden pillboxes before we approached were worse. The wrinkles and the volcanic rocks north of Airfield Number 1 could be overcome only the hard way, on foot. It seemed to the men who had to do the overcoming that there was no end to the process. A ravine would be taken; just over its forward edge there was always another ravine, usually steeper than the last, and containing even more caves.

What the Japs succeeded in doing was this: They built underground so well that they all but nullified our superior firepower. We could bomb and shell until our guns sizzled and our pilots dropped—one day we shot 25,000 rounds of 105 and 155 artillery shells; altogether we probably put 40,000 tons of high explosives on the island—but when our barrage lifted and our infantry advanced the Japs were back in position, firing their machine guns and mortars.

At times it was agonizing to realize that we progressed so slowly and at so high a price, in spite of our superior strength. For all our technical skill, we had on Iwo no method and no weapon to counteract the enemy's underground defense. The Japs made us fight on their own terms. We could beat them on their own terms; we could kill four for one; we could make them take as many casualties as we took (and their casualties were nearly all dead). But the men fighting on Iwo Jima frankly thought that price too high. The Japs didn't seem to mind dying; we preferred to live.

Whatever medals the Japs had to pass out should have been given to the Iwo commander, Lieut. General Tadamichi Kuribayashi. (His body was never identified.) He built the most hellish defenses in the Pacific, if not in the history of warfare. He killed a lot of Marines. "The Japs have a good sense of the ground," said Admiral Turner in a classic understatement.

The hopes we had of a quick victory melted away slowly. One day it seemed that only a few more days would be required; next day it seemed that surely a break would come somewhere; a week later our progress was still being measured 50 yards, 100 yards, 300 yards, at a time. Kuribayashi never gave the order for the battle-ending *banzai* attack. His men stayed in their tunnels and their molehills to the deathly end, and we had to go in and dig them out or burn out or seal them in. There was nothing else for us to do. It was brave men against Jap cunning and Jap steel.

Motoyama Airfield Number 2 was as tough as any other objective. The 23d Marines, badly depleted after taking the northern end of Number 1, turned to assault the ridges and soft-rock embankments between the first and second fields. This distance between the two fields was only about a mile, but it seemed a thousand miles to the men who had to face the heavily armed, cleverly emplaced Japs. By the time its men had covered most of this long mile the 23d had lost very heavily; it had supplanted the 25th as the hardest-hit Fourth Division regiment. The 23d was relieved, to rest and reorganize; 700 replacements of the 2,500 the Fourth Division had brought along were sent to the 23d at this point. Its relief was Colonel Hartnell Withers's 21st Regiment of the Third Division.

The Fourth Division on the right and the Fifth Division on the left had drawn up slightly beyond the southern end of Airfield Number 2. They could advance no farther until the center was cracked. Colonel Withers's assignment was to take the airfield in the middle; as tough an assignment as any regimental commander ever faced.

The defenses in the center were most formidable. All around the southern end of the airfield the Japs had built concrete blockhouses into the sand, and had surrounded them with smaller pillboxes. Behind every mound of earth there were Japs with rifles and hand grenades. Mortars from the entire northern end of Iwo poured shells into the American lines.

The 21st knocked out some fortifications, but its first day's advance could be measured in yards. "It was pitiful," Lieut. Colonel Eustace R. Smoak, the regimental executive officer, said later; "we would go forward, then we would be mowed down." Next day was no different. The First Battalion, attacking on the right, lost two commanding officers in two days (Lieut. Colonel Marlowe C. Williams, Major Clay M. Murray). The Second lost three rifle-company commanders. On the third day the Third Battalion relieved the First and managed to cross the airfield at its narrowest part, the center of the X-shaped runways. The battalion assaulted a ridge on the other side, was knocked off, assaulted again, and stayed. For its advance of about 600 yards the 21st had paid about 600 casualties. But the center of the line had been brought even with the flanks. The battle for the east and west ends of the airfield went on.

On D plus 5, Colonel Howard N. ("Red") Kenyon's 9th Marines went into the line to relieve the 21st, and the Third Division commander, Maj. General Graves B. Erskine, assumed the center command (till then the 21st had been attached to the Fourth Division). General Erskine had taken over the Third Division in the fall of 1944, after the Guam battle. At 46 he was the youngest general in the Marine Corps. For three years he had been "Howlin' Mad" Smith's chief of staff. A soft-voiced Louisianian with cold, blue-green eyes, Erskine was known in the Corps as a hard man and a strict disciplinarian; recently he had court-martialed artillery men for firing short in training, killing some of their own infantry. But he was known as a man with a stern sense of fairness. During Iwo, many a Marine mentioned that he had come to approve of the "Old Man's" strict measures; they paid off in battle.

In the Third's attack through the center there were numerous examples of heroism against very great odds. None was greater than that of Captain Francis L. Fagan, a brilliant young officer from the University of Wisconsin (where he made Phi Beta Kappa). On D plus 5, Captain Fagan, commanding G Company of the 9th Marines, led a combined tank-infantry attack against a strong enemy hill on the west side of the airfield. He directed the tanks against many pillboxes; he went in front of the infantrymen to show them where to attack. A machine-gun bullet wounded him, but he kept going. Next morning he led a hand-to-hand charge against the position. His tanks and infantry knocked out more than 30 pillboxes before Fagan was mortally wounded early in the afternoon of the second day. "We've got to lose a company to take that place," one of Fagan's superior officers had said. The company was not lost—not more than 50 per cent. It might have been, but for Francis Fagan.

Private Wilson D. Watson of Earl, Arkansas, a Browning Automatic rifleman, was in a squad of G Company, 9th Marines, which was held up by several Jap pillboxes on D plus 6. He ran to one pillbox, killed the men in it. He rushed to a second, blew it up with a hand grenade, shot the Japs who fled from it. With his squad he dug in for the night. Next morning he ran up a hill in the face of intense fire, firing from the hip as he advanced. At the top he had to stand erect to fire at the Japs on the downward slope. That's what he did. He held that hill alone for 15 minutes, until the rest of his platoon joined him. Official reports credited him with killing over 60 Japs.

There were many other heroes in this Third Division march against the center. Lieutenant Raoul J. Archambault assumed command of K Company after Captain Rodney Heinze was hit. Reorganizing his scattered, depleted company, Archambault led a bayonet attack against a Jap-held mound. Twice the fire became too hot and he had to retire with his men; the third time K Company stayed. The position was held through the night. Captain William E. Evers of I Company, 9th Marines, and Captain William K. Crawford of K Company, both of whom were killed, led their men in heroic charges in the February 25 attack on the upper end of Airfield Number 2. Pfc. Ralph H. Crouch, of

Arlington, Virginia, a company runner for B Company, 9th Marines, got a message for one of the platoons. He was shot through the belly, but he crawled the rest of the way and delivered the message before he died.

Pfc. Robert Fransko was a flamethrower operator. On D plus 7 a company of the 9th's First Battalion was held up by an emplacement on a ridge which had contained a dual-purpose gun, but now contained mortars and machine guns. Fransko ran across a field of fire 40 yards wide, let go several bursts into the main entrance of the cave, frying the Japs there. He walked through the main tunnel, spraying his flame into other openings. He picked up a bazooka, fired nearly a dozen rounds at an approaching Jap tank, one of the few mobile tanks the Japs had (most of their tanks were buried deep into the earth, and used as armored pillboxes). After he knocked out the tank, Fransko was wounded in the right arm. Ordered to the rear, he carried an empty flamethrower for refilling; it might be needed.

Lieutenant Dominic Grossi was a platoon leader in Archambault's company, the first to cross the center of the airfield on D plus 4. Grossi lost all but 12 of his men in the charge across the strip, but the rest kept going up the high ground which had to be seized. Knocked off the high ground, Grossi again led a bayonet and grenade charge up the slope. This time they stayed. Grossi lived until March 8.

Major Holly H. Evans of Texas City, Texas, was commander of the Third Division's tank battalion. He was confronted with a problem which apparently had no solution; his tanks could not advance along the rugged ground on either side of the air-strip; yet he knew they might be knocked out if they tried to use the runways. He tried the runways, anyway. Very quickly the Japs' mines and 57-mm. and 47-mm. high-velocity guns knocked out nine of Evans's tanks. But the commander walked through intense fire to the forwardmost of his remaining tanks, reorganized them, and continued the attack which helped the 9th Marines to take the high ground on the west side. The tankers' spirit was best illustrated by an incident of March 1; Lieutenant Charles Hubbard Kirkham, of Sweetwater, Alabama, and his gunner, Corporal Robert J. Schwimmer of Saginaw, Michigan, were in a tank whose tread was blown off by a mine. Two men were wounded; the third was ordered to evacuate them. Kirkham and Schwimmer stayed in their tank, though they were forward of the front lines. With their 75 and machine gun they destroyed three planted Jap tank pillboxes, three ammunition trucks, and several machine-gun nests. Finally, the two Marines fired all their ammunition, and ran for cover. Five minutes later the Japs who had been trying to blow up the tank succeeded.

Such deeds as these, taken by themselves, might indicate—as hero stories often indicated—that we swept the Japs before us in a series of mighty blows. Such was not the case, of course. The point is; *without* such examples of leadership and of inspiring individual heroism we probably would not have advanced at all. The Third Division's greatest feat was the taking of Airfield Number 2 and the central ground north of that field. Thereafter, it moved faster than either division on its flank, and a platoon of A Company, 21st Marines, was the first to break through to the sea, on D plus 17.

But even with the Third Division the battle seemed to grind very slowly. Whenever I saw the division, which was not often, the process of advancing seemed tortuous. On the late afternoon of D plus 6 I was at General Erskine's CP. It was on the reverse slope of a revetment, just beyond Airfield Number 1 and it was still under mortar fire; a Marine was wounded 50 yards away as I arrived, and he cried softly as he walked by, supported by two comrades.

General Erskine was not satisfied with his division's progress, though all but the northern end of Airfield Number 2 had been captured by that time. The General was a hard man to satisfy. He wanted to try a night attack. So he called in Colonel Kenyon, the 9th Marines' red-faced perspiring commanding officer.

The General wanted to know if Kenyon's men were prepared to make a night attack. Colonel Kenyon wiped his forehead and said: "I think they might, but it's pretty late in the day to pull it on the men. They're mighty tired."

Erskine reflected for a moment, and said: "When I was in France in the last war I did patrols. Once, I remember, I went out with 38 men and four of us came back. My company c.o. then told us to go on another patrol; he told me to go throw a rock at that German machine gun, so they would shoot at me, and we could spot it. I did what he told me. The Jap fights to the last man, but I'm sure we're a better man than the Jap is."

A big, dark captain named Oscar Salgo was called in. Said the General: "You're the reconnaissance company commander. I want you to go through the Jap lines in a night attack and blow up and burn out some of these pillboxes that are holding us up. Are you prepared to do it?" Salgo said he would try it, but he would like to know just which pillboxes needed to be knocked out.

So, late in the afternoon Salgo took his platoon leaders and senior noncommissioned officers to investigate the pillboxes at the north end of Airfield Number 2. It turned out that there were many pillboxes holding up our advance there—not just a few, as the map indicated. The night attack had to be postponed.

But General Erskine never abandoned his idea that night attacks would work against the Japs. In the early morning darkness of D plus 16, without any preliminary bombardment, the 9th and 21st Marines began advancing. The Japs were taken completely by surprise. The line advanced several hundred yards before the enemy discovered what was happening. The only trouble was that the Japs thus bypassed started shooting up the Third Division from the rear.

Even after Airfield Number 2 was captured, there was almost continuous sniper fire on it, as there had been on Number 1, and as there always seemed to be, wherever we fought the last-ditch Japs. I discovered this on March 1, when I started walking up the Third Division's central area with Bill Marien, a broad-beamed, 250-pound Australian correspondent.

We passed the 21st Regiment CP, a captured concrete blockhouse about half way between the two airfields, and stopped to examine a roped-off area containing about 40 of the big Jap kettle mines which had caused our tanks so much trouble. There were "Safe Lane" signs along the paths which had been cleared of mines, and the jeep ambulances were rolling steadily to the rear with their wounded. On top of one jeep containing three litter cases a corpsman lay precariously, holding a plasma bottle in an effort to keep his patient alive. Other jeep ambulances, empty, were tearing along the narrow, sandy road in the other direction. On Iwo, it seemed, there was always an insatiable demand for ambulances and litters.

As Marien and I climbed the embankment leading to the lower end of the airfield, a sniper's bullet whizzed overhead. We walked a few feet farther, and the sniper shot again, closer this time. We ducked into a shell hole on the edge of the airfield, waited there ten minutes. When we stuck our heads up the sniper fired again, and we ducked again.

At this time a company of Marines walked along the airstrip, headed in the same direction we had been traveling until we were forced to take cover. This entire company walked past our shellhole, and the sniper fired not once. But when they had passed we rose again, and the sniper

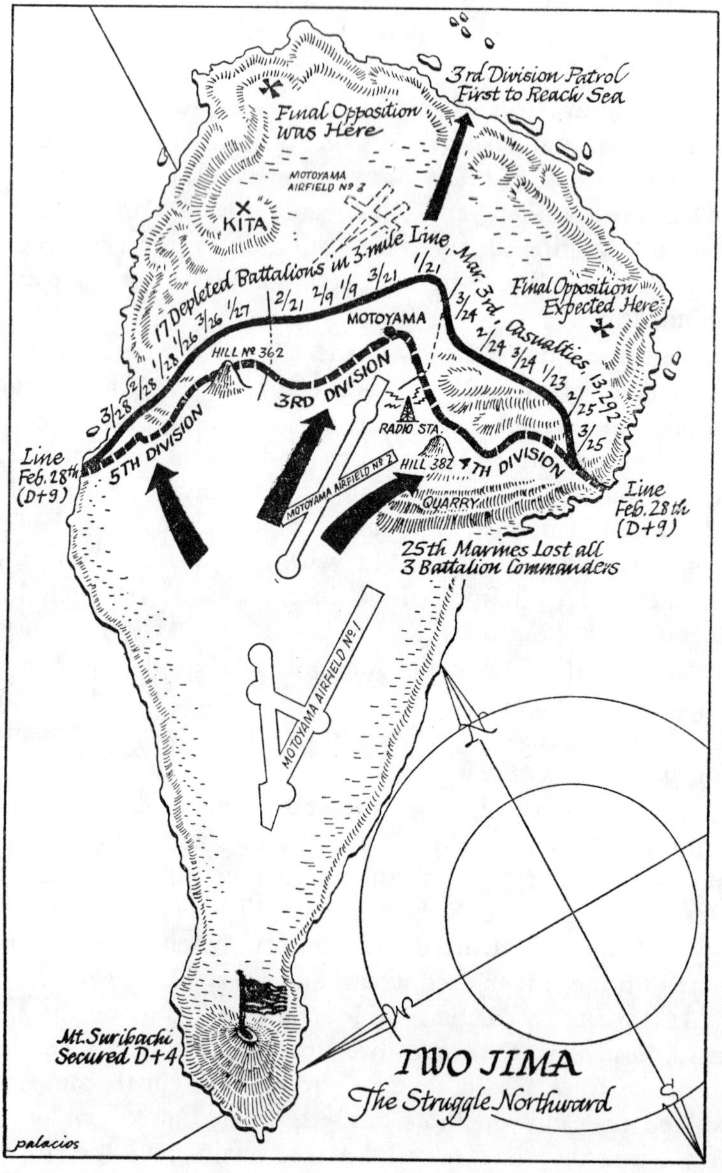
3rd Division Patrol
First to Reach Sea
Final Opposition
Was Here
MOTOYAMA
AIRFIELD No 3
KITA
17 Depleted Battalions in 3-mile Line, Mar. 3rd, Casualties, 13,292
3/28 2/28 1/28 1/26 3/26 1/27 2/21 2/9 1/9 3/21 1/21 3/24 2/24 3/24 1/23 2/25 3/25
Final Opposition
Expected Here
MOTOYAMA
HILL No 362
3RD DIVISION
5TH DIVISION
RADIO STA.
HILL 382
4TH DIVISION
Line
Feb. 28th
(D+9)
MOTOYAMA AIRFIELD No 2
QUARRY
Line
Feb. 28th
(D+9)
25th Marines Lost all
3 Battalion Commanders
MOTOYAMA AIRFIELD No 1
N
S
Mt. Suribachi
Secured D+4
IWO JIMA
The Struggle Northward
palacios

fired again. Since the firing seemed to come from the west, we slipped off the airfield and walked down the east embankment. Marien concluded sadly: "I guess I'm too fat. The Jap thinks I'm a Marine general."

We walked the length of the airfield past a dozen dead Japs and Marines, then crossed to the west side. Now we were at the rear CP of Lieut. Colonel Wendell H. DuPlantis of 3/21, who had just moved forward 700 yards, near what had been the village of Motoyama. It had been rugged going all morning. A mortar shell had just landed among a group of men, killing the battalion communications officer, Lieutenant Charles T. Jones, and several others, and wounding many more, including Major Minetree Folkes Jr., the battalion's headquarters company commandant.

The aid station was set in a small pocket enclosed by 15-foot-high hills. Doctor Marvin Courtney, a 27-year-old surgeon from Chicago, was bloody to the elbows. With the aid of Doctor Howell Carter, also 27, of Grinnell, Iowa, an A Medical Company surgeon, he had already performed seven operations that morning, including a tracheotomy and several amputations. (Major Folkes's right leg had been blown off). The aid station was empty of patients at the moment, but there would soon be more. Company I urgently needed six litter bearers, and none was available.

I spoke to the regimental chaplain who was in the aid station, Lieut. John P. Lee, a Northern Baptist of Glendale, California. He said mortar shells had just killed four men in Motoyama and wounded 30 others, many of them severely. "You can't tell when they will hit," he said "last night I was walking along there with a man, and a mortar shell hit 20 feet away. It pierced the leg of my companion, and blew the foot off another man. God has been good to many of us. I don't know how we have managed to come as far as we have, except I know the spirit of these men is wonderful. Last Friday [D plus 4] was the worst. They would get up on the airfield, then they would get knocked off. Then they would make it again."

As we walked back to 21st regimental headquarters along the west side of the airfield, Marien and I stopped near some engineers who were probing the road for mines. There was a Jap ammunition dump, 35 boxes of 25-mm. shells, each box containing 72 rounds. That amounted to 2,520 rounds. And it was two-thirds empty. It was the mortars that were causing most of the havoc among our troops, not the smaller artillery. And on March 1 we still had taken little more than half of Iwo. For instance, General Erskine told us that his casualties now amounted to 1,546.

Before the battle ended they would total over 4,000, and there would be only one company captain, Donald M. Beck, to last out the battle alive and unwounded. One of the lasting memories I had of Iwo was talking to the Third Division personnel officer, Major Robert Kriendler, in a blacked-out tent on the night of March 8. He said, sadly: "So many of these casualty reports indicate what green troops we are having to use. They get killed the day they go into battle as brand-new replacements. Seventeen years old—four months, six months, after they've enlisted—and they are dead. When I see a Marine whose number is over 900,000 I know he has died when he was very new, and probably very young."

Severe as the casualties were in the Third and the Fourth Divisions, they were considerably lighter than the Fifth's. The Fifth was in action only once in World War II, but the price it paid was horrible, 8,935 casualties.[1] Even this figure does not tell the whole story; 258 received a second wound, and nine were wounded in three separate actions. (Of these brave men who carried on in spite of a second or third wound, 55 died). By adding 1,275 officers and enlisted men who were evacuated sick (usually with severe gastric and

[1] 8,360 if "Died of Wounds" cases are subtracted from the list of "Wounded."

respiratory diseases) it was possible to get an idea of the manpower shortage which confronted General Rockey, especially when it was considered that 70 per cent of his battle casualties were in the front-line infantry regiments.

Iwo never seemed to end for the Fifth Division. D Day produced 849 casualties, and the next three days 557, 534, and 467 more. For the next few days losses dropped to an average of 250, but by D plus 11 and 12, when the reports came in from that bloody rock called Hill 362, the division casualties shot up again, to 394 and 494. As late as D plus 23, two days before Iwo was declared secure, the Fifth lost 327 men. And there were more than 500 casualties after the island was declared ours, from D plus 26 to D plus 35. The worst of the tail-end fighting was in the "badlands" to the north where steam poured out of fissures in the rocks of this inferno. There were companies with five or six men out of 200 who had landed, platoons with not one man left, battalions with a handful.

Hardest hit of the battalions in the Fifth Division was 2/26, which landed with 37 officers and 917 enlisted men. During the battle 40 officers (108 per cent) and 911 enlisted men (99 per cent) were killed or wounded. Replacements, of which there were 14 officers and 251 enlisted men, were, of course, included in that figure, and among the replacements 10 officers and 134 enlisted men were battle casualties.

The odd feature of the experience of Second Battalion, 26th Marines' casualties was this—it did not get into the line until D plus 3. It had landed at 1630 on D Day, was sent to the west side of the island to the rear of the front lines, to provide depth and beach security. For the five days between February 22 and February 27, the battalion attacked in the center of the division zone, taking heavy casualties from Japanese positions on the high ground on either side. On February 23 the battalion commander, Lieut. Colonel Joseph P. Sayers, was hit by shrapnel in the arm and side.

213

He was succeeded by Major Amadeo Rea, who was an inspiration to his outfit throughout the rest of the battle.

By March 2 the battalion had been reorganized, and was again committed. On March 3 the battalion was launched against the heights of Hill 362, just northwest of Airfield Number 2, and its position was held after an attack spearheaded for 600 yards by Company F. The battalion lost 152 men that day.

From March 6 to 9 the battalion was in reserve. When it was committed once more, on March 9, it stayed in the line eight days while advancing a few hundred yards a day up the rugged northernmost end of the island. On March 16 2/26 was pulled out of the line for the last time until it boarded the transports March 25. Several times during its advance up the west side of Iwo, 2/26 had seemed almost to reach the breaking point. It had had to borrow attached 37-mm. platoons, engineer platoons and many headquarters personnel, use them as riflemen. But the battalion stuck it out, and Colonel Chester B. Graham, the 26th Marines commander, commented later, "On getting a little rest and hot food, morale surged back into these men and a phenomenally high spirit of comradeship and pride in their organization became evident."

Although 2/26 suffered heavier casualties than any other battalion on Iwo, the Fifth Division's losses in all regiments were fantastically high; the infantry battalion which came off lightest lost 54 per cent. B Company of the 28th Marines, which broke through to the west side of the island on D Day under the leadership of the gallant Captain Dwayne E. Mears[2] of Bakersfield, California, furnished an example of

[2] Captain Mears hit the beach where the blockhouses were thickest, was seriously wounded, but continued leading his men until the fortifications were knocked out. He assaulted a Jap machine-gun emplacement with a pistol, was shot again, in the throat. Then he used hand signals until the Japs on southern Iwo had been isolated. He died of his wounds on D plus 1.

the severity of the losses; the company command changed eight times, the company's second platoon's leadership changed 11 times (five lieutenants, one gunnery sergeant, one sergeant, two corporals, one private first class, and Private Dale O. Cassell Jr. of Sacramento, who served three days until he was killed March 14).

CHAPTER THIRTEEN

DIVISION HOSPITAL

A NOTE ON THE WOUNDS AT IWO JIMA: BY THE END OF JULY, 16,163 wounded had been reported to Washington headquarters. Of these, 1,233—nearly eight percent—had died of wounds, as opposed to the World War II average of three to four percent. This is what was meant when it was said that the mortars the Japs used on Iwo were murderous.

Of 5,409 casualties (including 1,634 dead) which were analyzed in the Fourth Division, 1,377 (25 per cent) were caused by gunshot wounds, 4,132 (75 per cent) by artillery and mortar fragments. A high 20 per cent of the total were head wounds (due to the vertical nature of blast arising from soft volcanic soil), 35 per cent extremity wounds, 4.87 per cent abdominal, and 22 per cent multiple. There were eight cases of pubic and testes wounds. Those figures are necessarily incomplete; 140 died from causes unknown, and the injuries of 225 were unknown when these figures were compiled one month after the Iwo battle had ended. Not included are 695 cases of combat fatigue and 75 cases of psychoneuroses in the Fourth Division.

This hospital was not high on a hill, as a hospital should be. It was built low into the embankment beside the airfield, to afford maximum protection from Jap mortar and artillery fire. It was not white and shiny and antiseptic looking. Instead, it was made of dark-green tenting. Inside, the air was stuffy with stale cigarette smoke which mingled with the smells of dirt and blood and the sweat of men who had been in the grimmest of battles for twelve to sixteen days without much chance of washing their faces, let alone changing their clothes.

This was the Fourth Marine Division hospital, which had been set up four days after we landed, despite mortar fire which still fell in the area. It consisted of two long tents and several smaller tents set in the bulldozed embankment ditches, plus two operating rooms about ten by twenty feet. These operating rooms were really cisterns the Japs had built to catch the rainwater as it ran off the airfield. They had only tenting for a roof, but their sides were solid concrete which would protect the patients and doctors from all but a bulls-eye hit topside. The rawboned, red-faced division surgeon, Commander Richard Silvis, was proud of his operating rooms; they even had concrete floors.

Shortly after eight o'clock on the evening of D plus 15 (March 6), Dr. Silvis and I crawled through the blacked-out entrance and walked down the gangway into the cistern-operating room on the side of the roadway, next to one of the runway strips. On the first table, beneath the big non-shadow electric lamps, lay a Fourth Division captain, Walter A. Coakley Jr. of Brooklyn, who had been a Jap machine gunner's target about three hours earlier. Dr. John W. Harper held up the captain's slashed, liver-colored spleen, which had just been removed, and said: "Here's another spleen, Dr. Silvis; these bullets tear 'em up. We also took out a piece of kidney and he has a bullet through his diaphragm and lung. He asked for a priest right away."

Silvis pulled back the eyelid of the gravely wounded man and said: "He looks pretty good, though." Then he turned to me and said: "This is a very serious case, but he has a chance. A healthy young man takes a lot of killing—a 45-year-old man couldn't live through an operation like this one."[1]

At the next table a private first class was about to have a piece of shell fragment removed from his kidney. Like the

[1] Despite his brave fight for life, Captain Coakley died eleven days later.

captain, he was receiving, through a tube in each arm, whole blood which had been packed in ice in pint bottles at San Francisco, and flown some six thousand miles in the hope of saving life.

"This whole blood is wonderful stuff," said Dr. Silvis, "much better than plasma when they have severe hemorrhages." One of the bottles of blood had the name of its donor written on the label. I meant to write down the name of the donor, so I could tell him one day that he helped save a life, because the private first class was still alive and getting well when I heard of him five weeks later. But I never did.

Two surgical teams, three doctors to a team, worked in each cistern. Before going to the next cistern we crossed in the darkness to one of the long tents, the receiving ward where patients were brought first. Medical corpsmen were unloading stretchers from jeep ambulances in which the wounded men had been driven from their battalion aid stations at the front lines. They negotiated the double-blackout flaps of the tent, and after they got inside they set the stretcher-borne patients on the ground.

A medical corpsman recorded each case at the tent entrance. At the head of the row of seven stretcher cases lay a tow-headed youth with a bloodily bandaged left arm in a splint. He asked for a cigarette, then told the corpsman his name (R. N. Cardinal), his serial number, his rank (private first class), his unit (F Company, 23d Marines). Under "S or A" (stretcher or ambulatory) the corpsman wrote "S," and under "Diagnosis" he wrote "Wounds, multiple fragments, left arm and leg."

At one end of the long tent there were eight operating tables, and beyond that were an x-ray machine and a big refrigerator for serums. The wounded were placed upon these tables, or upon other tables nearer the entrance, and examined immediately. If necessary, whole blood or plasma was administered, perhaps for the third or fourth time, since plasma is also given at the battalion aid stations and even in the jeep ambulances during the ride back to the hospital. The simpler operations were performed right there in the receiving tent. The complex cases were for the cistern-operating rooms.

The Marine on the first table, Field Music First Class Carlton J. Hopkins, had no serious wound, but he had been shot through the back and through the left arm. Doctor Howard Johnson of Uniontown, Pennsylvania, was rubbing sulfanilamide powder into the hole, about the size of a quarter, in his arm. The next man had been shot by a sniper, whose bullet sliced through the belly's frontal layer, hit a pair of wire pliers fastened to the man's belt, and went out the other side. This man was describing his wounds as he was being x-rayed.

At another table, Captain John W. Key, commander of the Division Reconnaissance Company, lay with a bullet through his right forearm. The splint on his arm had been fashioned from the limb of one of the scrub trees which dotted northern Iwo Jima. Captain Key said: "I got out light. Most of the boys in my outfit got it in the head."

"Where are you from?" asked the doctor. "California," said Key. "Know anybody in Florida named Key?" "No," said Key.

Key glanced at his arm and said, "Well, anyway, I won't have to write any letters now." The captain was not wounded seriously, but he typified something I have always noticed about wounded men—they nearly always find something to be cheerful about. Blinded men are thankful they didn't lose their arms; armless men are grateful to have their eyes.

One man from E Company, 23d Marines, who had a Polish name, lay on a stretcher near the doorway, his eyes and face covered. One of the doctors lifted the blanket from his face and said to Silvis: "I think we had better send him to corps. They are better fixed to diagnose eye cases, and it looks as though this fellow will lose one, maybe both of his eyes."

A very pale and dirty Marine, Pfc. Basil Carbis of Los Angeles, had been placed on a table near the entrance. A corpsman was adjusting the rubber tube carrying whole blood to his arm. Dr. Silvis looked at him and said: "See his lips? He's washed up." Then he turned to the corpsman and said: "Let's give him another bottle and put it in the femoral, the blood can run in faster than it can through the arm." The surgeon explained to me that the femoral is a big vein in each groin. It is quite deep, and not easy to find with the needle. But soon he had found the femoral vein in both groins and blood was pouring into Carbis, who needed it so badly.

One of the new arrivals had a broken leg, and the effect of his morphine had worn off. He trembled all over, like a cold, frightened child, and he moaned "ohhhh," took a deep breath, and moaned again as one of the doctors cut the temporary bandage off his leg. Of about 75 men in the big tent, he was the only one making any conscious noise. It seemed remarkable that in the midst of so much pain there was so much calm.

There were a few ambulatory cases sitting on stretchers, or on the edges of cots. I spoke to one of them whose hand was bandaged, a corporal from E Company, 23d Marines. I asked if his hand were badly hurt. He said: "No; that's shrapnel I got several days ago. Today I got concussion."

More than half the receiving tent, like the whole of the other big tent, was designated as a "recovery ward." After men had been operated on, in either the south end of the receiving tent or in one of the cisterns, they were brought in, and placed on cots in the recovery ward. They stayed there pending evacuation by hospital ship or by airplane; at this late stage of the battle the troop transports, which earlier had carried nearly the entire burden of hospitalization and evacuation, had ceased operating in such capacities. Some of these wounded who lay on the cots had "light" wounds like broken legs or arms, and they would be evacuated tomorrow or next day. Others, despite the best efforts of many skilled men, would die and lie forever in the alien volcanic ash of Iwo.

One man, a corpsman, died as we stood beside his cot. One minute his heavy, rasping breath could be heard throughout the tent. The next he was quiet, so the sheet was pulled over his head and he was borne outside the tent to await transportation to the cemetery in the morning. Commander Reuben Sharp of Camden, New Jersey, the medical battalion c.o., said: "When he was brought in here we didn't think he would last two hours. We gave him everything—oxygen, a lot of whole blood. Wagensteen apparatus, and he lasted five days. But he was licked from the start."

A blond boy, a corpsman, smiled as the doctor passed his cot. He said, "Doctor, I want to apologize for the way I acted." He had been operated on in the afternoon after he was brought in from the front. He had a bullet through the upper abdomen and a shell fragment in the forearm. His card said his condition was "generally good." The cot opposite held a wounded man who was vomiting. A chief pharmacist's mate walked over there and said to the corpsman attending the sick man, "God damn it, I told you not to give him too much water, just a sip."

I stopped at another cot, where lay Pfc. Alonzo Applegate of Bay Head, New Jersey, another man from E Company, 23d (which had caught particular hell on this day). He was sleeping and snoring. I read his ticket: "Multiple fragment wounds left foot, left leg, left hand, elbow and buttocks and lumbar area. 40,000 units penicillin."

It was now after nine o'clock. The corpsman who kept the

records at the north end of the tent told me 183 cases had been admitted during the day. Some new patients had just arrived. On the first operating table now there was a big Marine with a huge neck and bulging biceps, Pfs. Lewis I. Elliott of Millville, New Jersey. His barrel chest heaved mightily as he fought to breathe and live. Blood was flowing into his left arm while Pharmacist's Mate Third Class Billie K. O'Neil of Arkansas held a drainage tube in his throat. O'Neal said: "One of his main arteries was hit. The interal hemorrhage is so great he seems to be drowning in his own fluids. Not much chance for him." Half an hour later the big fellow had lost his fight against death.

Another man was brought from the operating room and lifted from the stretcher to a cot. He was just coming out of the anesthetic. He shifted uncomfortably, and moaned, "What's under me?" The corpsman beside him said, "Believe it or not, a mattress." Doctor Johnson said: "Many men come in here with a sense of relief. The battle is over for them and they figure they're lucky to get out of it alive. One of my corpsmen came in today, shot through the leg and heel; he was very happy about it."

I ducked out of the tent into the dark. Then I went across the road and climed down into No. 1 cistern, where two doctors had been working on the belly cases. Doctor Silvis was there now to relieve another surgeon for a spell. He was standing beside the operating table which held Carbis, the same dirty-faced Marine, who had been fed blood through the femoral veins when he arrived in the receiving tent. The two tubes from dark-red bottles still poured blood into his groins, but he was smoking a cigarette now. Silvis said, "I put lipstick on him"—meaning that color had returned. Silvis added an aside: "I think I'm going to save that guy; he was really washed out; I thought I'd never get enough blood in him. But you can't be conservative; you've got to pour it in. In 20 minutes I'll go into his belly and tell you whether he'll live."

They had cut Carbis' clothes off now, and there was a cluster of guts as big as two fists sticking out of the left side of his abdomen, though the hole itself was thumbsized. "There's a lot of pressure inside the stomach, and it forces the guts out," said Silvis.

At the other table in the cistern three doctors were more than halfway through operating on a badly wounded first lieutenant, also from the 23d's E Company. He had caught shell fragments in the belly, but he was also wounded in the face, his left leg had about 30 wounds, including "one you could put a baseball through," his right arm was fractured. Even his dogtag was covered with blood. The doctors were cutting into his belly first. The other wounds could wait. Doctor Paul Giddings of Augusta, Maine, was the surgeon. Doctor Robert Cahill of Springfield, Massachusetts, was assisting him, holding a tube which sucked the excess blood out of the eight-inch-long belly opening. Dr. Leonard Brandman was the anesthetist. This was the eighth belly operation this three-man team had performed since eight o'clock in the morning; each case took about two hours.

When they had finished with the lieutenant, these three doctors paused for a cigarette. I asked Doctor Giddings if he knew Major Merriwell Shelton of Augusta. He did. It seemed like a long time ago, and a long way off, but I had seen Doctor Shelton operating on soldiers on Attu in circumstances quite similar to those of Doctor Giddings's operations on Marines on Iwo.

Dr. Cahill said: "The mortality in belly cases is generally 70 per cent, but we ought to save half those we've operated on today. All the patients are young and strong and they've got a will to live, which makes a lot of difference. I'm afraid we'll lose that lieutenant, though.[3] He was living on borrowed time while we operated."

[3] He was right. The lieutenant died aboard a hospital ship after a few days. A month after the battle, eleven of the Fourth Division doctors' 45 belly cases had died of wounds, 21 were definitely living, and 13 had not been located among the various Pacific hospitals.

A corpsman wiped the blood off the rubber pad where the lieutenant had been lying, to get it ready for the next case. Doctor Giddings inhaled his cigarette smoke deeply, and said: "The surgeons in this division have been together since the Fourth was formed. They were at Roi-Namur, Saipan and Tinian, but they all agree they have never seen such wounds as they bring into the hospital here."

Commander Sharp came in and said two more belly cases had just arrived, and that one would be sent to each cistern. Doctor Silvis and his assistant, Doctor Andrew Weaver, and his anesthetist, Doctor Charles Saint, had already donned their white gowns and masks and had gone to work on the dirty-faced Marine, Carbis, whose cluster of guts was sticking out. Sharp watched them a few minutes and said: "Look at that. First, they take out the spleen, then they resect [cut and mend] the small bowel, then they sew up the rent in the colon. In civilian life any one of these would be regarded as a major operation." Before the three doctors finished they removed a total of nearly two feet of gut which they tossed into a wastebasket. (Said Silvis, "People have more gut than they need, anyway.")

In addition to the two operating tables, there was a cot in the cistern-operating room. On it lay a husky young lieutenant who led the machine-gun platoon of E Company, 24th Marines. In his neck he wore a circular rubber device with a hole in it. His larynx had been hit, and he was kept in the operating room because the necessary suction apparatus was there. He slept only fitfully, and was conscious most of the time. He could hear what was going on, but he could not talk, of course. Once in a while he would tug at someone passing his cot, and motion for a pad of paper. Once he wrote, "Did you say you are going to give me penicillin?" When the corpsman nodded he wrote "water." One of the doctors said it would be all right to give him a little water. Another time he pulled at my field jacket, and wrote: "Can you help my breathing somehow?" I motioned to the corpsman, who came over and connected the whirring suction machine and put a tube in the hole in the device in the lieutenant's throat. "He's getting along all right and they'll build him a fine artificial larynx," said the corpsman. (But the corpsman was wrong; the lieutenant died two days later).

Doctor Silvis' operation required two hours and twenty-five minutes. While waiting for him I walked through the dark to the other long tent that was known as the recovery ward. There was none of the bustle of the receiving ward or the operating cisterns. Most of the postoperative patients were sleeping quietly in the two rows of cots. One of the corpsmen, Pharmacist's Mate Second Class Bernard Levine of Union, New Jersey, opened a can of orange juice and said, "I'll show you the sword I got this morning." He brought over a finely polished Japanese officer's sword.

"A Marine gave it to me," said Levine. "This Jap sneaked through our lines and was on top of the Marine before anybody saw him or had a chance to shoot him. A BAR man killed the Jap, but he left the sword sticking in the Marine's back. I pulled it out and treated him, and sent him back to the hospital. He said he wanted me to have the sword."

The recovery ward cases ranged from slightly wounded to very serious. One man wore a plaster cast which covered him from toes to chest. His right arm had been amputated about six inches below the shoulder. He was the only amputation case in the ward, but one of the doctors told me there had been quite a number. There had been several cases where two limbs were lost, and two cases where three limbs had been amputated. One of the latter cases had died after being evacuated; the doctor did not know whether the other had lived or not.

It was now twenty minutes after midnight, and the receiving ward, having received nearly all the cases that would come in before morning, was also less active. Total admissions for the day had now reached 207, and only one new case came in while I was there for the last time. He was from an amphtrac outfit. This man, Pfc. Gordon E. Diggs, of Paris, Texas, had stepped on a land mine, probably a planted aerial bomb, near the cemetery (three miles behind the front lines). Although he had had a full grain of morphine, he was in extreme agony, and he pleaded with the doctors: "Please can't you put me to sleep; my God, my feet feel numb." We could see why. One of his feet had been blown off just above the ankle, leaving a piece of charred bone protruding from beneath a hastily applied bandage. In addition, his other leg was mangled, and his hands and arms had been badly torn and burned black by the flash of the explosion. He said, "Goddlemighty, doc, I think I must have gone forty feet high when I stepped on the thing." In a few minutes he stopped groaning, and when the doctor gently sought to turn his black and bleeding arm, Diggs said bravely: "Go ahead, Doc, turn 'er over. I'm all right now."

Doctor Silvis was just finishing his operation when I returned, and the Giddings team was about halfway through its ninth belly case. Silvis said he thought his man Carbis had a pretty fair chance,[4] though the belly had been worse than expected; its wound evidently had been caused by an explosive bullet.

Once during the operation the hospital's generator had stopped briefly, and it had been necessary to turn on the battery lights, but no time had been lost. Doctor Silvis took off his white gown and put on his khaki shirt, and when we started through the blackout flaps I noticed that the concrete floor was lightly covered with blood.

[4] He was alive and doing well in the Naval Hospital, Oakland California, **four** months later.

CHAPTER FOURTEEN

THE TOP BRASS

BETWEEN BATTLES I CAME TO KNOW MOST OF THE MEN WHO ran the Central Pacific war; some of them I knew well, some only slightly. The Nimitz command sprawled over a vast area, from the Aleutians in the north to the New Zealand ports in the south, from the west coast of the United States to Okinawa, a total of 65,000,000 square miles of blue water and islands. By the winter of 1944-45 there were 21 admirals and generals of four-star and three-star rank serving under Nimitz. They commanded an incomparable fleet, several dozen air and naval bases, six Marine divisions, and six Army divisions. Six months before the end of the war Admiral Nimitz had more than 5,000 airplanes among his instruments of war.

The white-haired man who sat at the top of this vast empire was one of the calmest men I had ever met. There was nothing impetuous about Chester William Nimitz. Shortly before we sailed for Iwo Jima, a few days before the Fleet Admiral's sixtieth birthday, I asked one of his closest advisers what he considered Nimitz's secret of success. He thought a long time, then replied, "A sunny disposition and an unruffled demeanor, induced by excellent health."

Exercise was almost a fetish with Nimitz. At his headquarters in Pearl Harbor, and later in Guam (where he moved into a hill-top cottage the Seabees built for him in January, 1945), he used to get up at 0530, walk a half hour at a brisk pace, eat breakfast, then walk the mile to CINCPAC headquarters. By 1630 he left his immaculate desk and took a long walk or ran the legs off several younger men in a tennis game. In the evening he indulged his fondness for symphonic music, his prime hobby.

If Nimitz ever worried, he kept his worries to himself. Once I asked him what stood out in his mind as the low point of the war, mindful of the lean days in early 1942, when it seemed that the Japs might sever our line to Australia, and of the darkness of late 1942 when the Navy was down to one serviceable aircraft carrier *(Enterprise)* and it seemed that the Japs might knock the Americans off Guadalcanal.

But Chester Nimitz thought the first 24 hours of the war were the worst. On Sunday, December 7, 1941, he was at his home on Q Street in Washington, listening to the New York Philharmonic Orchestra. He was chief of the Bureau of Navigation. When word came to him of the attack on Pearl Harbor, he walked to the Navy Department with his assistant, Captain John F. Shafroth (later a rear admiral commanding a battleship division). After he reached the low-lying "temporary" (since World War I) headquarters building on Constitution Avenue, he found that the news became progressively worse. When telephone communication with Pearl Harbor had been re-established, Rear Admiral Claude C. Bloch, commander of the Fourteenth Naval District, read the returns to Admiral Harold R. Stark, then Chief of Naval Operations. The assembled admirals heard the bad tidings roll in like thunder.

When the time came to select a successor to Admiral Kimmel, Nimitz was the logical choice (he had been second choice a year earlier when Kimmel was picked). Nimitz demurred; he suggested that the Pacific command should go to Vice Admiral William S. Pye, Kimmel's temporary successor. But Nimitz got his orders. Wearing civilian clothes, he boarded a train, rode to San Diego, and flew from there to Pearl Harbor.

He arrived on Christmas Day and found the Pacific Fleet staff steeped in gloom. Actually, he found two staffs, the one he inherited from Kimmel, and another which Admiral

Pye had assembled. "There were too many people and too much pessimism," he told me a long time later. His first problem, as he saw it, was to restore confidence. When he saw how much damage the Japs had inflicted, he, himself, didn't feel particularly confident, but he shook off the gloomy mood, and went to work at the bottom of a long ladder.

Nimitz's orders were to hold the Midway-Samoa-Australia line at all costs, and he had very little to hold it with. Fortunately, the Japs had not quite caught the carriers as well as the battleships when they bombed Pearl Harbor. The carrier raids of early 1942 were set up to feel out the Japs and keep them guessing. Admiral Halsey struck at Marcus, Wake, the Marshalls and the Gilberts in raids that were not in themselves militarily significant, but they served their purpose. Nimitz believed that the American people owed a great debt to Halsey for those strikes ("Halsey was the right type—and he delivered"). They meant a great deal to morale, especially in Pearl Harbor.

In Nimitz's view (and in the views of most Navy men), the turning point of the war came at Midway. "That was where we felt the Jap strength, and we knew what to expect; never again did I have any doubts about the outcome of the Pacific war," he said in 1945.

Admiral Nimitz used to insist on the virtues of the balanced fleet. He praised the new battleships (his carrier pilots called them "the most expensive anti-aircraft platforms ever built"). In interviews he always pointed out the value of the old battleships like *Pennsylvania, Tennessee, Nevada, et al.* whose high explosive shells paved the way for troops' landing on heavily-fortified islands. A submariner himself, Nimitz would recite the heroic achievements of the submarine men, who sank 1,256 Japanese ships before the war ended, and lost 52 of their own craft. Then he would point out the indispensability of the destroyers.

As he had to, the Admiral believed in every part of his balanced fleet. His censors took stories about the Admiral to him for approval.[1] In one such story I wrote: "But the *Essex*-class carrier is undoubtedly the heart and soul of the Pacific fleet." Admiral Nimitz changed "heart and soul" to "mainspring."

Despite his sunny disposition, Admiral Nimitz was cautious in whatever predictions he made. (The admirals never forgot Halsey's toe-stubbing prediction that the Japs would be defeated in 1943.) In October, 1944, Admiral Nimitz broadcast to the New York *Herald Tribune* forum: "We fully expect to win, but we know the road to victory will be long and rough." That fall he spoke to the American Legion: "But if the Japanese have 'no room for optimism' we Americans have no room for overoptimism. With each westward advance, new problems arise associated with supply of distant bases. These problems are not to be solved overnight. We also expect that as we draw closer to the heart of Japan we will run into tougher and more compact defenses . . . We have not yet come to grips with the main bodies of the well trained Japanese Army in spite of the virtual annihilation of some garrison forces stationed on Japan's outer island fortresses . . . We are opposed by a tenacious and savage enemy, worshipping false gods and false ideals—and willing to die for them." That speech was made before Iwo and Okinawa were invaded and before the final Japanese surrender, which Admiral Nimitz could foresee no more than anybody else in the Pacific in 1944.

The first Nimitz in America was Charles, a sailing-ship master who arrived from Bremen at Charleston, South Carolina, in 1844. Two years later Charles Nimitz went with other German settlers to Fredericksburg, Texas (named for Prince Frederick). There he built a hotel with a boat deck,

---

[1] MacArthur's censors did likewise. The General once struck out the word "aloof" when a correspondent used it to describe him, and substituted "remote."

a bridge, and various maritime appurtenances which caused it to be nicknamed "the Steamboat Hotel." Charles Nimitz's son Chester married Anna Henke, but Chester died in the fall before his son Chester, Jr., was born February 24, 1885. The young widow married her late husband's brother, William, and moved to Kerrville. Young Chester Nimitz's early life was divided among Kerrville and Fredericksburg and Wolf Creek Ranch, which belonged to Uncle Otto Henke.

Despite his nautical background, Chester Nimitz absorbed much Army lore from soldiers stationed in the San Antonio-Fredericksburg-Kerrville area. He wanted to go to West Point.[2] But Congressman James Slayden of the Twelfth District had only an appointment to the Naval Academy. Of tow-headed Chester Nimitz, who finished seventh in the class of 1905, the *Lucky Bag* said: "A man of cheerful yesterdays and confident tomorrows."

In 1908 Ensign Nimitz was assigned to submarines, which were then regarded "as a cross between a Jules Verne fantasy and a whale." His first submarine commands were tiny gasoline-burners, *Plunger* and *Narwhal*. Before World War I, Nimitz went to Germany to study diesels; in 1912 he wrote an early and excellent text book on submarines.

Nimitz served on the staff of Admiral Samuel S. Robinson, commander of Submarine Forces Atlantic Fleet in the war. He attained the grade of commander. After the war, when Admiral Robinson became Commander-in-Chief of the United States Fleet, Nimitz became his aide and assistant chief of staff. By this time, Nimitz's fine sense of balance and rigid application to duty had marked him as a man who would go far. He had a flair for administration, and the invaluable ability to reconcile conflicting temperaments

[2] Several outstanding figures in World War II went to the "wrong" academy. Examples: Lieut. General Lesley J. McNair, whose youthful ambition pointed toward Annapolis; Fleet Admiral William D. Leahy, who aspired to West Point.

within his command. "He's the sanest man I know," was a designation applied frequently to Nimitz.

In 1926 Chester Nimitz, on the eve of becoming a captain, was directed to establish the Naval Reserve Training School at the University of California. He spent three years there, and liked it. During the war years Mrs. Nimitz (she was Catherine Vance Freeman of Wallaston, Massachusetts, before she was married to Nimitz in 1913) lived in Berkeley, and during his brief visits from the Pacific, Nimitz might be seen hiking, in civilian clothes, across the university campus. Admiral Nimitz sent his four children (three daughters and a son, Chester, Jr., Annapolis '36, also a submariner) to Catholic schools because he liked the firmer discipline to be found there.

For six years prior to Pearl Harbor, Admiral Nimitz was stationed in Washington, as assistant chief, then chief, of the powerful Bureau of Navigation, excepting one year between the jobs when he went to sea as Commander Cruiser Division Two, and Commander Battleship Division One. When the call came to command the Pacific Fleet, Nimitz was ready for the job.

By the time the war was three years old, Nimitz had almost as many jobs as Jesse H. Jones had midway in the New Deal. He was commander of the paper organization called the First Fleet, military governor of the Gilbert and Ellice Islands, of the Marshall Islands, of the Marianas, Peleliu, Ulithi. But for purposes of naval communications he was CINCPAC (Commander in Chief Pacific Fleet) and CINCPOA (Commander in Chief Pacific Ocean Areas). Originally the two jobs were intended to carry separate staffs. But the same staff of Navy, Army and Marine Corps officers came to serve the combatant Pacific Fleet as well as the administrative and supply units within the Pacific Ocean areas.

Chief of staff to Admiral Nimitz in the later stages of the Pacific war (he succeeded Admiral Spruance in 1943) was

Vice Admiral Charles H. ("Soc") McMorris, who had been Kimmel's war-plans officer and had commanded the surface task force in 1943's eerie Battle of the Komandorskies. Deputy chief of staff and war plans officer was one of the Navy's brightest young admirals, one upon whom Nimitz leaned heavily—Forrest Sherman, who had commanded the *Wasp* when she sank. Admiral Sherman[3] longed to get back into combat with a carrier group, but Nimitz would never let him go.

Nimitz's operations officer was Commodore James B. Carter of Arkansas.[4] His intelligence section was headed by an Army officer, Brig. General Joseph J. Twitty, and his logistics section by another, Maj. General Edmond H. Leavy. Personnel and training were not assigned to a staff spot, but were allotted to the vast service force of Vice Admiral William L. Calhoun (who was succeeded in 1945 by Vice Admiral William W. Smith). Like Vice Admiral John H. Towers, Deputy CINCPAC, Admiral Calhoun kept his headquarters in Pearl Harbor instead of moving westward to Guam.

The vastness of his command was Nimitz's big burden. His subordinate commanders included many another noncombatant officer: Vice Admiral John Henry Newton at Noumea, Commander South Pacific; Lieut. General Robert C. Richardson in Hawaii, Army Commanding General Pacific Ocean Areas; Vice Admiral Charles Lockwood in Guam, Commander Submarines Pacific; Vice Admiral George Murray, Commander Air Pacific; Vice Admiral Frank Jack Fletcher in Adak, Commander North Pacific Area. Mindful of his far-flung domain, Nimitz once courageously conceded, before the Texas Society in Honolulu: "If there is anything bigger than Texas, it is the Pacific Ocean."

[3] Not to be confused with Rear Admiral Frederick C. Sherman, who commanded the old *Lexington* when she sank, and had a carrier group throughout most of the war.

[4] Not to be confused with Commander Worrall Carter of Service Squadron Ten.

When he moved to Guam, Admiral Nimitz, a ruddy, husky man (five feet nine, 181 pounds) went informal; he quit wearing long khaki trousers, donned shorts. But his moments of informality were rare. The Admiral was frequently the despair of his public relations men; it simply was not in him to make sweeping statements or to give out colorful interviews (he sometimes upbraided his officers if he thought they were claiming more damage than they had inflicted; consequently most Navy estimates of battle damage after 1942 were probably conservative). Nimitz conceived of war as something to be accomplished as efficiently and as smoothly as possible, without too much fanfare.

Whenever he was tempted to delve into the unnecessaries he usually came off badly. He was photographed dancing with a hula girl at Waikiki, posing with a gooney bird at Midway. He was persuaded to go on the air personally to read his communique announcing the invasion of Okinawa. For some reason, he withheld the announcement until more than 12 hours after the landing—until 10 o'clock Sunday evening. Then he went to the microphone. But in the United States it was five o'clock to eight o'clock Sunday morning—the worst possible time to expect a listener audience.

There was one facet of Admiral Nimitz's character which received little public comment during the war: his patience in dealing with General MacArthur. Nimitz had barely begun plotting his Central Pacific campaign when the Southwest Pacific General stormed angrily and publicly about "island hopping." Said he (in September, 1943): "My strategic conception for the Pacific Theatre contemplates massive strokes against only the main strategic objectives, utilizing surprise and air and ground striking power, supported and assisted by the fleet . . . Island hopping . . . is not my idea of how to end the war as soon and as cheaply as possible."

General MacArthur issued several communiques from the Philippines during the Iwo battle whose implication was not lost upon the Central Pacific commanders. For example, concerning the recapture of Corregidor, MacArthur said March 1: "A total of 3,038 troops overcame an enemy of a strength of approximately 6,000 troops. A strongly fortified island fortress, defended to the point of annihilation by a well-equipped, fanatical enemy ... was reduced in a period of twelve days by a combination of surprise, strategy and fighting technique, and skill, perfectly coordinated with supporting naval and air forces. Four thousand two hundred and fifteen enemy bodies have already been counted, while many hundreds have been sealed in tunnels and caves where they were buried alive or blown to bits, and several hundred killed while attempting to escape by barges or swimming. Eighteen prisoners were taken. Our losses were 136 killed, 531 wounded and eight missing—a total of 675."

In his communique of March 10, while the Marines battled savagely to blow up the caves of Iwo, General MacArthur described how he handled the interlocking caves on Luzon: "Our method of attack consisted in preliminary saturation bombardments by air, artillery and all infantry weapons, calculated to confine the enemy within the tunnels. When this has been accomplished a small demolition group from the infantry moves in with white phosphorus grenades and flamethrowers and demolitions of several hundred pounds of explosives are placed inside the entrance to the lateral and blown to close the opening.

"In this manner the four or five laterals are sealed off and the vertical shaft then blown from the top. Each cave with its laterals can hold about 25 men. When trapped in this way, the enemy is suffocated to death and destroyed without taking any compensating toll from our troops. As an example, a brigade of the First Cavalry Division in 48 hours in the attack now developing took 137 caves and blew 446 of the outlets to these caves, with practically no loss to themselves, while the enemy's loss is estimated at several thousand men. Similar methods have been used throughout the New Guinea and Philippine campaigns. Slow progress of the attack is allowed by these methods but an enormous saving in life and material is affected."

The implication was plain: MacArthur could take heavily fortified positions by using certain weapons, without losing any men, while Nimitz—who used the same weapons—well, look at Iwo.

MacArthur issued a statement August 5 (the day before the atomic bomb was dropped on Hiroshima) saying he had extended his Pacific Army command to the Ryukyu Islands (which Nimitz's forces had captured). Thus, MacArthur said, the Ryukyus joined the Philippines as "a great semi-circular base which is being forged under the primary responsibility of General MacArthur for the final conquest of Japan." The statement was generally interpreted in the United States as the final announcement of MacArthur's assumption of the supreme Pacific command, which he had been forced to share throughout the war with Nimitz.

To Nimitz, MacArthur's statement meant no such thing. Next day he replied with a stiffly formal "clarification:" all the naval installations on Okinawa and all the naval forces around Okinawa were still part of his command—as they had been since the Joint Chiefs of Staff had turned over to Nimitz the Seventh Fleet (which MacArthur had controlled), and had turned over to MacArthur the Tenth Army and other Army units which had been Nimitz's. Perhaps Nimitz was finally prodded into answering MacArthur because the General had refused the invitation to return the Admiral's visit. (MacArthur sent his staff instead.)

With the end of the war Nimitz seemed to become a little less conservative. Arriving in Toyko Bay to play second fiddle in MacArthur's surrender ceremony, he staked his claim to winning the war: "We have seen an island empire, its Army almost intact, well-equipped and with a large air force—but no Navy—brought to surrender before any invasion assaults had taken place. That was brought about by seapower, spearheaded by carrier-borne aircraft and aided by the excellent work of our submarine force. This seapower has made possible . . . the movement of Army and Marine troops, the seizure of bases for land and airpower, and bases for the fleet itself. It is the same seapower that made possible the use of the atomic bomb by seizure of bases from which our planes using weapons of that type could operate. Without our seapower we could not have advanced at all. What has been accomplished is the result of teamwork of the very highest order . . . in emphasizing seapower I am not detracting from other branches of the service. But it must be obvious to everyone that no matter how much Army and airpower we have, we can't get started without bases in the direction of the enemy; these must be taken and protected by naval vessels."

The General's memoirs (and the Admiral's, if he writes them) should make interesting reading.

For most of the last year of the war we indulged in a bit of pleasantry designed to fool the Japs—and we often wondered how successful we were. Apparently we had two vast fleets in the Pacific, the Third and the Fifth. Actually, of course, the two were composed of the same ships. When Admiral William Frederick Halsey Jr., took them out, they were Third; when Admiral Raymond Ames Spruance and his staff replaced Halsey and his staff, the ships became the Fifth. Not until the occupation of Japan began did Nimitz actually divide the fleet.

The basic combat unit of the fleet in 1944-45 was the Fast Carrier Task Force, usually composed of 12 to 14 big *Essex*-class carriers, six or eight *Independence*-class light carriers which had been built from cruiser design, eight or ten new battleships, 20 or 30 cruisers, and several dozen destroyers. (More often than the Navy dared admit, the size of the Task Force depended on how successful the Japanese suicide flyers had been.) Neither the old battleships nor the escort carriers could be used; they were too slow, and were relegated to supporting amphibious landings. Also, the remaining old carriers, the *Enterprise* and *Saratoga*, were outdated; they could not turn and maneuver with the Fast Carrier Task Force. But they carried on nobly as night-fighter carriers. We had come a long way since the *Big E* and the *Sara* were our principal offensive naval weapons.

The Fast Carrier Task Force had its own alternating commanders (Mitscher of Task Force 58 with Spruance; and McCain of Task Force 38 with Halsey). The fleet commander generally rode within the task force, leaving its detailed operation to the task force commander. The idea of having two fleets was simple: Halsey and McCain would execute a plan of battle while Spruance and Mitscher worked out the plans for future operations, which, when they took over, they would carry out. Then the roles of the planners and the battlers would be reversed.

In Spruance and Halsey, Admiral Nimitz had two fleet commanders who were as different as two Naval Academy graduates could possibly have been. Spruance was quiet; Halsey was noisy—a sort of seagoing Patton. Spruance had an ingrained distrust of publicity. Halsey could not have thrived without it. Spruance shied away from anything ostentatious; he kept a small staff, and he preferred an old cruiser (the ill-fated *Indianapolis*) as his flagship. Halsey rode the biggest things afloat, the new battleship *New Jersey* and later the *Missouri*, and the more men he had around him the better, he thought. With his brilliant, popular chief of staff, Rear Admiral Robert B. ("Mick") Carney, and with his other officers, Halsey kept up a running banter; all the Halsey men seemed always to be having a hilarious time.

One day, in December, 1944, I saw Halsey at Ulithi in his office on the *New Jersey,* rocking back and forth in a swivel chair. He was nude except for a pair of khaki shorts. That night he went ashore on Asor Island, made a pre-movie speech to the shore-based enlisted men, who loved him. It was along the lines of the usual Halsey theme: "We're going to show those yellow bastards what God damn fools they were for starting this thing." I could not help thinking how impossible it would have been for the austere, correct Spruance to make such a speech.

Admiral Spruance had recently been designated Commander Central Pacific, after a period as Nimitz's chief of staff, when I walked into his office one day in October, 1943, and asked to see him. His secretary, a lieutenant who doubled as a signalman, came back with the answer, "Admiral Spruance desires no personal publicity." But I finally arranged to see him next day.

I found him a middle-sized, iron-gray man with a seaman's clear blue eyes. If his hair hadn't been well combed he would have resembled the late Will Rogers. I also found him, to my surprise, pleasant, humorous, and easy to talk to. He was proud of his Hoosier background (though he was born in Baltimore and spent some of his youth in New Jersey). His great-grandfather had gone to Indiana as a Methodist missionary among the Indians.

Early in his post-Annapolis career Admiral Spruance had been sent, with three other officers, to Schenectady to study electrical engineering. ("There wasn't much instruction; it was mostly absorption.") He had helped to build the battleship *Pennsylvania.* Since I had recently been on the *Pennsylvania* in the Aleutians, I asked why they built her decks so low; people were always cracking their heads on beams. The Admiral explained that she wasn't built that way; the *Penn-*

sylvania had had about six inches of armor added when she was reconditioned, hence the low ceiling. "But it's a disadvantage sometimes, being tall," the Admiral said. "I knew a Marine officer once who was nearly seven feet tall, and he had a hell of a time. On the ship they had to build an extension for his feet that went into the next room."

Spruance was not nearly so well known to the headline-reading public as was Halsey, who announced that he was going to ride Hirohito's white horse when he got to Tokyo, and who told his flyers at the war's end: "Cease firing, but if you see any enemy planes in the air, shoot them down in friendly fashion." Such was the nature of "Bull" Halsey. Actually, Spruance put in more time as fleet commander than Halsey did.

Spruance was in command during all the Central Pacific landings, from Tarawa through Okinawa, except the Peleliu appendage. Halsey covered the Philippines landings and contributed immeasurably to the subsequent campaign. In September, 1944, Halsey had finally gone back to sea as Third Fleet commander, after more than two years of shore duty, mostly in the South Pacific. When one of Halsey's flyers was shot down off Leyte, was rescued by guerrillas, and returned to the fleet, he reported that the Japs were weak in the Central Philippines. On the strength of this flimsy but creditable report, plus some other intelligence, Halsey sold MacArthur on the idea of invading at Leyte in October instead of Mindanao in December.

Halsey was to have had the first carrier crack at Tokyo, November 15. But the revision of the Philippines campaign cost him that plum. When MacArthur invaded Leyte he ran into rains which made airfield construction all but impossible. Land-based planes could not protect the Leyte beachhead, and Halsey's carriers had to be called back. Meanwhile, the Second Battle of the Philippine Sea took place; the *kamikaze* pilots were playing havoc with Halsey's carriers, and the *kamikaze* threat off the Japanese islands loomed even larger. The first Tokyo strike had to be postponed until February, when Spruance again was in command of the fleet.

Both Halsey and Spruance had their hindsight critics. The criticisms, which could be evaluated only in the light of complete documentation, reflected the north-and-south estimates of the two men. Generally speaking, the colorful Halsey was a sailor's admiral. But many a Navy man said of him, "My God, he's going to get us all killed!" There was nothing cautious about "Bull" Halsey, as proved by his successful prowl into the South China Sea in January, 1945, and his beating his chest up and down the coast of Japan during the last weeks of the war. Halsey let himself get caught in two embarrassing typhoons, one in December, 1944, another in June, 1945. Rightly or wrongly, he was criticized by many Navy officers who thought he could have avoided the typhoons by using more discretion. The Second Battle of the Philippine Sea in October, 1944, caught Halsey midway between the two theaters of action. Two Jap battleships escaped off Cape Engano, Northern Luzon; four other ships got away from the Leyte Gulf area to the south. Luckless Admiral Halsey, with his fast, new battleships, could have finished off one group or another if he had not left the northern area so soon, or if he had departed sooner.

On two historic occasions Spruance was suspected by some of being over-cautious. At the Battle of Midway he did not attempt to track down the Japs' surviving ships; at the First Battle of the Philippine Sea he might have dashed faster and farther to the west to sink the Jap fleet or whatever portion of it was west of Saipan. (As it was, the damage to the Jap Navy was done by planes which could not make it back to their carriers before dark.) But on both counts I have heard Spruance defended as strongly as he was attacked. At Midway we only suspected the true strength of the Jap Navy; a reckless jaunt might have exposed Hawaii and Midway to flank attack. At Saipan, Spruance conceived his true mission to be the protection of the landing forces; it seemed more than probable that the Japs had much of their naval strength in reserve to the north, strength that could have been thrown at Saipan if it had been left unprotected.

When Halsey commanded the fleet, the carrier pilots were almost invariably referred to as "Halsey's flyers." When the less spectacular Spruance was the boss they were "Mitscher's flyers." Two incidents at Saipan well illustrated Spruance's self-effacing nature: First, when he received a copy of *Time*—the first to reach the Marianas for several days—whose cover was adorned by his picture, he hid the magazine even from his devoted chief of staff, Captain Charles J. Moore, who knew the Admiral better than did anyone else ("it takes years to get to know Admiral Spruance," he once said); secondly, Spruance figuratively wrung his hands when Admirals King and Nimitz trumpeted the First Battle of the Philippine Sea as a great victory; he thought they were overplaying his achievement.

During the week before United States forces entered Japan, Admiral Spruance held his second personal press conference of the war. In Manila Bay he said exactly what Halsey would have been expected not to say, "I think the Japs fought an excellent war, considering what they had to start with." He also favored cutting down the size of the Navy, making Okinawa a United Nations base, rather than a strictly American base. After all, said the shy, frugal Admiral, "As I see the picture, the only countries with major fleets left are the British and ourselves. We're certainly not getting ready to fight each other."

The two Fast Carrier Task Force commanders, Mitscher and McCain, had at least one thing in common; both were grizzled, wry-humored little men. Both had their personal quirks; on his flag bridge Mitscher always faced aft ("I'm an old man now; I spent my youth looking ahead"); McCain wore the Navy's most outrageous headgear, a mechanic's cap surmounted by a black headband and a gold-encrusted visor. He also rolled his own cigarettes, which he lit with a silver lighter.

Marc Andrew Mitscher was born in 1887 in Wisconsin, but he grew up in Oklahoma, and got one of the Oklahoma territorial delegate's quadrennial appointments to the Naval Academy. Because his predecessor at Annapolis had the mellifluent name of Peter Cassius Marcellus Cade Jr., Mitscher as a plebe was required to roll it off his tongue whenever an upper-classman entered his room. Hence Mitscher's lifelong nickname, "Pete." John Sidney McCain was "Jock." He was born on his father's plantation near Carrollton, Mississippi, three years before Mitscher.

Mitscher took up aviation a few years after he finished at Annapolis, and became Naval Aviator Number 32. That endeared him to World War II carrier pilots, who attached considerable importance to the question, "How long has the Admiral been flying?" McCain, on the other hand, was past 50 when he took up flying, in 1935. During the war I heard it argued dozens of times that the older admirals who largely controlled naval aviation were not progressive enough, and just as often I heard the countering argument: If many senior officers, such as King, Halsey and Turner, had not taken up flying when they did, naval aviation would have been lost many years ago in a separate air force. For me the dispute was never settled satisfactorily; I only knew that naval aviation did a superb job in defeating Japan. I mentioned this observation to a 40-year-old captain after the Third Fleet's spectacular foray into the South China Sea in January, 1945. His answer was, "Look; the kids flying the planes off these carriers are so good they could pull any admiral out of a hole." I was still unconvinced, one way or another, about the importance of age in air admirals.

Mitscher had made a name for himself as captain of the *Hornet* when he took the Doolittle flyers to Tokyo in April, 1942, shifted to Noumea that fall as Commander Fleet Air South Pacific, to Guadalcanal as Commander Air Solomons, in April, 1943. After five months back on the U. S. West Coast, he arrived in Honolulu in January, 1944, as Commander Fast Carrier Task Forces Pacific. During the months from January to September his carriers blazed the trail through the Central Pacific. They paved the way for the landings at Kwajalein and Eniwetok, moved over to attack Truk in one of the most successful surprise strikes of the war, hit a few days later in the Marianas (four months before the invasion of Saipan), struck at the Palaus in late March, went south to Hollandia and to Truk again in April, and to Ponape in May. In June, Mitscher concentrated on Guam, Saipan, Tinian, Rota, and Iwo Jima; he also fought the Philippine Sea battle. In July he continued working over Guam prior to invasion, hit again at Palau and at Yap and Ulithi. By August Mitscher seemed established in the Western Pacific; Pearl Harbor was ages behind.

Mitscher continued commanding the fast carriers even after Halsey (*i.e.*, the Third Fleet) took over in September. But it was obvious that he was carrying too heavy a load; his weight dropped from 135 to 120. McCain had arrived in the Pacific from Washington in mid-summer as an observer; he rode with Mitscher's forces for many weeks.

Finally, in early November, five days after the Second Battle of the Philippine Sea, McCain assumed command of the Carrier Task Force.

McCain arrived soon after the *kamikaze* planes began their concerted drive to sink the United States Navy. He brought with him a solution: Make dive bombers out of the fighter planes; thus your dive bomber becomes a fighter itself after it has dropped its bomb. Chief proponent of the radical plan was McCain's tall, lean operations officer, Commander

John S. ("Jimmy") Thach, famed as a fighter pilot early in the war and as inventor of the "Thach Weave" fighter maneuver. Jimmy Thach was exultant: "This is one of those rare miracles where you get something for nothing; you drop your bomb, then you've got the world's best fighter." Jimmy was also philosophical about the suicide tactics of the Japs: "Every time one country gets something, another soon has it. One country gets radar, but soon all have it. One gets a new type of engine or plane, then another gets it. But the Japs have got the *kamikaze* boys, and nobody else is going to get that, because nobody else is built that way."

McCain's plan to ditch the dive bomber (by that time we had discarded the old SBD's and were using the new SB2C's) created a tempest among the carrier forces. The United States Navy had invented the dive bomber, and the whole production schedule was set for dive bombers as the main offensive weapon, leaving fighters for defense. But McCain sold the plan to Halsey. An *Essex* group came to mean 73 fighters, only 15 dive bombers (instead of 36), and 15 Torpedo bombers. When I arrived in Ulithi in December I met many dive-bomber pilots on their way back to take fighter training.

There were not enough Grumman F6 Hellcats to fill the increased demand for fighters, or enough Navy squadrons ready at the moment. But McCain could call on F4U Corsairs, which were quickly equipped as carrier-based instead of land-based planes, and he could call on Marine pilots who have been the only F4U pilots, and who were just beginning to practice carrier landings with a view to escort-carrier duty in support of amphibious operations. It was not long before the fighter squadron aboard an *Essex*-class carrier had grown so big it had to be divided into a fighter squadron and a fighter-bomber squadron, and there were enough fighters to keep a constant patrol over a vast target area. McCain had created something of a revolution in carrier tactics. The arguments about his being right or wrong were still going on when the war ended, but before then the Jap Navy, which was the target against which the dive bomber was most effective, had ceased to be even medium-good pickings.

Mitscher was back in command of the carriers for the first Tokyo strikes, the Iwo and Okinawa operations. The suicide planes hit two of his flagships within a week, the *Bunker Hill* and the *Enterprise*. But when he was relieved again by McCain in May, he went home protesting against a desk job. Admiral McCain did not get home until the war was over; by then he had worn himself out. A few days after he reached American soil he was dead of a heart attack.

CHAPTER FIFTEEN

THE AMPHIBIOUS BRASS

A FEW DAYS AFTER D DAY AT IWO JIMA THE JAPANESE RADIO devoted its commentary to castigating one man: "He is responsible for killing countless numbers of our younger and elder brothers on various islands throughout the Central Pacific area . . . This man Turner shall not return home alive; he mustn't and won't; this is one of the many things we can do to rest at ease the many souls of those who have paid the supreme sacrifice."

Aboard his flagship, *Eldorado,* Vice Admiral Richmond Kelly Turner read the Domei dispatch, rubbed his gray-cropped, balding head, peered over his steel-rimmed spectacles, and scribbled a "dead-pan" note to his immediate superior, Admiral Spruance: "Maybe you'd better come rescue me."

Turner had not always been so unpopular among the Japanese; in 1939 he had commanded the *Astoria* when that cruiser delivered the ashes of Ambassador Saito across the Pacific, as a gesture of international good will.

But that had been a long time ago, and Kelly Turner had become the Commander Amphibious Forces Pacific Fleet (COMPHIBSPAC). Admiral Turner probably knew more about amphibious operations than any other man in the world; he certainly had the most experience commanding the tough ones: Guadalcanal, New Georgia, the Gilberts, the Marshalls, the Marianas, Iwo Jima, Okinawa. His amphibious landings on the coast of Japan were, anti-climactically, unopposed operations for occupation purposes, but he had his plans ready for Kyushu (November) and Honshu (March) when the war ended so unexpectedly.

Until 1942, United States history was almost devoid of major episodes wherein our troops landed in the face of enemy fire. Commodore Esek Hopkins had 50 sailors and 200 Marines ashore at Providence Island, Bahamas, in 1776 and there had been bloody Fort Fisher on the North Carolina coast in the Civil War. But the failure of Gallipoli in World War I seemed to have discouraged all major powers (except Japan) from concentrating on amphibious operations. Wars simply had to be won, apparently, on land or on sea; certainly, not on the beachheads.

Some time between 1936 and 1938 Kelly Turner became interested in amphibious warfare, which gave at the time, little promise as a career. Turner, already past 50, was teaching strategy at the Naval War College. He was known as a brilliant but erratic and irascible officer; he had finished fifth in his class of 1908 and the four ahead of him had long since resigned or dropped into the obscurity of naval construction, as so many bookish graduates of Annapolis did. Turner carried to extremes the Navy idea of all-round experience. He had done his duty on battleships, cruisers, and destroyers. He had commanded his small ship, the destroyer *Stewart,* then he had been selected to go back to the Naval Academy as a postgraduate student in ordnance.

A "p.g. in ordnance" automatically became a member of the "gun club." Sometimes smart gun club members with low numbers eventually wound up as Chief of the Bureau of Ordnance, and, in turn, sometimes became Chief of Naval Operations. But in 1927 Turner decided he had squeezed all there was out of gunnery, and he abandoned it. At 42 he took up flying. His reasons for doing that were somewhat obscure, except that there was a new law saying only flyers could command aircraft carriers or naval air stations, and Kelly Turner was never a man to shy away from an opportunity to learn something new.

Turner's career in aviation was brief; he dropped it, for

all practical purposes, when he arrived at the Naval War College in 1935. His propensity for knowing everything and lecturing everybody made Turner an excellent teacher. He was mean, but he was good at stimulating his pupils' imagination. He spared nobody's feelings, but his critiques were described as masterpieces of strategy. In addition, he could read two dozen papers an evening, then discuss all of them next day, without further reference. This power of assimilation stood him in good stead later. During his war against Japan, Turner frequently amazed other officers with his offhand ability to memorize a two-inch book of operations plans.

On December 7, 1941, Turner, a rear admiral in charge of war plans, was pruning the hydrangea bushes in the garden of his home in Washington. He had just recovered from an attack of influenza. Admiral Stark telephoned to ask Turner to come down to the office. Turner went. There was an angry protest from Admiral Thomas C. Hart, in Manila; Turner had drawn up plans to withdraw the Asiatic Fleet from Manila Bay to the East Indies in case of war, and Hart didn't like it. Admiral Hart later admitted, Turner said, that the Turner plan which was followed was the only proper course; the insignificant Asiatic Fleet consisted of two cruisers, 13 over-age destroyers, 29 submarines, and two squadrons of PBYs in Patrol Wing Ten—hardly a match for the Jap planes and fleet.

It was while Turner was in Stark's office that the staff communications officer, Rear Admiral Leigh Noyes, dashed in with the famous intercepted flash from Hawaii which told that Pearl Harbor was under attack.

When Turner had arrived in Washington in 1940 he had hit the War Plans Office like a typhoon. "It was a rather leisurely existence up till then," the officer recalled later, "but Turner turned War Plans upside down. He drove everybody like a slave, but he worked like ten slaves himself. His system was to write chits—dozens every day—on his green memo pad. 'Do this,' 'Do that,' 'Believe you should look into this.' He was into everything and he wanted to know all there was to know about everything. Then he wanted to run it his own way.

"I'll give you an example of how Turner was into everything. One of the duties assigned to Harry Hill and Forrest Sherman of Turner's office was membership on Mayor LaGuardia's Joint Canadian-American Defense Board, along with Generals Stanley Embick and Joe McNarney of the Army. Their business was done in Canada, in New York, and in other places, but the green chits signed 'T' pursued Hill and Sherman. Pretty soon Turner was practically running the Defense Board. He never seemed to be able to find enough to do."

This inclination to assume all the burdens was as definite a Turner trait as his unquenchable thirst for knowledge. During the Pacific war he was often criticized for not delegating authority, but such an act on Turner's part would have been as unlikely as a dog delegating his bone. (He could not travel from ship to shore without telling the coxswain how to bring the boat alongside.) Amphibious warfare probably involved the most complex of all naval operations in the Pacific, but Turner held on to the final say-so in all matters, however minute. He kept a big staff; at Iwo, 102 officers, and he worked his key men relentlessly, men like his communications officer, Captain Charles Horne, Jr., his gunnery officer, Captain J. McN. Taylor, and his secretary, Commander William Mott. Turner himself, nonetheless, insisted on reading the 3,000 messages which flowed to and from his flagship in the course of a day in action. The staff invariably agreed on one point; the Old Man knew more about each job than the officer in charge of the job.

Soon after Pearl Harbor, Turner asked Admiral King (who had succeeded Admiral Stark) for the South Pacific amphibious command. He figured that any attacks would have to come up from New Zealand and New Caledonia, if they could be held long enough to mount an attack. During March, 1942, the plans for retaking Guadalcanal and Tulagi were first broached. But there were no troops ready, and, particularly, no ships. Guadalcanal was planned for November. Turner got ready to leave for New Zealand June 23, expecting to send the troops ashore five months later.

But President Roosevelt and the Joint Chiefs of Staff suddenly decided, on the basis of new intelligence, that Guadalcanal could not wait so long. The Japs had started building an airfield at Guadalcanal and a submarine base at Tulagi which might be the means of cutting the supply line to Australia. As Turner locked the door of his house in Washington the telephone rang; his successor, Rear Admiral Charles ("Savvy") Cooke, was calling to say that the first amphibious operation had been stepped up.

On June 30, Turner met Admirals King and Nimitz in San Francisco and got the word that he was to land the Marines on Guadalcanal little more than six weeks later. After that Admiral King ordered the operation advanced again—from mid-August to August 8—when he learned the Japs were about to send more reinforcements to the Solomons. Turner didn't reach Auckland until July 15. Two days later he assumed his command. Five days after that he sailed in his first flagship, *McCawley*. Sailing from New Zealand with him were enough transports, mostly ancient, long laid-up passenger ships, to carry the First Marine Division plus the First Raider Battalion. At about the same time the 2d Marine Regiment and the Third Defense Battalion sailed from Samoa. The two forces met on July 24 with two carrier groups under Rear Admirals Leigh Noyes and Frank Jack Fletcher. Forrest Sherman, then captain of the *Wasp* in the Noyes group, recalled the meeting: "I said, 'Oh, oh, watch me get a chit.' Sure enough, a destroyer came alongside with a message from Admiral Turner. He wanted to know if we could make a hundred copies of the only good photographs we had of our objectives."

The forces staged a rehearsal—"a very sorry rehearsal," said Turner later—from the Koro Sea in the Fijis. On August 8 (east longitude) the Marines landed against stiff opposition on Gavutu and Tulagi, and against no opposition at Guadalcanal. Kelly Turner had got his first troops ashore.

In the light of later operations, such a landing would have seemed amateurish. The preliminary naval gunfire and aerial bombardment would have looked puny compared to what preceded Iwo Jima. Only a few of the landing boats even had ramps. The DUKW, a wonderful truck that swam through the water and then ran on the land, had not been invented, the amphibious tractor (the "alligator") was still an experiment whose aluminum cleats usually came off.

Up to Guadalcanal, Kelly Turner had looked like a "fair-haired boy"; brilliant if gruff, always admired if sometimes detested. But he had to have a long, excellent record to survive Guadalcanal. The four cruisers sunk the night after his landing were part of his command, as the immediate screening force in all his operations was part of his command. The fact that the cruiser division commander, the British Admiral Crutchley, was at a meeting on the *McCawley*, did not relieve Turner of some responsibility for the loss of the cruisers. But, as Admiral King later reported officially "Because of the urgency . . . the planning was not up to the usual thorough standards. Certain communications failures . . . fatigue . . . generally speaking, however, we were surprised because we lacked experience." That night the Japs muffed their best chance to eliminate Kelly Turner. Fifteen miles beyond the sunken *Vincennes, Quincy, Astoria,* and *Canberra,* Turner's transports sat like so many ducks, with only a thin line of destroyers around them. But the Japs showed their usual inability to improvise beyond the immediate plan; they failed to follow through.

After this heart-breaking beginning, Turner decided to withdraw quickly his partly unloaded transports and cargo ships. Militarily, it was the only sensible thing to do. But it did not make him popular with the Marines on shore, who winced even after the war whenever they recalled the weevils in the captured Japanese rice they had to eat. They also recalled the hopeless fear they had of running out of ammunition. Admiral Turner insisted he left the Marines on Guadalcanal with 34 days' rations, those on Tulagi with 12 days' rations. It was, he said, other circumstances (daylight infiltrations and dusk bombings) which cut the Guadalcanal meals down to two a day. That was one of those arguments that probably never would be settled.

Turner made three more trips between Noumea and Guadalcanal, carrying a regiment of Marine or Army reinforcements each time. Each time he lost ships because the United States did not have enough ships and planes available to protect him. But he kept plugging, and he kept learning.

In February, 1943, after Guadalcanal had been declared secure, Turner set himself up ashore and planned the Russell Island invasion, 60 miles north of Guadalcanal. When he sent some Forty-third Division troops ashore, the last Japs had been gone ten days.

The New Georgia landings, some 200 miles north of Guadalcanal, had been planned for May 1. But the Attu battle 4,000 miles to the north claimed too much shipping. Finally, on June 30, Turner had enough to land Army troops at Rendova and Marine raiders at Viru Harbor. Two days later landings were made on New Georgia proper. The landings went off smoothly enough, but the New Georgia campaign ashore was no prize package. Turner finally relieved the Army division commander.

The New Georgia campaign led to two naval battles in Kula Gulf which cost us the cruiser *Helena,* and the destroyer *Gwin,* and damage to several ships, including the cruisers *St. Louis* and *Honolulu* and New Zealand's *Leander.* Turner's own *McCawley* also was ignominiously sunk, causing the amphibious commander to shift his flag to a destroyer. In the Solomons, Kelly Turner had done the best he could with what he had; he had made mistakes and he had learned from them. But the strategists changed their signals. To them it appeared that the South Pacific was not the place from which to wage the main offensive against Japan. In August, 1943, Turner was summoned to Pearl Harbor to command the Central Pacific Amphibious Force and the war of the toughest beachheads in history.

An amphibious landing involved much more than a given number of Marines or soldiers climbing down the nets of their transports and getting into small boats to go ashore to kill the enemy. The men on foot always paid the heaviest price in any amphibious operation. But there were a thousand things to be done before they could go ashore.

The planes—carrier-based or land-based, depending on distances—had to take out enemy planes, not only on the airfields of the objective, but also on all fields within flying range of the landing beaches. Before the combat-loaded troop transports arrived, the battleships, cruisers, and destroyers usually spent two, three or even more days shelling the beachhead. Fighters and bombers from the support group, and from the Fast Carrier Task Force at times, worked over the area until everything above ground was presumably destroyed. These planes and ships' guns were also used for support and for called fire after the troops had landed, supplementing the land-based artillery long after it got ashore.

All these supporting elements, as well as the transports, were part of Kelly Turner's show. He was boss of everything connected with amphibious operation; even land-based planes and planes from the fast carriers came under his control when they were used against his objective. Turner remained the boss of an operation until he turned over the objective to Commander Forward Area. Obviously, the coordination of these elements, the split-second timing of their strikes with the troops' action, required a man combining the qualities of a juggler, mathematician and high-powered executive. Turner was such a man. "Nobody but Kelly could get away with running a show big as this by himself," said a friend at Iwo Jima as he watched Turner pace the bridge of the *Eldorado* during 0500 General Quarters. The admiral wore an old bathrobe. He barked orders like a chief bosn's mate, stopping now and then to growl at the stupidity of slow-thinking people in general.

One of his staff officers showed me a routine message he had drawn up one day off Iwo. As usual, he had shown the message to Admiral Turner before sending. The Admiral put in three commas, took out one comma, changed "were highly pertinent" to "was pertinent." Sometimes he rewrote entire messages. Sometimes he merely changed their grammar. No poet himself, he sometimes edited the verse written by Bill Mott. And he read nearly all the stories written by war correspondents and filed through his flagship for radio transmission, though he had three or more censors. Turner rarely exercised his own censorship prerogatives; he simply wanted to know what the writers thought about the things that were going on.

Turner's enthusiasm for editing may have stemmed from his college days. He edited the *Lucky Bag* at Annapolis. Or he might have inherited it; his father was a printer on the Portland *Oregonian* when Kelly was born (the family moved to California when the boy was ten months old), and printers' sons frequently become editors.

Admiral Turner's severest test, perhaps, was his last. For the troops ashore, Okinawa was rough, but the soldiers and Marines had been through hell before. For the Navy, Okinawa was by far the costliest battle of the Pacific. There was doubt in some officers' minds as to whether the ships offshore could outlast the *kamikazes*. I saw Turner aboard the *Eldorado,* and asked what he thought. He lifted his eyebrows in surprise, and said: "Sure, we're going to take heavy losses, in ships and men. We knew we'd have to take on the whole Jap air force when we came here. But we'll be all right." He had had 22 ships hit the day before, including battleships, cruisers, transports, ammunition ships, and, particularly, his destroyers on the picket line.

Turner got his fourth star at Okinawa. This was appropriate recognition, but it was not equal to the accolade paid him at a conference of admirals shortly before he sailed to Okinawa. One of the admirals said, "They can replace me, and they can replace you," and, turning to a third officer, "somebody could fill your shoes, but there's nobody else who can do Kelly Turner's job."

Admiral Turner's command of the troops ended on the beachhead. Once they had landed, they were the tactical responsibility of the Army or the Marines (though the generals insisted that Turner sometimes tried to tell them how to deploy their troops, too). Turner's partner in the amphibious trek across the Pacific, until Okinawa, was the choleric old Marine, Holland McTyeire Smith.

It was an explosive partnership. Turner and Smith often went to the mat, but they usually came up friends. General Smith had a deep-seated suspicion that all Navy thinking was hidebound. He growled at the Navy assumption of omnipotence in all kinds of warfare, including fighting on shore. Turner was just the man for such arguments.

"Howlin' Mad" Smith looked and talked as Wallace Beery might, in the role of a Marine general. He was always demanding, and often profane. He could be kind, too. He fumed and he scolded, but when he laughed he laughed deep in the belly. He was enthusiastic, thoughtful, stubborn, a hard driver. Sometimes he scaled the heights of elation; again he walked hip-deep in despair. (Once he sent to the Marine commandant, General Thomas Holcomb, a list of generals he thought should be retired, to give younger officers a chance; Number 1 on the list was Holland Smith).

By 1905, Holland Smith, at 23, was a graduate of Alabama Polytechnic Institute and the University of Alabama, and for two years a practicing lawyer. He cared little for the law. He took down his shingle, said good-by to his mother and father (the latter also a Montgomery lawyer), and went to Washington. There he told his Congressman that he would like to try for a commission in the Army. There were no Army vacancies, but the Marines could use another second lieutenant. "What are the Marines?" asked Holland Smith. He took the commission.

During his training at the Annapolis "Schools of Application" (where civilians were turned into officers), Marine Smith met Ada Wilkinson of Phoenixville, Pennsylvania, at a dance. In 1909, when he returned from the Philippines, he married her. The Smiths, like all Marines, traveled. They lived in Bremerton, Seattle, Manila, Cavite, Shanghai, Puerta Plata, Norfolk, Newport, Port-au-Prince, Quantico, Philadelphia, New Orleans, Long Beach, San Francisco, Washington, San Diego. In one two-year stretch they moved 14 times.

By 1917, Captain Holland Smith set off for France, where he spent two years. He was adjutant of the famed Fourth Marine Brigade. Then he was operations officer for the First Corps, where he served with Army officers as well as Marines. He was at Soissons, Champagne, St. Mihiel.

In September 1939, when World War II was already under way, the First Marine Brigade started an amphibious training program. General Holcomb sent his assistant, Brig. General Holland Smith, to take command. To train some 5,000 men in amphibious landings, Smith and the Atlantic Fleet commander, Rear Admiral Ernest J. King, had to make and mesh their own rules. Navy gun crews had to be taught to fire at beaches instead of at ships; Marines had to learn how to scamper down rope cargo nets, what to do once they had splashed ashore. Combat loading had to be learned.

Equipment was more than a problem; there wasn't any. Holland Smith started practicing with two ancient ship's launches whose engines frequently did not work. He started experimenting together with Andrew Jackson Higgins, the boat builder, on a fast, high, stout-bottomed boat that could bounce over shallow reefs and hit the sand hard enough to get men into shallow water. He got Higgins to build a boat that would carry tanks into water shallow enough for them to roll ashore. He tried the amphibious tractor ("alligator") that Donald Roebling had invented for rescue use in the Florida Everglades.

Late in 1940, Holland Smith took his brigade and his single amphtrac to the Caribbean for seven months' hard training in beachhead landings. After he returned he was made a major general. Before the United States was at war, Holland Smith was a corps commander. He was training not only his Marines but also the First Army Division in amphibious operations. Later he trained the Ninth Army Division. In 1942 he was transferred to the West Coast, where he gave postgraduate courses in amphibious warfare to the Seventh Army Division (before it landed at Attu), the Third Marine Division (before Bougainville), and the five regiments which landed at Kiska. When his pupils went into action on Attu, Holland Smith was allowed to watch them from an airplane. Before the troops sailed from Adak for Kiska, Smith wanted a patrol sent into find out if the Japs had really pulled out. The patrol was not sent; Kiska turned out to be an Intelligence Section farce. Worse, in the fog some of the United States troops got into pitched battle, and more than 20 were killed before they realized at whom they were shooting.

With the opening of the Central Pacific in late 1943, "Old Marine" Smith finally got the combat assignment he wanted. As the top-ranking Marine in the Pacific, he commanded the Marine and Army troops which landed from Tarawa on to Iwo. He was in hot water often; he particularly became *persona non grata* to the Army at Saipan. But whenever Admiral Nimitz sent his ships and his troops toward Japanese-held soil he wanted Smith to go along; even to Iwo, where the three Marine divisions had their own corps commander in Maj. General Harry Schmidt. Lieut. General Smith, who had become Commander Fleet Marine Forces Pacific (a desk job), said, "I guess they sent me along just in case something happened to Harry Schmidt."

Okinawa brought in one of the Army's most colorful characters for the Central Pacific climax. Lieut. General Simon Bolivar Buckner, Jr., the ruddy-faced, white-haired "old man of the mountains," who built up Alaska's defenses, had hoped to lead United States troops into Japan from the north. In Adak in 1943 he spent nearly an hour telling me the virtues of a campaign against Japan from the Aleutians.

But the descent from the north was not to take place. Instead, Buckner in mid-1944 was called to Hawaii after four years in Alaska and the Aleutians, and ordered to organize the Tenth Army. Not until Okinawa did the Central Pacific offer enough land mass to warrant the use of more than a corps of troops.

At Okinawa, Buckner was enthusiastic, eagerly anticipating the final landing on Japan. After it was over he wanted to get back to his beloved Alaska, where he could retire to his hunting and fishing. He had recently bought a farm at Homer, on the Kenai Peninsula, where he could grow outsize vegetables and berries "as good as Matanuska." The farm abounded in wild life—brown, black and grizzly bears, grouse, ptarmigan, ducks, and geese, trout, salmon, king crabs, and clams.

As he rolled these words off his tongue one day aboard Kelly Turner's flagship off Okinawa, General Buckner told me: "I expect it will take me a solid year to catch up with my hunting and fishing. And I'll be so far away from things I won't be able to exercise a retired general's prerogative of swearing that the new Army has gone to hell since he got out of it." But Simon Bolivar Buckner never got to his happy hunting grounds in Alaska. On June 18, just two days before his Okinawa victory was declared complete, a Jap shell ended his life.

Buckner's successor was the gray-haired, rotund commander of the Third Amphibious Corps, Maj. General Roy Geiger, only Marine ever to command an army. But his command was brief. Soon after Okinawa was secured, General MacArthur relieved him and gave the job to General Joseph Stilwell, who would have led the Tenth Army into Japan. Geiger, promoted to lieutenant general, went back to Hawaii to succeed Holland Smith as Fleet Marine Force commander.

CHAPTER SIXTEEN

ON TO OKINAWA

March 22

"OPERATION ICEBERG" WAS THE NAME GIVEN TO THE OKINAWA invasion by the men who came up with code names. After eleven days in Guam, following my departure from Iwo, I was on the way to "Operation Iceberg." During the two-hour ride on the TAG plane from Guam to Ulithi, I could think of only one thing: Here I am going into another bloody landing, where a lot of fine young men will die, and God knows when it all will end. I had not cherished the idea of going to Okinawa; after Iwo I thought I had seen enough bloodshed for one man to see in a lifetime. But Okinawa looked like the most important operation of them all, the logical conclusion to the Central Pacific campaign—and it is true that war is a horribly fascinating thing, however much a man may hate it.

March 24

Ulithi was one of our big secrets of the later stages in the Pacific war. It had been mentioned casually from time to time, ever since its unopposed capture (by the 323d Regiment of the Eighty-first Infantry Division)[1] was announced in September, 1944, soon after the Peleliu landing. Stories were written about the paralytic king, Ueg, and his 300 natives who lived under the care of a Navy doctor and chief pharmacist's mate on Fassarai, one of the coral sandspits which were strung around the anchorage like so many beads.

[1] Nearby Fais Island, a Jap radio station captured in January, 1945, cost three killed, six wounded.

But the war was nearly over, and the fleet had moved out, before it was possible to write that Ulithi had been the main anchorage of the United States Pacific Fleet.

Ulithi was a series of flat, palm-dotted islands strung onto a necklace-shaped atoll, 110 miles east of Yap (still held by the Japs at the war's end), 400 miles southwest of Guam—and 4,000 miles nearer the war than Pearl Harbor. The great Ulithi anchorage, 112 square miles, could hold nearly 1,000 ships of the United States Fleet.

For Navy purposes there were three main islands: Falalop, out of which a 3,300-foot airstrip was carved to accommodate Marine fighter planes which protected the $20 billion worth of ships, the Navy planes stored there as carrier battle replacements, and the transport planes which shuttled between Guam and Peleliu; Asor, the second island, headquarters of the ATCOM (atoll commander), short, jovial Commodore Oliver Owen (Scrappy") Kessing; and the recreation island, Mogmog, which was in a class by itself. When the fleet was in, Mogmog would sometimes accommodate 15,000 sea-wobbly sailors who had been at sea for weeks or months. On Mogmog they could swim, play basketball, curse the sand and everything else in the tropics, and drink (beer for enlisted men, blended whisky for officers). There was a thatched, 100-foot bar for junior officers, a 50-foot bar for lieutenant commanders and up; a third, and better, lounge (in Chief Ueg's former "palace") with primitive chairs for admirals. In December and January, between carrier strikes on the Philippines and the Asia coast, I had seen as many as 20 admirals there.

But Ulithi's chief function was to supply the fleet with "bombs, beans and bullets." In the anchorage floated the "crockery fleet"—concrete barges storing the million items needed by a thousand ships—the barges were sometimes called "the green dragons." Fast supply ships and fast and slow tankers shuttled from the United States to Ulithi, bringing oil, meat, screws, tires, and flour to these warehouse-barges, which, in turn, unloaded their supplies onto carriers, battleships, cruisers, destroyers, and countless amphibious vessels.

Ulithi was the main base of Service Squadron Ten, "the world's largest naval-supply operation." This morning some correspondents went to call on its boss (COMSERVRON 10), thin, bald Commodore Worrall R. Carter, on board his floating office, the auxiliary ship *Ocelot*. Commodore Carter was proud of Ulithi: "We can do anything a naval base can do."

"Admiral Nimitz calls us his secret weapon," said Commodore Carter. "We've got six types of naval repair ships, one of them for radio and radar alone. Supplies are brought out and unloaded onto the 'crockery fleet.' Then the supply ships scoot right back. Commercial tankers come out and unload into Navy tanks (which go out to meet the fleet), then they scoot back. The Japs didn't belive such an operation was possible; they thought in terms of fixed bases, limiting ships to 1,000- or 1,500-mile range."

Ulithi could drydock no ships larger than destroyers (the floating drydock for battleships was at Manus), but the anchorage had tenders which made emergency repairs on bigger ships like the bomb-blasted carriers *Franklin*, *Ticonderoga*, and *Intrepid*. The badly damaged big ships could be made ready at Ulithi for the trip back to Pearl Harbor or the West Coast.

The necessity for a floating base became apparent when the Navy started its push across the Pacific. Admiral Nimitz had ordered Service Squadron Ten formed in October, 1943. Vice Admiral Calhoun, his supply officer, assigned the job to Carter. Makin had been selected as the first atoll to accommodate the floating base, but plans to use Makin were abandoned. When Kwajalein was captured, one of the unoccupied Marshall atolls, Majuro, was picked for Service Squadron Ten's first home.

"We didn't know much about it at first," said Commodore Carter, "and we had no idea the operation would grow so fast as we stepped up the push across the Pacific. At Majuro we had to have four destroyer tenders; we couldn't get them then, but now we have eight. We asked for 20 small boats; we had 36 before we left Majuro, and now we have over 200. The basic idea of floating bases was not new; we simply had never tried it. Now we are taking care of 600 amphibious ships alone."

The Truk and Palau carrier raids early in 1944 were the first operations serviced by SERVRON 10 at its Majuro base. After Kwajalein, Eniwetok was found to be less heavily defended than had been expected, so this westernmost Marshall atoll was selected as the second main advance base for the service squadron. (For the Marianas operation the Saipan amphibious ships staged from Eniwetok; the carriers and the Guam transports were serviced at Majuro, which continued operating for several months. Majuro declined as Eniwetok, Saipan and Ulithi, farther west, rose in importance.)

"We made some mistakes," Carter confessed; "once we had to unload a thousand tons to get to eight-inch ammunition when it was badly needed in the Marianas for bombardment. Sometimes things looked tight in the Marianas operation. It was delayed, and it was big. We were in the growing stage. We had a temporary shortage of oil; not an actual shortage, but bad timing delayed the oil's arrival. The Marianas was the first amphibious operation SERVRON 10 handled; it wasn't included in the original plan. But now we figure we can handle anything. We've learned about issue loading and we've learned timing.

"We thought it would be risky in these atolls which have so little protection from the weather. Some typhoons have scared hell out of us, but fortunately have caused little damage. We had over 50 knots of wind here last winter, but we lost nothing but small boats. Once we lost a 'crockery fleet' off Saipan."

Just why the Japs paid so little attention to Ulithi we did not know. In November some midget submarines fired torpedoes through an opening in the net guarding the anchorage, and sank a tanker. Not until March 11 did the suicide planes come, though they might have made one-way trips from Truk or the Philippines at any time. Then there were only two. One dived into the carrier *Randolph*. In the twilight the other mistook one of the small islands for a ship, found it unsinkable. After that the Japs left Ulithi alone.

March 25

Today the correspondents learned some details about the invasion of Okinawa. The briefing this time was not aboard Admiral Turner's flagship; the *Eldorado* had gone on to Leyte to accompany the other corps of the Tenth Army (the XXIV). We in Ulithi who were to be assigned to the III Amphibious Corps boarded small boats at Asor Island, and were taken to the *Panamint,* a command ship (AGC), which flew the flag of Rear Admiral Lawrence Reifsnider.

Actually, the operation against Okinawa had begun, although L day was a week away. In Ulithi's big anchorage there was already evidence to indicate that the cost might be high; the correspondents' boat passed the carriers *Enterprise, Wasp,* and *Franklin* which had been hit March 18 and 19 off the coast of Japan, with more than 1,500 casualties. It seemed to us beyond human belief that the shattered *Franklin* could have made port—but there were many times in World War II when the men who man the ships rose to unbelievable heights.

The tall, urbane Admiral Reifsnider greeted the correspondents, and introduced the corps commander, portly Maj. General Roy Geiger. Then he turned the briefing over to his intelligence officer for Task Force 53, Lieut. Commander Samuel R. Sutphin, who explained the strategic significance of Okinawa ("a foot in the door for the final poke at the Japanese Empire"), the gigantic logistical problem (6,200 miles from San Francisco, even 1,200 from Saipan or Ulithi, but only 330 from the Japanese home islands), and the unprecedented danger from Japanese airpower ("there are at least 100 airfields within range of Okinawa").

"This is the biggest thing yet attempted in the Pacific," said Sutphin, "all the forces available in the Western Pacific are involved except those in the Philippines and the Aleutians. The 20th Bomber Command in China is furnishing weather reports. The 21st Bomber Command in the Marianas is operating against Honshu, and especially Tokyo, from L minus 22 to L minus 6. The Fourteenth Air Force in China started flying search and reconnaissance, and neutralizing Canton and Hongkong, on L minus 14. The B-24's of the Strategic Air Force have as their mission the neutralizing of the Nansei Shoto. The Army Air Force in the Southwest Pacific is neutralizing Formosa with B-24's and B-25's and keeping 55 airfields knocked out. It is also stopping shipping off the China coast.

"The British Navy joins up with us on this one. A task group consisting of two battleships, four carriers, two light cruisers, three anti-aircraft cruisers, and eleven destroyers will hit Sakashima Gunto off northern Formosa from L minus 6 to L Day, and on L minus 4 the British will also bombard Miyako Jima. Task Force 58, which is already operating in Japanese waters, will go in close against Kyushu to cover the landings. The fast carriers are protecting the minesweepers now as they move into the target. Okinawa is heavily mined, something like the North Sea in the last war.

"The submarines are patrolling the outlets to the Inland Sea. We will land on the Hagushi beaches on the lower west coast of Okinawa. On L minus 8 actual fire support began when a squadron of old battleships and light and heavy cruisers and destroyers began shelling the beaches. On L minus 6 the western attack force hits Kerama Retto,[2] the islands just southwest of Okinawa, which we don't think are heavily defended; there are a copper mine and a populaton of about 4,000 on Tokashiki. The Seventy-Seventh Division is landing on the islands to reconnoiter them. Kerama Retto gives us an immediate protective anchorage for re-arming and refueling, and a seaplane base; we expect to have PBM's operating there by L minus 3.

"On L minus 3 the underwater demolition teams start clearing the approaches to the western beaches. On L minus 1, one battalion of 155's and one of 240's go into Keise Shima, off the southwest corner of the island, to set up long-range land-based artillery which can cover almost all the landing area. The Seventy-seventh Division is handling that job, also. April 1 is 'Love Day,—that is, L Day, the official designation for the Okinawa landing."

Sutphin explained that Okinawa would be rugged terrain for fighting. "It is very mountainous, with steep, sharp hills from north to south. The entire island is reef-bound, with reefs as bad as any—like Saipan and Guam—250 to 550 yards wide, and loaded with niggerheads. There is not much water over the reefs; the timing of the amphibious tractors will be difficult. The beaches are small and shallow, and the exits from them are not good. There are terrible swells, but the weather odds—sea, surf and swell—are two to one in our favor. There has not been a typhoon in April in ten years.

"The landings will be from Point Bolo (Zampa Misaki) along the beach southward to a point three miles north of the principal city, Naha, which has a population of 65,000— or had. The III Corps will land on the northern half of the landing beach, the XXIV Corps on the south. On

[2] "Retto" means a small group of islands.

L Day a demonstration group consisting of the Second Marine Division will sail up and pretend to start landing on the south coast of Okinawa, to draw the Japanese troops down there.

"Okinawa will be the first heavily inhabited enemy island we have invaded. The population is about 450,000, and we have no reason to believe they are any different people from the mainland Japanese. We expect resistance to be most fanatical."

After Lieut. Commander Sutphin had finished, Colonel Walter H. Wachtler, the bald, drawling operations officer for General Geiger's III Corps, continued the briefing. The troops on Okinawa, the Tenth Army, would be under the command of Lieut. General Simon B. Buckner, consisting of the III Corps and Maj. General John R. Hodge's XXIV Corps. The III had in it the First Marine Division (Maj. General Pedro del Valle) and the Sixth Marine Division (Maj. General Lemuel Shepherd). The XXIV Corps was made up of the Seventh Infantry Division (Maj. General Archibald Arnold) and the Ninety-Sixth Infantry Division (Maj. General James L. Bradley). The Seventy-Seventh Division, whose primary duty was securing various small but vital islands around Okinawa, was commanded by Maj. General Andrew Bruce. In addition, there were two divisions, the Second Marine (Maj. General Thomas Watson), in floating reserve at the target, and the Twenty-Seventh Infantry Division (Maj. General George Griner), in floating reserve at Ulithi.

Said Colonel Wachtler: "The two assault corps will land simultaneously abreast, III on the left XXIV on the right. In the III Corps sector the Sixth Marine Division will land on the left, the First Marine Division on the right; in the XXIV Corps sector the Seventh Division will land on the left, the Ninety-sixth on the right. The main effort will be made on the right [the southern end of Okinawa], since most of the enemy is supposed to be in the south. But it may develop that a large percentage is in the III Corps area.

"The initial objective is to drive rapidly across the island and to pocket the enemy force. The Sixth Division will pinch out the Yontan Airfield. Phase One ends at the neck of Chimu Wan. Beyond that, it depends on what the Japs do. There are supposed to be 65,000 Jap troops on Okinawa, at least 16,000 of them in the III Corps sector. But there is some controversy over that.

"We do not know whether the civilians will be armed. We suspect there are a police force and a home guard made up of natives. We know there are caves by the thousands, and pillboxes, bunkers, and trenches. The defense will be tough—and probably worse than that. The terrain is most difficult. The latest photos indicate prepared artillery positions of 24 guns each; the Japs may be considering the employment of mass artillery for the first time."

At the end of the briefing, nobody could have felt overconfident. "Scrappy" Kessing had arranged a farewell party back on Asor Island for the correspondents, and it was welcome. There was a band and there were even women—about 70 nurses from the six hospital ships in the anchorage, plus two women radio operators from a Norwegian ship.

March 26

At 0900 the correspondents boarded picket boats at the Asor Island dock, preparatory to leaving for their assigned ships. Commodore Kessing had a Negro sailors' band playing their own "boogie-woogie" version of sad farewell music. The commodore himself came down to see the forty-odd correspondents and photographers take off for the next landing. So did Lieutenant L. A. Newcomber, commander of the Sixth Special Seabee detachment which had built most of Ulithi's installations, and Coast Guard Commander Jack Dempsey, the former heavyweight champion.

"Keep your head down, Ernie," somebody shouted at Ernie Pyle, the great little man who had seen so much of the European war before coming to the Pacific to land on Okinawa with the First Marine Division. "Listen, you bastards," said Ernie to a group of reporters in one of the picket boats, "I'll take a drink over every one of your graves." Then he turned to Jack Dempsey, who weighed approximately twice as much as he did, and put up his fists in mock belligerence: "Want to fight?"

The picket boats made the rounds of the various transports in the anchorage, dropping off one correspondent here, another there, until all had been distributed. Jay Eyerman, the *Life* photographer, and I had been assigned to the Coast Guard transport *Cambria,* which carried the headquarters of the Sixth Marine Division.

The Sixth was already considered a prime outfit. As a division, it was going into action for the first time, but a little more than half of its men were veterans. The 4th Regiment, commanded by one of Annapolis's great athletes, Colonel Alan Shapley, was 70 per cent veterans; it was formed by the old Raider battalions which became famous in the South Pacific war, and, according to one estimate, included two complete All-American football teams. The 22nd Regiment (Colonel Merlin F. Schneider) was scarcely less famous. It had fought well at Eniwetok and, teamed with the 4th as the First Provisional Brigade, had spearheaded the invasion of Guam in July, 1944. The 29th Marines (Colonel Victor F. Bleasdale) had been added for the Okinawa invasion as the third infantry regiment of the new Sixth Marine Division, but not even the 29th was completely green; the First Battalion, 29th, had fought with the Second Division at Saipan and had captured the peak of Mount Tapotchau.

Commodore Herbert Knowles, the crusty veteran of

twelve amphibious landings who had his transport squadron flag on the *Cambria*, said of the Sixth's headquarters: "There is the smoothest working staff I've ever seen. They know what they want; they know how to load a ship. They don't have to go ask the general every time a decision has to be made."

Maj. General Lemuel Shepherd, the division commander, had indeed gathered an excellent group around him. His assistant division commander, Brig. General William T. ("Johnny") Clement, had been on Corregidor from the beginning of the war until he came out on one of the last submarines. Then he had served in London and, recently, as commandant of Marine Corps Schools at Quantico, Virginia. Shepherd's red-headed chief of staff was Colonel John C. McQueen, who had been a staff officer in the Pacific since the war's beginning and had served with Holland Smith at San Diego and in the Aleutians.

The Sixth Division operations officer, Lieut. Colonel Victor H. Krulak, was, like all Naval Academy coxswains, called "Brute." A stocky blonde about five feet five inches tall, Krulak had commanded a parachute battalion in the non-airborne Choiseul invasion, where he reportedly stuck razor blades into the trunks of palm trees to discourage tree-climbing Japanese snipers. Of Okinawa, the "Brute" was fond of saying: "Now we're getting into the residential area. The Japs may decide to fight the Battle of Japan here."

General Shepherd had many competent staff officers, including Lieut. Colonel Thomas E. Williams of Intelligence, a reserve who had been on duty since 1940; Lieut. Colonel August Larson, a big, lumbering, but smartly efficient supply officer; Lieut. Colonel Elby D. Martin, Jr., signal officer, Major Eliott B. Robertson, who had to build more roads—in the Sixth's northward Okinawa push—than any other Marine engineer of the Pacific war; Captain Don S. Knowlton, the division surgeon, and many others. Shepherd had chosen his staff carefully, and he had built up one of the best I saw in the war against Japan.

Even before he received a division command, Virginia-born "Lem" Shepherd was considered one of the "fair-haired" officers of the Marine Corps. He had attended Virginia Military Institute, had come out of World War I with a Navy Cross, a DSC and two Silver Stars. In 1935 he commanded the Marine detachment at President Roosevelt's Warm Springs, Georgia, home.

Shepherd had been regimental commander of the 9th Marines of the Third Division in 1943. At Cape Gloucester he was assistant commander of the First Division, and as a brigadier general he welded the 4th and 22d Marines into the First Provisional Brigade for the Guam invasion. He had also commanded the Marine Corps Schools, where he enhanced his reputation at a teacher of tactics; he was always known as a "schools man." His friends believed that Shepherd's uniformly high standard of performance, plus his general popularity, marked him as a likely candidate for Marine Corps Commandant.

March 28

The Seventy-seventh Division's landings on Kerama Retto were reported successful. Tokashiki had been secured, and on Aka the fighting was reduced to sniping; on Zamami there was still sporadic opposition. Enemy killed were estimated at 292 (an incomplete figure), and the number of prisoners was 49, including one officer. Twelve women had been found strangled in a cave, and one was found buried alive. The Kerama Retto seaplane base was already established, and the first planes were due tomorrow.

Many Jap suicide boats were, as we had feared, in evidence. They were described as 20 feet long, armed with a mine or bomb, and manned by one man.[3] Between 15 and 20 suicide

[3] Generally, the suicide boats were a failure at Okinawa. The Japs evidently had counted heavily on them. More than 350 were found in Kerama Retto alone.

planes attacked the naval force on the 26th and 27th, and twelve were shot down, while six crashed into our ships. Floating mines had been found in waters west of Okinawa. A carrier pilot had been shot down over Okinawa, had been rescued by a destroyer and observation planes. He reported that the Japs on Okinawa were directing artillery fire from caves in the ground. (There was no doubt in our minds that the Japs intended to put up a terrific fight for Okinawa.) The suicide planes were going to be a problem beyond anything we had yet faced; already a minesweeper had been sunk, two destroyers had been hit, and the battleship *Nevada's* Number 3 turret had been knocked out (eleven killed, 49 wounded). The aerial photographic officers had revised upward their estimate of the number of Jap troops on Okinawa, to 70,000.

I spent several hours listening to Radio Tokyo, which was already claiming the sinking of a battleship, six cruisers, seven destroyers, and a minesweeper. The two "Zero Hour" announcers (both men) interspersed their claims with banter and with recorded music. "The Zero Hour," one of them said, "is broadcast for all you American fighting men in the Pacific, particularly those standing off the shores of Okinawa, because many of you will never hear another program."

"Here is a good number for you boys, 'Going Home'; it's nice work if you can get it . . . Here's one for the boys off Okinawa; listen and enjoy it while you can, because when you're dead, you're a long time dead . . . A little juke-box music for the boys and make it hot, because the boys are going to catch hell soon, and they might as well get used to the heat."

The Japs' radio propaganda was not very successful. The few sailors who sat around the communications room acted as bored as men who had seen a Grade B movie three times. "Don't fail to tune in again tomorrow night," said the Japanese announcer, who had just told the sailors that they would not be alive by tomorrow.

March 29

It was not difficult to understand why the Navy considered Okinawa the most important target of the Pacific war. The mileage chart (in nautical miles, of course) was impressive. From Naha, Okinawa's capital, the distance to Pearl Harbor was 4,040, to Saipan 1,210, Guam 1,230, Iwo Jima 740, Manila 790. But enemy-held territory was mighty close: Shanghai 450, Hongkong 780, Formosa 330, Kagoshima (on Kyushu 360, Nagasaki (on Kyushu) 410, Korea 540, Tokyo 845. There were plenty of bases from which *kamikaze* planes could be flown against our ships off Okinawa.

Okinawa, the intelligence booklets told us, was 60 miles long, three to ten miles wide. Two possible fleet anchorages were Nakagusuku Wan (Bay) and Chimu Wan. Eighty per cent of the northern two-thirds of the island was heavily wooded; the same area of the southern one-third was planted in sugarcane and sweet potatoes. The island abounded in flies, mosquitoes, mites, rats, and poisonous snakes. Among the Marines on the *Cambria* the snakes probably caused more concern than the Japs; the deadly *habu's* bite was supposed to be immediately fatal,[4] and the habu, in photographs, was a very wicked looking creature.

March 30

Today, L minus 2, Radio Tokyo raised its claims of sinkings to 30 ships, including ten battleships, six cruisers, ten destroyers, and two transports. Casualties on ships off Okinawa already amounted to 33,000, said the voice from Tokyo, adding angrily: "The American people did not want this war, but the authorities told them it would take only a short while and would result in a higher standard of living. But the life of the average American citizen is becoming harder and harder and the war is far from won . . . No

---

[4] It developed that Intelligence was overly concerned. Late in the Okinawa battle some Marines finally found a *habu,* cut it into filets, fried and ate it.

amount of air raids can weaken the will of the Japanese people, and when the American Navy comes to the shores of Japan . . ."

It was only a day and a half until H Hour, and the ship began rolling in moderate seas. "How is the weather?" was a question anxiously asked dozens of times a day. A typhoon, or even a slight shift in the weather, could cost 10,000 lives. In all the Central Pacific invasions we were favored by fine D-Day weather—but there still could be a first time . . .

One of the underwater demolition men, Lieutenant Charles H. Withey, reported on what was found on the Sixth Division beaches when his men swam into shore under covering gunfire yesterday: Pillboxes behind the beaches by the hundreds, small arms fire from everywhere, and very few exits from the beaches which our vehicles could use. The underwater demolition teams had already cleared most of the posts from the shallow water.

From Kerama Retto the Seventy-seventh Division now reported killing 331 Japs and capturing 100, including the lieutenant in charge of the suicide-boat unit. He told his captors there were 700 suicide boats in Okinawa. The Seventy-seventh reported its own casualties as 29 killed, one missing, 78 wounded. Another intelligence report told us that the destroyer *Halligan,* sunk four days ago by a mine, had only one officer and 150 men to survive.

March 31

Late in the afternoon, when we were about 50 miles south of the southern tip of Okinawa, and preparing to turn west of Kerama Retto, many more ships which had been out of sight came into view. Six escort carriers appeared to the right of Commodore Knowles's four columns of ships. Astern of the Sixth Division's transports were the 24 transports carrying the First Marine Division. Farther back were the transports which had brought the Seventh and Ninety-sixth

Divisions from Leyte. Our protecting destroyers extended far into the horizon on either side.

The weather had turned much warmer. Visibility was unlimited, and the sea was smooth as glass. We sailed into a setting sun obscured only by a thin line of slate-gray clouds. "Looks like a typical Hawaiian evening," said one of Knowles's staff lieutenants as we watched the peaceful end of L minus 1, "but tomorrow a lot of good men are going to be dead."

Aboard the *Cambria* there was the usual final preparation for going into combat. Men packed and repacked their gear, oiled their rifles for the last time, donned their battle dress, and counted the invasion currency which had been issued them; it was a new experience, counting in yen and sen. The message from General Shepherd was read over the "bullhorn" by his provost marshal, Lieut. Colonel Floyd Stephenson. It was simple and brief. The key sentence: "I know you men of the Sixth Division will uphold the proud traditions of your Corps." The ship's chaplain, Father Keating, and the division chaplain, a red-headed Episcopalian, Donald Mayberry, said brief prayers which did not dwell too long on the prospect of imminent death for their listeners.

CHAPTER SEVENTEEN

THE UNBELIEVABLE LANDING

April 1

NOTHING STRANGER OCCURRED IN THE PACIFIC WAR THAN THE Tenth Army's Easter Sunday landings on Okinawa. Soldiers and Marines stepped ashore with slightly more opposition than they would have had in maneuvers off the coast of California. Merely to say that they were bewildered was to gild the lily of understatement.

Where was the withering machine-gun fire? Where were the 320-mm. mortars, the nine-inch rockets? Where were the Japs? They were not defending the west coast of Okinawa, from Zampa Misaki down toward Naha.

But the suicide planes were at work. One came over at 0130, seven hours before H hour, and was shot down by one of our destroyers. There was another General Quarters aboard the *Cambria* at 0515. By the time I reached topside a plane was burning on the water, a mile ahead. At 0530 another Jap plane was shot down by our Combat Air Patrol, Commodore Knowles informed me. At 0605 I saw a flaming plane plummet toward the water three miles to port. Many times before daylight the sky around us was pierced by anti-aircraft tracer bullets, but no enemy plane got within shooting distance of the *Cambria*. The Japs caused some damage to our ships; the transport *Hinsdale* and two LST's, all carrying troops of the Second Marine Division which was making the demonstration south of Okinawa, had been hit. But casualties were light.

In the division's operations room aboard ship, the news dawned on us slowly. The leading waves of amphtracs hit the beach at 0837. The new T-6 tanks, with their 30-foot-long pontoons which were blown off by a small explosive charge when the tanks reached water shallow enough, had trouble at first, but they were soon reported landing in order. At 0846 the first two waves of 2/22 were reported on the beach, without having been fired upon, but that message could have been a mistake.

A few minutes later the 22d Marines were reported moving off the beach without casualties; the 4th Marines' command post was on the way into the beach; at 0920 the reserve battalion of Schneider's regiment was ordered to land and close the gap between the two assault battalions, and the First Division troops on Yellow Beach were reported 400 yards inland and standing up. Then we knew we had made an unopposed landing on the island that was supposed to have been tougher than Iwo.

With the Seventh and Ninety-Sixth Divisions farther south the story was the same—one assault battalion of the veteran Seventh (of Attu, Kwajalein, Leyte) had landed alongside a seawall; its men stepped from their amphtracs as easily as if they had been on a pleasant fishing trip. Then the Seventh had knocked out a solitary machine-gun pocket and captured Katena Airfield.

The capture of Yontan Airfield was accomplished by the 4th Marines with a few shots from isolated snipers. Casualties: two killed, nine wounded. At 1000 I wrote in my notebook: "This is hard to believe."

Just why the Jap general decided to abandon the beaches we did not learn immediately. Possibly he expected reinforcements; perhaps he had been badly deceived by the demonstration of the transports and landing craft at the southern tip of the island; but it seemed impossible that he could have been fooled so badly. Did he think we planned only a perimeter beachhead, as we had established at Bougainville? Did he withdraw to the south because his defenses were stronger there, as he proved amply in the next twelve

OKINAWA

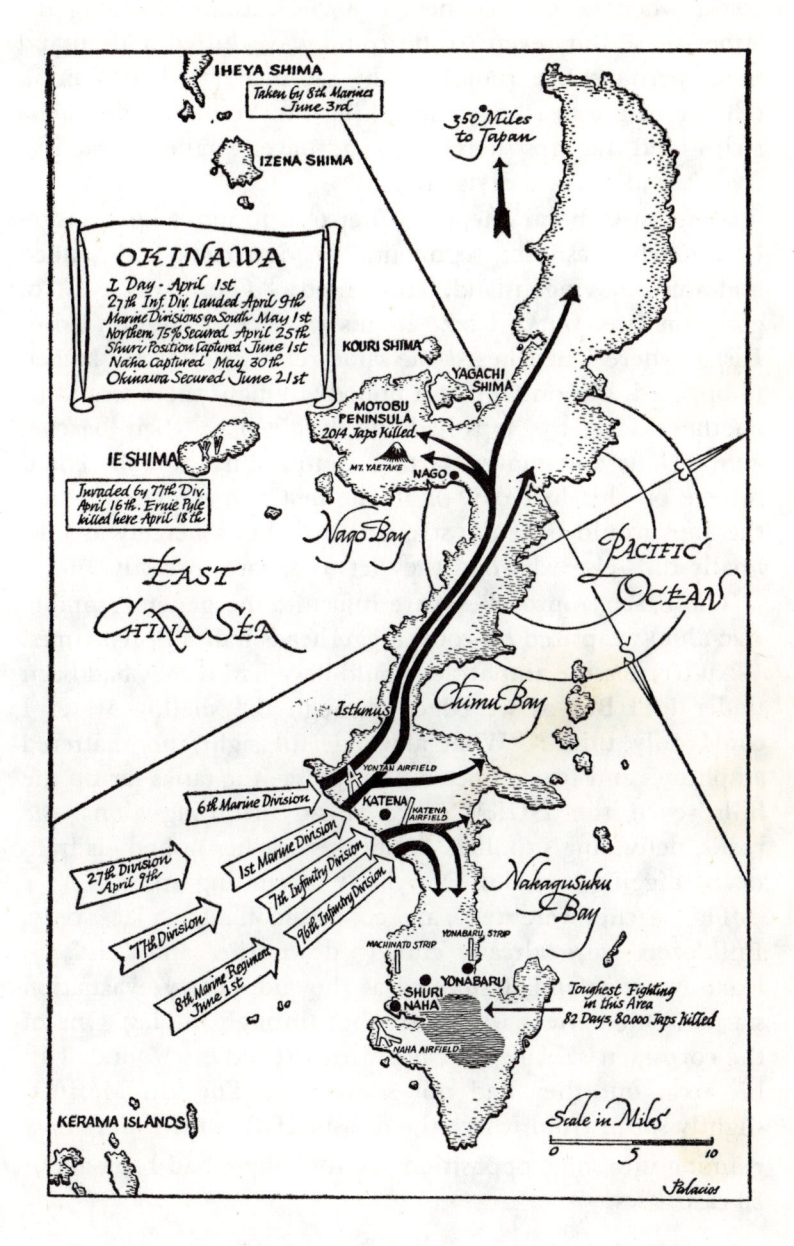

L Day - April 1st
27th Inf. Div. Landed April 9th
Marine Divisions go South May 1st
Northern 75% Secured April 25th
Shuri Position Captured June 1st
Naha Captured May 30th
Okinawa Secured June 21st

IHEYA SHIMA — Taken by 8th Marines June 3rd

IZENA SHIMA

350 Miles to Japan

KOURI SHIMA

YAGACHI SHIMA

MOTOBU PENINSULA 2014 Japs Killed
MT. YAETAKE
NAGO

IE SHIMA — Invaded by 77th Div. April 16th. Ernie Pyle killed here April 18th

Nago Bay

EAST CHINA SEA

PACIFIC OCEAN

Isthmus

Chimu Bay

YONTAN AIRFIELD
KATENA / KATENA AIRFIELD

6th Marine Division
27th Division April 9th
1st Marine Division
7th Infantry Division
77th Division
96th Infantry Division
8th Marine Regiment June 1st

Nakagusuku Bay

MACHINATO STRIP
YONABARU STRIP
SHURI
NAHA
YONABARU
NAHA AIRFIELD

Toughest Fighting in this Area
82 Days, 80,000 Japs Killed

KERAMA ISLANDS

Scale in Miles
0   5   10

Palacios

weeks when he exacted nearly 40,000 casualties among the Americans? But, even so, he could have killed a thousand men, perhaps five thousand, by sacrificing a battalion in defense of the beaches approaching the Yontan and Katena strips—and the Japs theretofore had never quailed at sacrificing a battalion, or a division.

At noon General Shepherd prepared to move his division headquarters ashore; regimental headquarters had landed and were moving inland. He smiled: "There was a lot of glory on Iwo, but I'll take it this way." I was reminded of Kiska, where I had heard the same remarks after we landed unopposed. But on Okinawa nobody thought there would be another Kiska; the Japs had simply given up their beaches above Naha and moved farther south. What nobody could foresee on this first day, or in the first two weeks, was that the Japs would have the strength to fight as fiercely as they finally did—else why had they let us ashore so easily?

The beach approaches were difficult; the general's amphtrac almost capsized on coral niggerheads half a dozen times. What trouble the amphtracs would have had if they had been under fire! But as we edged through the shallow water I could only think: "What a wonderful sight; no shattered amphtracs and broken boats. We can see the tanks far up the hills; even the DUKW's are already running along the roads, delivering supplies. Along the beaches nobody is frantically digging foxholes. Everybody is standing up."

The beaches were steep, and accessible in a few places only. Bulldozers were already cutting down the sandy cliffs to make roads inland. I stopped at the shore-party evacuation station. One patient was there, shot through the leg. One of the corpsmen said he had heard of two others wounded in his area, but they had not shown up. The 4th Marines, slightly south from where the division CP landed, were now running into some opposition; by 1300 there had been about 30 casualties.

The bizarre feature of the low hillsides was the hundreds of burial vaults. These keystone-shaped vaults, of coral blocks, were built into the hillsides. They were neatly kept, about ten feet by ten feet, and about six feet high. Inside each vault there were steps, and on these steps were placed ironware or earthenware urns, 18 to 36 inches high. In these urns the Okinawans deposited the skulls and bones of departed relatives. Just inside the entrance of one of the vaults there was a small casket made of slats. It contained the body of a recently dead Okinawan. After three years, the Intelligence booklet had told us, the natives gathered the bones and placed them in the urns.

The soil near the beachhead was poor, a thin layer of topsoil over coral, in which potatoes, stunted sugarcane, and a wheatlike grain were planted. Open-air fishermen's shacks were hung with nets beneath roofs made of bamboo sticks and mud covered with red tile. The only smell of death on the Marines' beachhead came from two goats which had been killed several days ago by bombs. The hundreds of goats which remained alive were scrubs, not more than half-size. Okinawa was not a rich country, we could see.

The first Okinawans we saw confirmed this impression. By mid-afternoon hundreds of civilians began pouring through the American lines. These were not the fanatical civilian opposition we had half expected; these were the most miserable people, I thought, who inhabited the earth. They averaged no more than five feet in height. They were undernourished beyond description. They seemed much darker than most Japs I had seen, and the old men usually had heavy beards, denoting their hairy Ainu ancestry. One 70-year-old man was one of the most pitiable of God's creatures. He had been bayoneted by the Japs, I was told, before they evacuated Hanza village. Like many of the Okinawans, he wore a filthy blue smock. As a medical corpsman treated him, he tried repeatedly to rise from the stretcher, in an unknowing, fearful manner.

Among the surrendering Okinawans, however, one ominous feature was noticeable; there were no young men, and very few young women. Willingly or not, the able-bodied Okinawans undoubtedly had been conscripted. "They are all under six or over sixty," commented Lieutenant Spencer Silverthorne, one of the Sixth Division's Japanese-language experts.

In mid-afternoon I found the command post of husky, blue-eyed Colonel Alan Shapley. "This is a happy Easter," he said; "what the hell do you make of it! No mines, practically no snipers, the anti-aircraft guns were dummies. We had hoped to take the airfield some time tomorrow. So what? We walk aross it standing up."

Colonel Shapley was moving his CP a mile farther inland and northward, to the end of the Yontan Airfield. I walked with him. The Jap pillboxes we saw were only half-heartedly constructed of scrub-pine logs, lightly covered over with sand and coral. (How different from the pillboxes of Tarawa and Iwo!). They seemed to have been abandoned long ago. As we reached the top of a low hill we turned and looked at the scene off Okinawa's western beaches. There were about a thousand of the 1,400 ships involved in the Okinawa operation. As far as we could see there was the sheer power America had finally brought to bear against Japan.

"Some of my men were disappointed because there was no opposition on the beaches," said Shapley; "they had been built up to a high pitch of combat efficiency, and they were bound to feel let down. But they will get a bellyful of fighting before this thing is over."

Around the edges of Yontan Airfield lay a dozen blasted and strafed and shattered and burned Jap planes. Inside the domed coral hangars—one plane to the hangar—were several other planes which had been unable to hide from low-level strafing attacks. The airfield itself was barely pockmarked, and the engineers would have it ready for landings after a few hours' work.

It was 1600 before I saw a jeep ambulance bearing a wounded Marine from the front lines, on the hillside beyond the airfield. He had been shot by a sniper. The corpsman attending the wounded man said he had already administered two bottles of plasma.

On the way back to division headquarters I noticed a stunted Okinawan horse which was carrying a grinning Marine's pack. "The first real pack horse I've ever known," one of the Marines guffawed. On "Love Day" on Okinawa men could laugh.

My deadline was next day, so at 1900 I headed out to a ship to write my story about the Okinawa landing. It was no use. Half a mile offshore the ships in the harbor began to pierce the sky in a million places with the mightiest night display of anti-aircraft fire I had seen. The transports put out their smoke boats, which soon had a wall of fog over the area. Every sailor on a thousand ships had been alerted against Jap suicide boats, and I was not eager to try, after dark in a small boat, to get through that smoke. I spent the night on a little LCC control boat, Number PA52-49.

Captain Walter Zebkowski, the corps liaison officer who was with me, agreed that it probably was a wise decision. Throughout the night there was sporadic firing into the water from various ships. On our LCC the sailor on guard with a tommy gun had a fine time. Whenever an object drifted nearby he fired a dozen rounds or so, just to make sure. The object always turned out to be seaweed.

April 2

When I arrived aboard the *Eldorado* I learned that suicide planes had hit several ships last night, including the old battleship *West Virginia*. The Japs' failure to defend the west beaches was as much a mystery as ever. Admiral Turner only smiled wisely, and said: "We hit 'em where they ain't, although they had been there."

Some staff theorists believed the transport demonstration off the south beaches, coupled with heavy naval gunfire on the eastern beaches, had really pulled the Japs away from the western beaches. One of the civilian internees (an unreliable breed) said the Japs had deserted the western beaches only on the afternoon before we landed. Another said the Japs had made up their minds last October that when we landed, we would land on the southern beaches; therefore, those were most heavily defended.

In the afternoon, when I had filed my copy with Commander Paul Smith, Turner's public-relations officer, I went over to the *Cambria*, which was anchored not far from the *Eldorado*. By 1500 on L plus 1 there were only 19 wounded in the *Cambria's* sick bay, and only one of these was a serious case. In the entire transport squadron there were but 55. What a contrast with Iwo at the same stage!

April 3

At General Shepherd's new command post in one of the small villages I learned that the 4th Marines were running into stiffer opposition as they drove inland over the wooded hills. One of the regiment's outstanding company commanders, Thad N. Dodds, had been killed last night, and another, Nelson Dale, had been reported wounded. Total casualties in the regiment were about 100, a third of them in a single platoon; 265 Japs had been killed.

Shortly after noon, with Correspondents Alwyn Lee and Jay Eyerman, I set out to join the division reconnaissance company in what might have been a minor mission or a major fight. The company was assigned to proceed north, then to cut across the narrow neck of the island to Ishikawa, or until it ran into major opposition. In other words, the company was to find out where the Japs were.

The company loaded onto tanks and into amphtracs along the western shore road, and started north. About three-quarters of these Marines were new men, though their tall, husky company commander, Major Anthony Walker, the only Yale man I ever knew with a bulldog jaw, had been a Raider in Colonel James Roosevelt's old battalion. The 18-year-old Marine in the amphtrac next to me complained: "Not a man in the company has fired a shot yet; all we did was take about 500 civilian prisoners yesterday." I said maybe he would get to shoot on this trip. He said, "I hope so; I'm tired of carrying all this ammunition."

We passed through three small villages made up of thatched huts, which had burned, and tile-roofed huts, which hadn't. The Okinawa rolling hills were intensively cultivated, and they made quite a pretty picture. As we pushed up the narrow road I was struck by one sight. A presumably bloodthirsty Marine, on his way to kill the enemy, leaped off an amphtrac and ran ahead. Then he picked up a little goat before the amphtrac ran over him, and tossed the animal lightly to the safety of an embankment, where he landed on both feet. Again, the column slowed while the lead tank came almost to a halt, in order to let an old, old man cross the road. This litttle old man was barefoot. He was dressed in a straw hat, a blue coat, and no trousers whatsoever. Over his shoulder he carried a stick to which was tied a small bundle wrapped in a very dirty scarf.

Farther up the road we stopped to talk to another old man. The interpreter said his name was Tonaki Takara, his age 67, and he had been a school teacher. Mr. Takara told us there were no Jap troops between us and Ishikawa, but he was wrong.

When we turned east to go inland and across the island, the recon company executive officer, Lieutenant William J. Christie, of Orange, New Jersey, passed along the instructions: "Everybody get down now. If we run across anything, clear the amphtrac and attack from the sides." One of the Marines in our amphtrac said, "I guess this is it." Christie said to me while the column was stopped, "Did the general tell you what to expect?" I said yes. He said, "Well, we don't know what to expect, but I believe we'll soon run into some Japs." It was not very reassuring. The Japs would undoubtedly be in ambush. We were wide-open targets, sent out as such to feel out the enemy.

Before we had progressed a mile after turning east we found that the road had been blown up. The Marines unloaded and went forward on foot. But such an emergency had been foreseen. A tank 'dozer, one of the great American weapons of the Pacific war, chuffed up, lowered its blade, and within a few minutes the road was filled in and vehicular traffic was resumed.

When we were nearly three-quarters of the way across the Ishikawa Neck, Major Walker ordered the company to unload again. Then he assigned the platoons to spread out for about 300 yards on either side of the road, and walk through the undergrowth. The procedure resembled nothing so much as a quail hunt, without dogs.

It was 1700 and the sun was low. Major Walker said, "I'm going back; it's too late to start a fight tonight." He had no more than spoken when a Nambu machine gun started chattering. We looked to a hill about 600 yards to our right, and there, plainly outlined on the hilltop, were several hundred Japs. They did not attempt to conceal themselves. They just looked, and we just looked.

Then the Japs started firing in earnest. The first mortar shell went "ker-whi-i-ip!" about 50 yards beyond the road where the tanks and amphtracs had been parked. Another hit a little closer. The recon company scurried to its vehicles, which swung around quickly and headed back whence they had come. As the tanks and amphtracs rumbled westward, the Japs kept firing. Their aim was very poor. None of the 25 mortar shells they threw at our column came within 25 yards of the road. I was very glad to accomplish our mission and retire, even if not very gracefully. We had found the Nips and the two battalions of the 22nd Marines, which had followed us, could take care of them tomorrow much better than our single company could tonight.

On the way back our amphtrac explored a new road and got itself bogged in a rice paddy. In the hillsides near the rice paddy there were dozens of caves in which the Japs had stored rice and much ammunition. Why they had deserted such defenses baffled us more than ever.

General Shepherd was pleased with the progress of the operation. The 4th and 22nd Marines had covered almost as much ground today as on the previous two days. Supplies were being unloaded rapidly. The First Marine Division was almost all the way across the island, and the Seventh Infantry Division was "already dangling its feet off the seawall on the other side." The Ninety-Sixth, which had the extreme right flank, was finding opposition more intense as it probed in the direction of Naha. The Sixth Division's L plus 10 line was reached this morning. Artillery observation planes were already using one of the runways on Yontan Airfield, and the first Grumman fighter from a carrier had made an emergency landing.

April 4

"Colonel, please send us a dead Jap. A lot of my men have never seen one. We'll bury him for you," said Lieut. Colonel James Brower, the 12th (artillery) Marines' executive officer, this morning to Gus Larson, the supply officer. That was how scarce the Japs seemed on the fourth day on Okinawa.

General Shepherd and Colonel Larson made an inspection trip around the Sixth Division beaches this morning, and I went along. The trip was a revelation. The Americans' superb engineering equipment had transformed the beaches. The underwater coral niggerheads which had partly obstructed the approaches to Okinawa had been blasted by demolition men. DUKWS and amphtracs were chugging ashore, ladden with supplies. LST's and LSM's hung their ramps on the coral beaches, and many vehicles poured out with ammunition, water, food, switchboards, power plants, tents, troops, and typewriters.

No longer were the smoothest beaches the only unloading points. Where there had been steep sand dunes, even cliffs, there were now double-laned gradual inclines, thanks to the bulldozers. Scaling ladders brought ashore in the assault waves were now telephone poles. The DUKWS and amphtracs were now going far inland to unload their cargo; the front lines had advanced so far northward a heavy strain had been placed on the supply lines. All along the beaches the pioneer battalion of Lieut. Colonel Samuel Shaw was organized with assembly-line efficiency.

"These are the men who never get the credit they deserve," said Shepherd; "the men up front have a better chance of getting some rest early in the battle. Most of these men have not slept for three days, but they know they are doing a job that's got to be done." The general proudly watched his working men, pondered a few minutes, and said, "You know, we ought to take a couple of armies from here and go straight to Japan pretty soon; they can't stop us."

We stopped at one of the civilian camps where the miserable, downtrodden Okinawans were kept in custody until it was safe to return them to their homes. Of 1,200 in this particular camp, 500 were in the process of being sent back to their thatched huts and their few square yards of farmland, their stunted goats and pony-sized horses. Many of the Okinawans had leprosy, and many others suffered from lifelong malnutritional diseases. Perhaps one in a hundred of the internees showed a trace of belligerence; one woman said, defiantly, "My son is in the Army in Japan." Even those who had believed the Japs when they said the barbarous Americans would murder them were now grateful for the food they received: captured Jap rice, some K and C rations. One gold-toothed woman of about 50 clasped her hands under her chin and bowed low as she thanked the general for the treatment she had received.

General Shepherd stopped at the division cemetery, where a working detail was digging graves with picks and shovels. To me this was something new; every battle I had seen in the Pacific produced so many casualties so quickly that graves had to be dug with bulldozers. Four men of the Sixth Division had been buried; 17 other shroud-covered bodies lay on stretchers nearby, awaiting burial. At the graveyard site the sparse soil was mostly coral and the digging was tedious, hard work. The general thought of moving the cemetery, but this was so pretty a spot, with a view westward to the sea beyond the low, rolling hills, he did not give the order. I never found out whether the Sixth Division cemetery was moved, but I felt sure it was. Before Okinawa was over, more than 1,500 of the division's men had given their lives in its capture. But on this fourth day nobody could foresee the terrible weeks that lay ahead.

April 6

The weather had finally turned. Rough weather had slowed the landing of supplies to almost nothing on the fifth day. But the first four days had been sensational: the Tenth Army had hoped to unload 25,000 to 30,000 tons each day, but had actually unloaded an average of 60,000 tons. The transports and LST's were about four-fifths discharged. Casualties in the five divisions on Okinawa, including the island-hopping Seventy-seventh, were reported at 175 killed and less than 1,000 wounded.

By this time it was obvious that the Japs would make their initial major effort against our ships anchored off Okinawa. About 40 ships had been hit, including Admiral Spruance's flagship, the *Indianapolis*. The destroyer transport *Dickerson* had been damaged beyond repair by a suicide plane, and had to be sunk. LCI 82 had been sunk. Mostly, the ships had stood up well under their damage, which was a tribute to their builders. Casualties in the Navy were estimated at 790, an average of about 20 per damaged or sunken ship.

The *kamikaze* had become Japan's most lethal weapon against the United States Navy. At last the Japs had put their mania for suicide to effective use. We could knock down 80 per cent or more of the Jap pilots before they ever reached our ships; the Hellcat and Corsair pilots in Spruance's force took care of that many. The pilots from Turner's protective force shot down others after they got in range of the ships off Okinawa, and anti-aircraft gunners on the ships blasted others out of the sky. But some got through to carry out their missions, and often they did tremendous damage. About one-seventh of the Navy's total casualties in World War II was sustained off Okinawa (9,731 men), and the destructive weapon was the *kamikaze*.

Early in the war Jap pilots had occasionally dived their planes into our ships, but *kamikaze* as an organized movement apparently began about October 15, 1944. That was Radio Tokyo's story, as I heard it aboard the aircraft carrier *Essex* the following January. On October 15, according to the story, Vice Admiral Masabumi Arima flew his torpedo plane into an American aircraft carrier, lest "the traditional spirit of the Japanese Navy be spoiled." Thereafter Radio Tokyo daily intoned the names of "hero gods," who were promoted (posthumously, of course) two or three ranks instead of the customary one. Japanese journalists interviewed little boys whose ambition was to grow up and become suicide pilots. The whole nation, including the war workers, said the Japanese propagandists, had gone on a "special attack corps" basis.

When I arrived in the Pacific early in December, the Navy

talked about the "green hornets" to the exclusion of almost everything else. The suicide pilots were supposed to wear: (1) white robes, (2) yellow and green tights, or (3) black hoods. Some said they were manacled to their cockpits. It was no wonder there was so much "scuttlebutt" about the suicide pilots. Nothing could have been more awesome than to see a human being diving himself and his machine into the enemy; nobody except the Japanese could have combined such medieval religious fervor with a machine as modern as the airplane. The early *kamikaze*—the word means "divine wind"—attacks were not as successful as they became later off Okinawa, but their potentiality as a force to destroy the Navy caused great concern.

Before the beginning of the year several of our carriers, including the *Franklin* (its first hit, not the second and more destructive), the *Essex*, the *Lexington*, the *Intrepid* and a few others, had been put out of action, some briefly, some for several months. The Leyte, Mindoro and Luzon campaigns in October-January brought damage to well over 100 United States ships; more than half of them were hit by suicide planes. When the battleship *New Mexico* was hit by a *kamikaze* in January, the British Lieut. General Lumsden was killed, and so was my friend and colleague, William Chickering.

The first suicide attack I saw was on January 21, southeast of Formosa, just after the Third Fleet had come out of the South China Sea. The victim was the carrier *Ticonderoga*, on which I had spent the month of December. From the *Essex* in the same task group, I saw the ordeal of the *Ticonderoga*. At 1209 the five-inch anti-aircraft guns opened up, and the bell clanged for "general quarters." Everybody rushed topside. The nearby *Ticonderoga* was billowing black smoke 300 feet high. Seven planes had sneaked through. Six were shot down by AA fire. The seventh crashed through the *Ti's* flight deck. She was badly hit.

At 1253 more bogeys were reported on the starboard side. "Here they come!" somebody yelled. As I watched the burning *Ticonderoga*, the AA guns on a dozen ships opened up at once. Five Japs fell flaming into the sea, but the sixth, though he was burning in three places, plowed unwaveringly into the middle of the smoke, and a huge billow of orange-red flame reached for the sky.

It seemed inevitable then that the *Ti* would sink, but heroic damage-control work, as in so many other cases, saved the ship. The *Ticonderoga* lost 143 men killed or missing. Two hundred and two others were wounded, including the famed captain, Dixie Kiefer, who had his right arm mangled and his body punctured by 65 small bomb fragments. Many of the victims were men I had come to know and like during the month I had spent on the *Ti*.

But April 6 was probably the biggest *kamikaze* day of the war. During a 24-hour period the Japanese sent nearly 500 planes from Kyushu airdromes in an effort to knock the Americans out of Okinawa waters. The flyers from Mitscher's Task Force 58 shot down most of these planes, but an estimated 116 suicide-bent pilots got through. Hellcat and Corsair pilots from Turner's Task Force 51 Combat Air Patrol knocked down 55 more. Sixty-one managed to get through to the amphibious force, including the picket boats on the line 50 miles forward and the ships anchored in Kerama Retto. Of these 61, the anti-aircraft gunners shot down 39. The other 22 completed their mission by crashing into our ships.

The peaks of these attacks came between 1630 and 1900. I was on the *Eldorado*, idly looking through a porthole, when I saw a Jap plane diving toward an LST offshore to the south. Terrific streams of ack-ack poured toward the plane from every ship within two miles. When the Jap was 300 feet from his target he flamed, winged over, and fell into the shallow water.

In the next half hour I saw two more suicide planes shot down within two miles of the ship. At 1715 I boarded an LCVP to go over to the *Panamint*, with John Lardner and with some 25 soldiers who were shore-bound. We were about halfway between the *Eldorado* and the *Panamint* when a twin-engined Jap bomber came diving over the hills of Okinawa; it was heading low and directly toward our small boat, it seemed. The Jap was no more than 200 feet above the water when the pumping of the 40's and the cackling of the 20's finally brought results. His plane started flaming, and he smacked into the water, about 100 yards from our small boat. He barely missed a cargo ship and the hospital ship *Comfort*.[1] Burning gasoline scattered far across the water as the plane hit.

The Japs caused a lot of damage in their 22 hits. The brave little ships on the picket line—destroyers, destroyer escorts, and LCS's—were hit hardest. The *Bush*, *Colhoun*, and minesweeper *Emmons* were sunk. Two destroyers, the *Leutze* and the *Newcomb*, shot down three *kamikazes*, but were hit by four others (one plane skidded from the deck of the *Newcomb* then crashed into the stern of the *Leutze*). These two cans had 175 casualties. Eight other destroyers and three minesweepers were damaged. Two ammunition ships, the *Hobbs Victory* and the *Logan Victory*, were blown up. The tug *Yuma* performed one of the heroic deeds of the day. She put men on the burning *Hobbs Victory*, at Kerama Retto, to fasten a tow line, then in the midst of explosions and spreading nitric acid, towed it out to sea.

Any mention of suicide planes was taboo for six months. In our news stories we simply had to ignore one of the most lurid stories of the war, or of any war. On April 13 (east longitude time) Admiral Nimitz finally removed the restriction. But half an hour after he approved the release, Franklin

---

[1] The *Comfort* was not always so lucky. Three weeks later a suicide plane crashed into the defenseless, white ship, killed 29, wounded 33.

Delano Roosevelt died—and the *kamikazes* made quite small news.

The admirals nearly always depreciated suicide planes as effective weapons. Admiral Mitscher, for example, said, "They don't worry us very much." (This in spite of the fact that he and Admiral Spruance each had two flagships hit by *kamikazes.*) Whatever the admirals thought, I knew the sailors were worried, and so was I.

April 8

The ship's mimeographed news sheet told of a bill in Congress to appropriate $122,900,000 to dig up American dead from battlefields over the world and return them to the United States for reburial in national cemeteries. This seemed to me a mistake. Nobody could speak for the dead, and men who were about to die rarely spoke of death because each hoped, even when fighting against hopeless odds, that he would live. I had seen a lot of men die in World War II —good men. I talked to some of them within five minutes of their going, to many of them within a few hours of the time when they drew their last breath of Pacific air. I did not recall that any man told me what he wanted done with his body.

But I felt morally certain—as certain as anyone could feel about something about which he did not know the definite answer—that these men would have preferred to have their bones lie where their comrades interred them.

There was no way to find an answer, and, of course, the final decision lay with the next of kin. I began to ask men on and around Okinawa what they would want done with their bodies if they were killed. The results of my poll were interesting:

A junior grade Navy lieutenant said: "Good God, what will they think of next? Why not give that money to the widows and children?" A half dozen of the men pointed out that it would be cruel to subject the dead men's families to a second attack of grief coincident with the arrival of the bones. An Army major said: "We think the Okinawans are odd because they let the bodies of their dead lie three years before picking up the bones and putting them in a jar. But I wonder if their system doesn't make better sense than digging up bodies and sending them 7,000 miles to be planted again?"

I took a small boat over to the *Comfort* and asked the skipper, Commander Harold Fultz, and the ship's 205th Medical Complement Commander, Colonel J. F. Linsman, for permission to talk to some of the wounded. The wounded men were almost unanimous. A sergeant from the Seventy-seventh said: "It wouldn't be right for the families, and when it's over and you get a burial there's no use to take 'em back." Another sergeant from the Seventhy-seventh, who had machine-gun bullets in both legs, said: "It would be a waste of money, and besides, after a couple of days on Leyte our men would be eaten up by maggots." A sailor was scornful: "Cheap politics!"

A Marine major who had received multiple wounds, including one fragment through the mouth, could speak only with difficulty, but he said: "Most of my men say 'when I'm dead, leave me where I am.' The more intelligent say it would be too much trouble to move a lot of bones." A second lieutenant said: "The cemeteries out here are okay if they are well kept. A man doesn't want to be disturbed after he is dead." One seaman from Connecticut, whose ship had been hit by a suicide plane, was one of the two (of 40 I interviewed) who would have wanted his bones taken back home for burial.

The Catholic chaplain on the *Comfort* and the Protestant on the *Eldorado* both were against removing the men's bodies. Said the Catholic: "It is surprising how few men talk of the prospect of dying. But I don't believe the men would want to be dug up." The Protestant: "To remove the dead would be definitely an isolationist gesture—like locking ourselves in." One of the surgeons who had operated from 0530 yesterday morning until 0530 this morning, Major Edwin B. Eckerson, of New York, said: "It's silly. I was in the last war, and they didn't want it then. I don't believe the men's families would want it now, and I know very well most of the men themselves don't."

A Navy commander on the *Eldorado* smiled, and said: "I guess they never heard of Rupert Brooke's poem: *'If I should die, think only this of me; that there's some corner of a foreign field that is for ever England'*."

Casualties ashore were rising, especially among the Army divisions on the southern line, where the intensity of the opposition was increasing. The Tenth Army's figures tonight showed casualties as follows: First Marine Division 356, Sixth Marine Division 361, Seventh Division 550, Ninety-Sixth 775, Seventy-Seventh 273, XXIV Corps troops 138, III Corps troops 35. But the severe fighting on Okinawa was yet to come.

April 9

Ernie Pyle and I were in a room aboard the *Panamint*, writing stories. I told the little gray correspondent I had decided to go home after a few more days. He said he was tired of combat, too. "I'm getting too old to stay in combat with these kids," said Ernie, "and I'm going to go home, too, in about a month. I think I'll stay back around the airfields with the Seabees and engineers in the meantime and write some stories about them."

As I got ready to leave the *Panamint* I couldn't find the mess treasurer, to whom I owed $2.50 for two days' chow. Ernie said he would pay the bill for me. He asked me to see about forwarding his mail when I got to Guam. That was the last time I saw him. Nine days later, when I was in Maui in the Hawaiian Islands, I heard he had been killed. I never learned which doughboy of the Seventy-Seventh Division persuaded Ernie to change his mind and go on the Ie Shima invasion off the west coast of Okinawa. But Ernie rarely refused a request from a doughboy, or any other friend.

April 10

Before I left Okinawa I made one more trip through the Sixth Division area, which now extended far to the north and through most of the Motobu Peninsula which sticks out like a thumb to the west. With Brig. General Merlin H. Silverthorn, chief of staff to General Geiger of the III Corps, I rode all day through the thickening mud, past hillsides which were terraced to their very top, and past innumerable rice paddies.

We stopped at the "university" in the town of Nago, where General Shepherd had set up his new CP, near the base of the peninsula. Silverthorn was an eager general. "I want to go up where there is some shooting," he said, But *I* was going home next day, and I had no desire to see any more shooting, or to get shot at. (That last shot is always the most frightening). I went along, anyway.

There had been sporadic firing on the peninsula, but apparently there were not many Japs in that area. We jeeped onward to the town of Nakasoni, to find that we were the first Americans in the town. "Well, we've captured a town all by ourselves," said the general. Nakasoni's remaining population consisted at the time of one very old man. The general insisted on driving to the end of Motobu, though I was ready to go back. I was thinking of that C-54 which would be taking off tomorrow from Yontan Airfield.

We came upon a cave near the tip of the peninsula. In it were some belts of a thousand stitches, a Jap petty officer's suitcase, many signal flags, some fencing equipment, and a small wooden box which the general said looked interesting. He tossed the box into the jeep beside me.

We made our tortuous way back to corps headquarters.

Six times on the 35-mile ride bulldozers had to pull us out of the two-foot-deep mud. I was glad to get back, and when I heard from General Silverthorn several weeks later, after I had returned to the United States, I had more reason. The general wrote: "The Sixth Division killed 2,000 Japs on Motobu Peninsula after we were up there. . . . That box we picked up turned out to be a new kind of infernal machine."

When I left Okinawa on April 11 it was expected that there would be considerable fighting, especially in the Army's southern area. But it was not anticipated that the III Corps would be sent to the south also. Okinawa, of course, turned out to be one of the costliest battles of the war: 21,400 Army casualties, 15,400 Marine, 9,731 Navy.

Not only was it necessary to put the Seventy-Seventh Division in the southern line, and the Twenty-Seventh, and the two Marine divisions. At the battle's end a regiment of the Second Division (the 8th) was called back from its base at Saipan, where it had been sent after Okinawa appeared to be not too tough. There had not been 60,000 or 70,000 Jap troops on Okinawa; there had been over 100,000, according to the official reports.

Okinawa turned out to be a protracted Iwo. This fragmentary report of the landing does not touch the bitter battles which were waged through Shuri Castle, Naha, Sugar Loaf Hill, Conical Hill, Yonabaru, and the fiendish defenses throughout the southernmost parts of the island. Okinawa was a great victory to cap the Central Pacific campaign. After Okinawa came the naval gunfire attacks on the coast of Japan, the 800-plane B-29 raids and, finally, the atomic bomb and the hasty entry of Russia into the war. Whatever illusions the Jap high command had about American fighting power and American fighting men disappeared at Okinawa, 330 miles from Japan.

APPENDIX A
SAIPAN: SMITH VERSUS SMITH

After pages 88-93 I should add some details about the Army-Marine controversy. Following the Saipan battle I returned to New York and was there when Holland Smith held his press conference in Washington September 9 (page 91).

I wrote an article, unsigned as all except overseas reports were, entitled "The Generals Smith" for the September 18, 1944, issue of *Time* and, burned up at the Heast newspapers' attacks on Navy-Marine Corps strategy, I went too far in questioning the courage of the Twenty-seventh Division soldiers ("froze in their foxholes."). Whatever the weaknesses of this inept National Guard oufit, I should not have done it and I'm sorry. The effect on the morale of the division, which was retraining by this time on the South Pacific island of Espiritu Santo, was devastating.

General George C. Marshall, the Army's chief of staff, would permit no public answer to the *Time* article, fearing exacerbation of an already ugly interservice situation. When I got back to Pearl Harbor Admiral Nimitz told me, December 4, that he had approved the demand of Lieutenant General Robert C. Richardson, Army commander in the Central Pacific, that my correspondent's credentials be withdrawn—in other words, that I be fired. "We [Army and Navy] have got to live together out here," said the ruddy, white-haired admiral. He assumed that I had been informed by Washington, but nobody had peeped to me or my editors.

Years passed before I saw a copy of the message, by then declassified, that rescued me. Admiral Ernest J. King, the bald eagle of Constitution Avenue was not one to mince words—one legend held that he shaved with a blowtorch—in his dispatch of November 17 to Pearl Harbor:

For Nimitz, eyes only from King:

As explained in my serial 003233 of 6 November to Chief of Staff Army, copy to you, there is no valid reason for barring Robert

299

Sherrod from your area. Mr. Sherrod desires to return to Pearl Harbor in near future. See that he is accorded usual privileges of an accredited correspondent.

I proceeded from Pearl Harbor to Ulithi and boarded the aircraft carrier *Ticonderoga* for the Fast Carrier Task Force's journey toward the Philippines to support General MacArthur's December 15 invasion of Mindoro. My friendly relationship with Admiral Nimitz never wavered because of the Generals Smith affair: at the end of the war he signed a letter of commendation for me and, after he became Chief of Naval operations, he invited me to lunch in his dining room in the Main Navy Building on Constitution Avenue.

With General Holland Smith it was different. He wrote me in Shanghai in December 1947 that he was writing a book and "letting my hair down" on the subject of Saipan, and also "paying my respects" to the Navy: "the weak-kneed Nimitz, the shy Spruance and Kelly Turner have let me hold the sack...The story will be brutal but the truth will be told."

So be it, I thought. We journalists relish controversy. But when he sent me a copy of his manuscript after I returned to Washington in 1948 I was dismayed. Obviously Howlin' Mad had given little thought to his choice of a collaborator, Percy Finch, an Australian war correspondent who had covered parts of the Central Pacific drive, or to verifying facts.

The manuscript reflected little research beyond General Smith's own files. It was riddled with errors, and many of his wartime opinions had been proven cockeyed. I enlisted the help of Lieutenant Colonel Robert Debs Heinl, Jr., head of the historical section at Marine Corps Headquarters and a prolific writer on military subjects. We did a hasty job of correcting the worst of the errors, and Smith replied in the summer of 1948: "In trying to write the story I got into trouble over my head. I realize from your letter and [Heinl's] comments that the book can be materially strengthened but frankly I am almost helpless to do anything about it myself."

General Smith had sold the book to the *Saturday Evening Post* (for $20,000) and the magazine excerpted from it three installments, beginning with "Tarawa Was a Mistake," (November 6, 1948), a theme he adamantly refused to change, despite all the evidence to the contrary. Considering the *Post's* long lead time, this first article had almost certainly gone to press while Smith was still talking about starting all over, with a historian as collaborator. Never mind, I said, you can still make corrections in the book, which is more important for posterity.

On November 1, Holland Smith called me from La Jolla. He had made his decision: "I'm fed up with it. It has upset me terribly. It's driving my family crazy. I'm going to turn the manuscript over to the publisher as is. I've let a couple of eminent men read it and they think it is all right. I'm not writing a history. I'm just trying to give credit where it is due."

I asked General Smith to excuse me from my promise to write a foreword for the book, which he titled *Coral and Brass*. His former aide, Mac Asbill, Jr., later a prominent lawyer in Washington, D.C., took over the foreword task.

General Smith and I corresponded occasionally after his book was published. I last wrote him April 16, 1965, congratulating him on his eighty-third birthday, and had a warm reply May 25: "I am confident that you know I have an affectionate friendship for you." He asked me to visit him again in La Jolla, where my wife and I had stopped over in 1946 when en route to China, but I never did. Things simply weren't the same after *Coral and Brass*. He died January 12, 1967, and was buried in the Fort Rosecrans National Cemetery with Marine howitzers booming a seventeen-gun salute.

Holland Smith made a great contribution to World War II, in developing amphibious tactics and equipment, in standing up for the Marines when the likes of Kelly Turner and Robert C. Richardson threatened their function if not their existence. He fully justified the cover story I wrote about him for *Time* in early 1944 during the Marshalls invasion. It is too bad Holland Smith felt a compulsion to get even when it was no longer necessary, and to seek the limelight when it was not appropriate.

APPENDIX B
THE IWO FLAG RAISINGS

The raising of two flags on Mount Suribachi is noted on page 191, but no mention is made of the controversy attending those events which continued for several years. The Marine Corps Historical Center's quarterly newsletter, *Fortitudine,* carried an excellent six-page article on the raisings by the director of Marine Corps History and Museums, Brigadier General Edwin H. Simmons, USMC (Retired), in the Fall 1979 issue. His newspeg was the death of Rene Gagnon, the last Marine in Joe Rosenthal's famous photograph of the *second* flag-raising—the one that is immortalized in Felix de Weldon's huge statue next to Arlington National Cemetery. (The corpsman in the photograph, PhM 2/c John H. Bradley, still lives, in Antigo, Wisconsin).

The next six issues save one (Spring 1980) of *Fortitudine* printed responses on the flag raisings, including four pages I wrote, winter 1980-1981, which stemmed from a visit to Tallahassee. While driving through North Florida in December 1980, I recalled that Monticello (pop. 3,000) was the home of the Sergeant Ernest Thomas who led the detachment from E Company, 28th Marines, that raised the *first* flag, an event that was photographed by Technical Sergeant Louis Lowery of *Leatherneck* Magazine, about 10:30 on the morning of February 23,1945. Some two hours later a larger flag, 56 by 96 inches, was brought up from *LST 799,* lying offshore. Photographer Joe Rosenthal of the Associated Press accompanied this patrol and, at the right millisecond, snapped the most famous photograph of World War II. Sergeant William H. Genaust, a Marine Corps motion picture cameraman, also recorded the event in another remarkable, but lesser known, bit of filming.

Platoon Sergeant Thomas was ordered out to the flagship of Vice Admiral Richmond Kelly Turner and greeted by—and photographed with—Lieutenant General Holland Smith. He was interviewed in a radio broadcast back to the States, as reported by Technical Sergeant Keyes Beech, a Marine Corps combat correspondent whose story was spread world-wide by the Associated Press: Thomas told how his platoon had lost seventeen men out of forty-six in scaling Suribachi on D-plus-3. He modestly insisted that he didn't raise the flag all by himself: "Those fellows who were with me ought to be here, too." So, Thomas's feat was well known back home, though not on Iwo. (I never heard of it until March 13, when I was back on Guam.)

Unfortunately, "Boots" Thomas, like so many of his comrades, met his fate in the meat grinder that was the northern end of Iwo. His remains were brought home and reburied in Monticello's Roseland Cemetery April 28, 1948, under a marker that tells the story of his tragically shortened life: "Ernest I. Thomas, Jr., Sgt. USMCR, Mar. 10, 1924-Mar. 3, 1945. Killed in action on Iwo Jima five days after raising the first flag on Mt. Suribachi." (Actually it was eight days.) Plans were being made to erect a memorial to Thomas alongside Highway 90 a couple of months later. His boyhood friend, Dr. James S. Sledge, had hoped to collect $100,000 for the memorial plaque, a bas relief taken from the Lowery photograph which shows Thomas front and center atop Suribachi. But Dr. Sledge proceeded with the $7,000 in hand.

The ceremony was held February 22, 1981, with a noteworthy cast: four members from Thomas's Easy Company, including Sergeant Richard Wheeler, of West Palm Beach, author of two books on Iwo, and Charles Lindberg of Richfield, Minnesota, sole survivor of the quartet Lowery photographed tying the flag to a piece of Japanese pipe (a similar pipe was also used in the second flag hoisting), Sergeant Robert D. Sinclair of St. Petersburg, an official of the Paralyzed Veterans of America, wearing a Silver Star insignia, and Lieutenant J. Keith Wells of Abilene, Texas, a Navy Cross recipient who commanded the Third Platoon of Easy Company. Major General David Twomey, commander of the Second Marine Division, came down from Camp LeJeune, North Carolina, and made a short speech expressing the regrets of Commandant Robert H. Barrow, who had accepted but had to cancel; also present were Charles Whitehouse, a Marine veteran who became ambassador to Thailand and Laos, and Don Fuqua, member of Congress for the Monticello district.

So Sergeant Thomas was finally recognized. It was high time, thought his brother and sister (twins), his friends and neighbors—perhaps not in the manner of the six who raised the second flag, with (for the three who survived) war bond tours, reception at the White House and the assembled houses of Congress. But recognition, which is what we all strive for, is terribly important.

It was the struggle for recognition that started the flag-raising controversy in the first place. Which was more important, the fact of planting the flag first or the image as conveyed by the Rosenthal icon?

When I first saw the Rosenthal photograph on Guam it was easy for me to accept the vociferous insistence of some Marines, including Louis Lowery, that Rosenthal had posed the figures. A picture that good *had* to be posed, or so it seemed to me. Besides, the Marines who were at the site (but not at the same time as Rosenthal—I didn't know that) said it was, in Lowery's phrase, "grand photographically but, in a sense, historically phony, like Washington crossing the Delaware." Lowery died three years ago, but when I published this information in *Fortitudine,* Winter 1980-81, he raised no objection.

A few years ago I found a copy of my March 13 cable among the papers of the late Roy Larsen, former Chairman of the Board of Time Incorporated, in the Houghton Library at Harvard.

"The planting of the flag didn't quite happen that way and the historical picture was a post facto rehearsal," I blithely cabled. I couldn't have been more wrong, and I blush even today.

Back in New York the editors of *Life,* experts in every facet of photography, had decided on their own that the Rosenthal shot must have been posed and refused for three weeks to run it. *(Time* not only published it at the first opportunity, in the March 5 edition—on the newsstands March 1—but led the magazine with it.)

After confusion set in, *Time* ran the "Story of a Picture" in its March 26 issue, and *Life,* same date, finally published Rosenthal's classic shot along with Lowery's and also Emanuel Leutze's painting, "Washington Crossing the Delaware," which shows the Father of His Country standing up in the boat; it was painted from models on the Rhine River years after the American Revolution.

After I learned how wrong I had been I blessed my good luck that neither magazine had exposed my ignorance. I had got away with something and possibly avoided a lawsuit. Then, some time in the 1960s, I saw Alan J. Gould, former top executive of the Associated Press, who told me something that my editors didn't communicate to me on Guam, or later: my dispatch did get some circulation.

For a while in World War II my company had an afternoon radio program on New York's WJZ—weekly, I believe—called "Time Views the News," which broadcast a version of my March 13 dispatch: "Rosenthal climbed Suribachi after the flag had already been planted... Like most photographers [he] could not resist re-posing his characters in historic fashion. He posed them and snapped the scene."

The AP got wind of the program, asked for a transcript on March 15 and sent a photo editor across Rockefeller Plaza to the Time-Life Building. He had no trouble convincing the editors that the broadcast was wrong. "Time Views the News" apologized to the AP and to Rosenthal, and even said they misunderstood my cable: I had not used the word "re-pose," which was more exemption that I deserved.

I was laboring under the misapprehension that Lowery's photographs would not be published until the next monthly issue of *Leatherneck*—actually, they also went out by radiophoto immediately—and I felt it was important that the public know that Rosenthal's film not be labeled the original flag-raising on Suribachi. I thought the implications of Rosenthal's picture were all wrong. Iwo wasn't a matter of storming the parapet and planting the flag there.

Iwo was torturous slogging northward on the porkchop-shape island, yard by yard, day after day. Suribachi was a symbol and it was nice to have our flag up there, but the action and the horror were up north, where three of the Rosenthal flag planters, as well as Ernest Thomas, gave their lives. The inaccuracy was quaintly compounded by the fact that the symbol of Iwo depicted the *second* flag raising, after the shooting had stopped up there. (Sergeant Thomas's detachment had a fire fight before they could prosaically raise the first flag.)

I sometime encounter veterans of Iwo who, like a radioman with the first patrol, Pfc. Gene Marshall *(Fortitudine,* Fall 1979) still regard the second flag raising as "posed, re-enacted, fake." They are wrong, of course, though some nagging doubts remain: Why would six husky men be required to raise a flag on a thin piece of Japanese pipe with a following wind?

I have long since accepted Joe Rosenthal's version as stated in a 1975 interview with Ben Frank, chief of oral history in the Marine Corps History Division: "All of the fortunate things that can happen in one picture happened together without any urging on my part." I apologized to Joe in my *Fortitudine* article ten years ago.

Of the clashes between British and French cavalry at Waterloo, John Keegan writes in his book *The Face of Battle* (1976): "A little inquiry reveals, in any case, that formations were much less dense and speeds much lower than casual testimony, and certainly the work of salon painters, implies." The renowned Iwo photograph is the salon painting of World War II.

APPENDIX C
CENTRAL PACIFIC BATTLE CASUALTIES *

M: *Marines* A: *Army*

	Area (Sq. Mi.)	Approx. Force	Killed or Missing	Wounded	Total	Estimated Jap Force
Gilberts						
Tarawa	1.68	M—17,000	988	2,164	3,152	4,000
Makin	2.15	A— 7,000	66	187	253	700
Marshalls						
Kwajalein	1.88	M—16,000	229	797	1,026	3,800
		A—18,000	177	1,037	1,214	5,000
Eniwetok	.5	M— 5,000	196	550	746	2,200
		A— 5,000	70	228	298	
Marianas						
Saipan	71	M—48,000	2,382	8,769	11,151	30,000
		A—20,000	1,059	2,696	3,755	
Tinian	32	M—40,000	416	1,735	2,151	4,500
Guam	206	M—40,000	1,484	4,957	6,441	18,500
		A—20,000	591	2,818	3,409	
Palaus						
Peliliu	6.25	M—25,000	1,241	4,883	6,024	10,500
Angaur	3.37	A—10,000	264	1,465	1,729	3,000
Volcanoes						
Iwo-Jima	8	M—61,000	5,517	13,697	19,214	22,000
Ryukyus						
Okinawa	450	M—50,000	3,112	12,297	15,409	110,000
		A—90,000	4,417	17,033	21,450	
						214,200
Marines Total		302,000	15,565	49,849	65,414	
Army Total		170,000	6,644	25,464	32,108	
Grand Total		472,000	22,209	75,313	97,522	

* No attempt is made here to include Navy casualties which are not usually compiled according to battles. An exception was the costliest Navy campaign of the war, Okinawa, where 4,907 were listed as killed or missing, 4,824 wounded—mostly due to suicide planes.

APPENDIX D
CORRECTIONS AND CHANGES FOR THE SECOND EDITION

Start with the title, *On to Westward,* taken from the verse at the begining of the book. In the first edition I wrote: "These lines are inscribed on a plaque in the cemetery at Tarawa. Their Marine author is unknown."

He was unknown to me, but he actually was Captain Donald L. Jackson, USMCR, intelligence officer of the Sixth Marine Regiment, the outfit I spent much time with on Saipan (Bill Jones of pages 100-105 commanded the First Battalion, Sixth). I met Don Jackson in 1948 in Washington, where he was the newly elected Representative, a Republican, from Santa Monica, California; he would serve fourteen years in Congress.

Throughout the text I call the enemy "Japs"; I would say "Japanese" now. Likewise, Chapter Two, "The Nature of the Enemy," while accurate in its interpretation of World War II fanaticism, would need a supplement on Japanese achievement since the war. Fanatical yes. Cruel, yes (it is still difficult for me to understand how the Japanese could let thirty percent or more of their prisoners die); but definitely not savages.

Page 5: General MacArthur and Admiral Nimitz, particularly MacArthur, had a great deal of trouble getting whatever they wanted from the Joint Chiefs of Staff. MacArthur detested the Europe-first strategy, and also fought against the opening of the Central Pacific (as noted on page 234). When some of Nimitz's staff officers agreed in January 1944 with MacArthur's plan to concentrate on the Southwest Pacific, we now know, Admiral Ernest J. King stormed at Nimitz "in indignant dismay," and put the Marianas back on the schedule. (Memo to Nimitz February 8, 1944, cited in my *History of Marine Corps Aviation in WWII,* page 265).

Page 10, thirteen lines from bottom: Saipan grows in importance as the historians plow their furrows. On the morning of July 18, 1944, Prime Minister Tojo "told his cabinet in a weary voice that he had decided to resign because of the loss of Saipan." (John Toland, *The Rising Sun,*

1970, page 527). "Almost unanimously, informed Japanese considered Saipan as the decisive battle of the war, and its loss as ending all hope for a Japanese victory." (U.S. Strategic Boming Survey, *Campaigns of the Pacific War,* 1946, p. 220).

Page 12, line 5—For adjusted figures on Iwo casualties, see entry at "Page 154."

Page 12, line 7—Although more than 20,000 airmen found safe haven in 2,000 B-29's landing on Iwo, General Curtis E. LeMay forgot to mention this overwhelming fact in his autobiography, *Mission With LeMay* (1965), inconceivable as it may seem.

Page 32: Biak is an island, not a peninsula. The movies shown were Merle Oberon in "The Lodger" and Errol Flynn in "Northern Patrol."

Page 52: "1000 hours," not "hour"

Page 58: Jim Crowe was alive and well in early 1990, having served many years as Chief of Police in Portsmouth, Virginia.

Page 59: After the war Saipan became a favorite resort for Japanese, particularly honeymooners. The island is dotted with Buddhist and Shinto memorials to the war dead.

Page 76, three lines from bottom: "lying" not laying"

Page 77, three lines from bottom: "sounds" not "sound"

Page 88: For more on Smith *v* Smith, see Appendix A.

Page 92, line 2: The official was Admiral Richard S. Edwards, CNO's deputy chief of staff.

Page 117, nine lines from bottom: "When we" not "When he"

Page 119, eleven lines from bottom: "Hospital" not "Hospitals"

Page 154, mid page: Total casualties for Iwo eventually reached 28,686 (Marines 25,851, Navy 2,798, Army 37). Of these 6,821 KIA or DOW (Marines 5,931, Navy 881, Army 9; this total includes 2,648 Marine Corps combat fatigue cases which are not always listed). In addition, the VII Fighter Command AAF had 44 killed and 88 wounded in the final organized banzai attack by 200 to 300 on March 26.

Page 166, line 5: By March 26, when VAC commander Harry Schmidt departed Iwo, the Marines had taken only 216 prisoners, but during April and May 867 more stragglers surrendered to the Army's 147th Infantry Regiment, which had arrived for garrison duty six days earlier (USMC Historical Division, *Western Pacific Operations,* 1971, pages 708-712).

If Major Wolf is alive and will send me his address I'll pay him ten 1990 dollars, which are worth far less than 1945 dollars.

Page 184, four lines from bottom: President Truman pinned a Medal of Honor on Colonel Chambers in the Rose Garden of the White House in 1950.

Page 191: For more on Iwo's flag raising, see Appendix B.

Page 200: Months afterward, in New York, Correspondent Lardner told me he felt a knot in his leg, and squeezed out a bullet.

Page 221, line 6: not "forever." Iwo's dead, like those of other battlefields, were dug up and buried again in national cemeteries or other places designated by their survivors.

Page 237, mid page: Nimitz wrote no memoir; MacArthur wrote his *Reminiscences* in 1963, but the book was not published until after his death at 84 the next year.

Page 240, twelve lines from bottom: Halsey sold the idea to Nimitz, who sold it to the Joint Chiefs of Staff, meeting then in Quebec. MacArthur was at sea en route to Biak, and it was his chief of staff, Major General Richard K. Sutherland, who radioed agreement—in MacArthur's name—to the stepped-up invasion.

Page 240, two lines from bottom: Renamed the Leyte Gulf battle by historians.

Page 245, nine lines from bottom: F4U Corsairs were also flown by U.S. Navy squadrons and, eventually, New Zealanders.

Page 258, last line: The number of soldiers killed on Kiska by their comrades was twenty-four.

Page 273, line 15: Okinawa was defended by approximately 110,000 Japanese troops.

Page 278, line 22, and map 279: "Kadena" is the correct spelling of the airfield.

Page 280, top line, and page 298, line 12: Tenth Army casualties were 7,613 KIA or MIA, 31,807 wounded, plus more than 26,000 non-battle casualties; Navy's Okinawa losses: 4,907 KIA or MIA, 4,824 wounded. (Morison Vol. XIV: *Victory in the Pacific,* page 282).

Page 294: My campaign to let the dead lie got nowhere beyond an editorial in *Life,* which raised the question but advocated no solution. It made no sense, anyway, to spot dozens of cemeteries on the many islands where Americans were killed: how would the graves be cared for? Seventeen thousand Pacific war dead lie in the national cemetery outside Manila, and 18,000 more (World War II only) near Honolulu but most of the remains were shipped back to the mainland to be interred at Arlington, Virginia, National Cemetery (175,000 graves from many wars) or other places of entombment.

Page 297, line 7: "Merwin," not "Merlin"

Page 298, line 9: The Sixth MarDiv had 213 killed, 757 wounded in overcoming the 2,000 Japanese defenders on Motobu, 14-19 April. It was smart of the Japanese not to reveal their presence by shooting at me and General Silverthorn and, unquestionably, it was lucky for us.

Readers will please note that the subtitle of the book has been changed from "War in the Central Pacific" to "The Battles of Saipan and Iwo Jima."

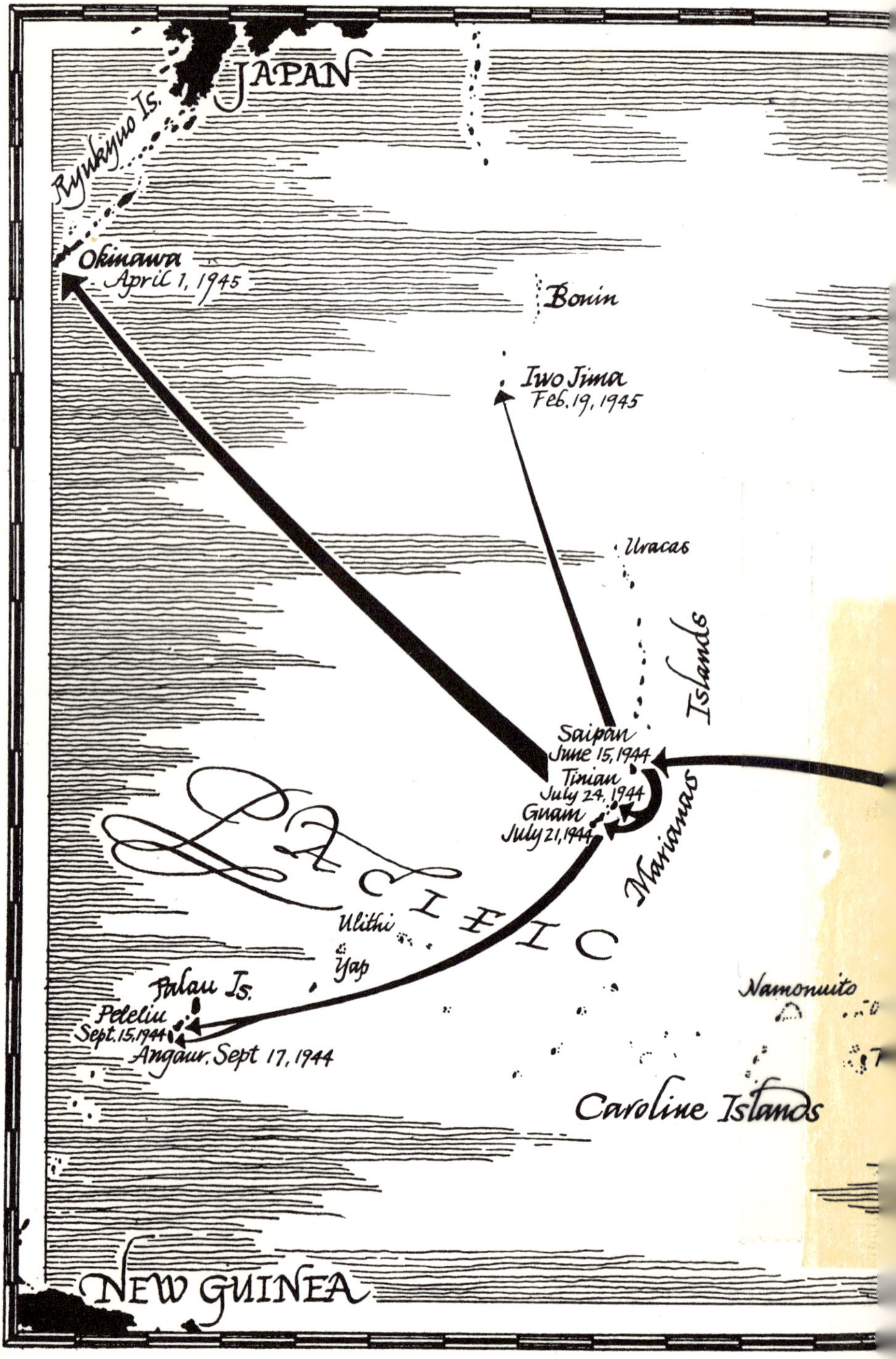

JAPAN
Ryukyuo Is.
Okinawa
April 1, 1945
Bonin
Iwo Jima
Feb. 19, 1945
Uracas
Islands
Saipan
June 15, 1944
Tinian
July 24, 1944
Guam
July 21, 1944
Marianas
PACIFIC
Ulithi
Yap
Palau Is.
Peleliu
Sept. 15, 1944
Angaur, Sept 17, 1944
Namonuito
Caroline Islands
NEW GUINEA